Culture, Mind, and Society

Series Editor
Peter G. Stromberg
Anthropology Department
University of Tulsa
Tulsa, Oklahoma, USA

Aim of the Series

The Society for Psychological Anthropology—a section of the American Anthropology Association—and Palgrave Macmillan are dedicated to publishing innovative research that illuminates the workings of the human mind within the social, cultural, and political contexts that shape thought, emotion, and experience. As anthropologists seek to bridge gaps between ideation and emotion or agency and structure and as psychologists, psychiatrists, and medical anthropologists search for ways to engage with cultural meaning and difference, this interdisciplinary terrain is more active than ever. **Editorial Board Eileen Anderson-Fye**, Department of Anthropology, Case Western Reserve University **Jennifer Cole**, Committee on Human Development, University of Chicago **Linda Garro**, Department of Anthropology, University of California, Los Angeles **Daniel T. Linger**, Department of Anthropology, University of California, Santa Cruz **Rebecca Lester**, Department of Anthropology, Washington University in St. Louis **Tanya Luhrmann**, Department of Anthropology, Stanford University **Catherine Lutz**, Department of Anthropology, University of North Carolina, Chapel Hill **Peggy Miller**, Departments of Psychology and Speech Communication, University of Illinois, Urbana-Champaign **Robert Paul**, Department of Anthropology, Emory University **Antonius C. G. M.Robben**, Department of Anthropology, Utrecht University, Netherlands **Bradd Shore**, Department of Anthropology, Emory University **Jason Throop**, Department of Anthropology, University of California, Los Angeles **Carol Worthman**, Department of Anthropology, Emory University

More information about this series at
http://www.springer.com/series/14947

David Lipset

Yabar

The Alienations of Murik Men
in a
Papua New Guinea Modernity

David Lipset
University of Minnesota Twin Cities
St Paul, Minnesota, USA

Culture, Mind, and Society
ISBN 978-3-319-84559-3   ISBN 978-3-319-51076-7   (eBook)
DOI 10.1007/978-3-319-51076-7

© The Editor(s) (if applicable) and The Author(s) 2017
Softcover reprint of the hardcover 1st edition 2017
This work is subject to copyright. All rights are solely and exclusively licensed by the Publisher, whether the whole or part of the material is concerned, specifically the rights of translation, reprinting, reuse of illustrations, recitation, broadcasting, reproduction on microfilms or in any other physical way, and transmission or information storage and retrieval, electronic adaptation, computer software, or by similar or dissimilar methodology now known or hereafter developed.
The use of general descriptive names, registered names, trademarks, service marks, etc. in this publication does not imply, even in the absence of a specific statement, that such names are exempt from the relevant protective laws and regulations and therefore free for general use.
The publisher, the authors and the editors are safe to assume that the advice and information in this book are believed to be true and accurate at the date of publication. Neither the publisher nor the authors or the editors give a warranty, express or implied, with respect to the material contained herein or for any errors or omissions that may have been made. The publisher remains neutral with regard to jurisdictional claims in published maps and institutional affiliations.

Cover illustration: Murik men's carvings at a sale for tourists.

Printed on acid-free paper

This Palgrave Macmillan imprint is published by Springer Nature
The registered company is Springer International Publishing AG
The registered company address is: Gewerbestrasse 11, 6330 Cham, Switzerland

For Diana, the huntress

Series Editor Preface

Psychological anthropologists study a wide spectrum of human activity: child development, illness and healing, ritual and religion, personality and political and economic systems, just to name a few. In fact, as a discipline that seeks to understand the interconnections between persons and culture, it would be difficult to come up with examples of human behavior that are outside the purview of psychological anthropology. Yet beneath this substantive diversity lies a common commitment. The practitioners of psychological anthropology seek to understand social activity in ways that are fitted to the mental and physical dimensions of human beings. Psychological anthropologists may focus on emotions or human biology, on language or art or dreams, but they rarely stray far from the attempt to understand the possibilities and the limitations on the ground of human persons.

Professor David Lipset describes men of the Murik Lakes region of Papua New Guinea, who find themselves caught in a sort of cultural limbo, suspended between their older ways and the wider world of a modern nation-state, a global economy and accelerating climate change. In particular, Dr. Lipset looks at the challenges of realizing masculinity in an environment in which neither precolonial culture nor modernity possesses an indisputable authority. In this cultural cacophony, men find themselves alienated not only from their social world but from their very selves. Yet—and in contrast to many studies of the march of modernity—Dr. Lipset does not depict his subjects as scrambling to adapt to a new hegemony.

In rich detail, he describes a number of social realms characterized by a multiplicity of cultural possibilities. While these possibilities leave no comfortable resting place, at the same time they provide opportunities for expression, dialogue and humanity.

Peter Stromberg

Preface

By way of introducing the topic of this book, I want to begin with a word about the meaning of its title and my relationship to it. As an American cultural and psychological anthropologist who is interested in various aspects of the relationship of tribal men to modernity, I have been doing fieldwork on this issue in Papua New Guinea (PNG) since I was a young man in the early 1980s. My research has primarily focused on men and masculinity among the Murik Lakes people, a rural society of coastal fisherfolk and traders who have been living with economic, religious and sociopolitical change since early twentieth century. Now from what I have come to gather, the *yabar* were venerated and feared as their most powerful ancestor-spirits in their precolonial Murik cosmology. Of all of the many ancestors in that archaic world, the *yabar* were attributed the greatest capacity to change the environment and persons. For example, two of them travelled widely in the coastal region, presenting people with outrigger-canoe technology, scattering mangrove propagules and leaving relics of their escapades along the coast. In Murik society even today, *yabar*-spirits use magic to make people terminally ill or just to cause a nagging cold.

Today, many Murik call white people *yabar goan* and *gnasen*, the "sons and daughters of *yabar*-spirits." I had always assumed that the extension of the term originated as a kind of a first-contact, millenarian association of Western wealth and agency with the ancestors of the kind that has been reported elsewhere in PNG and throughout the Pacific region. But upon occasion, I also heard rural Murik referring to middle-class Papua New Guineans as children of "*yabar*." During a casual conversation about the moral qualities of life in town in 2013, a senior widower offered up a rather unexceptional contrast, which nevertheless startled me for his use of the term *yabar* in noun form. Although it was late in the morning, Sailas had just gotten up, having spent the predawn hours out fishing in the bay in a little outrigger canoe his deceased wife had used. "You people," he remarked, "who live in *yabar* are all right. You are paid salaries. We have to [do subsistence] work in order to eat."

Not until that moment had I drawn the obvious inference. If PNG nationals were no less "sons and daughters of *yabar*" than expatriate whites, then *yabar* had become a vernacular term for a "modernity" that was indifferent to race or cultural background. *Yabar* had become a vision of modernity that referred to a bureaucratic market economy in which paychecks and salaries were distributed every two weeks, as well as, more generally, to a time and space in which people and the environment were subject to massive moral and technological transformations. Of course, Sailas was also criticizing life in *yabar* on ethical grounds. It was for him an immoral economy, a time and space lacking in love, nurture and support. More specifically, it was a time and space of masculine alienation where Murik men lacked the desire that might once have been felt and expressed for them.

The thesis of this book is that such ideas as "yabar" are part of a dialogue of masculine alienation from modernity which preoccupies Murik men. However, I take this notion of "dialogue of alienation" a step or two further. That is to say, not only do Murik men speak of and act in terms of their disaffection from modernity in PNG, their estrangement also extends to their own culture, which I will call their "archaic." Clearly, in Sailas' comment, *yabar* no longer denotes the ancestors at all. The term has been emptied out of all its former cosmological meaning. In this sense, "yabar" expresses not a single but a dual alienation. I want to make a stronger point, however, which is that even before its contemporary expressions of deprivation, and so on, masculinity was already an alienated subject position in and from the Murik archaic.

This argument arose from long-term fieldwork in dialogue with comparative and theoretical analyses; I must also acknowledge, however, that the concept of alienation is one in which I have a bit of personal investment. It is true that the Ashkenazi Jews from whom I descend found themselves on the margins of a Euro-American modernity to which they fled, while Murik men, like men throughout the developing world, find themselves on the edges of modernity, not because they were forced to relocate to them, but rather because the political, economic and cultural grounds of their lives shifted beneath them. As John Murray Cuddihy diagnosed in his extraordinary book *The Ordeal of Civility* (1987), Jewish intellectuals, having to conform to ambient expectations for emotion and thought that were foreign to them, answered creatively by making various kinds of social and theoretical "scenes" that kept the Gentiles at bay. But what is interesting is that–and this is the crucial point of overlap between them and the alienation of Murik men—modernizing Jewish intellectuals *were no less estranged from themselves* than they were from modernity. Thus Cuddihy observes that Jews were "caught between 'his own' whom he had left behind and the Gentile 'host culture' where he felt ill at ease and alienated" (1987: 4). Oddly perhaps, I share this sort of dual alienation with the Papua New Guinean men of the Murik Lakes who are the focus of this book. My ordeal as a man in the Diaspora and theirs in the *Yabar* are not identical of course, but I think the latter has helped me appreciate the former and *vice versa*.

When Murik men create new folk drama or debate rising sea levels, they speak of a time and space not of the self but of the other; however, following Simmel, Freud and Lacan, I view alienation, whether singular or dual, not as a position of helplessness and moping but as productive, if haltingly so. Certainly, composing this book has not been obvious or pleasant. But let me acknowledge the help and support I have received while doing the research for and writing it.

The fieldwork, which I began with my ex-wife, Kathleen Barlow, and the support of the Anthropology Department at UC San Diego, continued into the following decade with the support of the Australian Museum in Sydney, where Lissant Bolton and Jim Specht were then its primary sponsors. It went on in the early 1990s, now with the support of the Fowler Museum of Cultural Studies at UCLA, where Doron Ross supported a useful fieldtrip that became Chap. 5. I then did not return to the field until 2001, when, at the encouragement of my Minnesota colleague, Steven Gudeman, I undertook the first of seven fieldtrips, data from which informs this book. These received financial support from the Firebird Foundation of Portland Maine as well from the Anthropology Department at the University of Minnesota, specifically the Wilford Fund for Anthropological Research, the Imagine Fund in the College of Liberal Arts and from Travel Grants administered by Global Programs and Strategy Alliance.

A few incidents of fieldwork that primarily took place during 1993–2014 are scattered through this book. Practicing the Malinowskian method of long-term participant-observation, I appear in the villages, at meetings and feasts in Men's Cult Houses or breakfasting in peoples' houses. I appear standing with Murik informants in the parking lot of a hotel in the national capital as well as sitting behind a betel nut stall along a road in a provincial town. Perhaps, pulling together a coherent narrative from these events might prove somewhat interesting. But the overriding sentiment to which I want to call attention here is the generous cordiality of Papua New Guineans, fictive Murik kin, and many others in that great nation.

Too numerous to mention, I would like at least to make call attention to a few of the more important people. In Port Moresby, I regularly met with Elijah and Anna Ginau and Andrew and Anna Emang as well Stalin Jawa, Andrew's brother. Prof. Steven Winduo and the Right Honorable Sir Michael and Lady Veronica Somare were helpful. In Wewak town, the provincial capital of the East Sepik Province, I was a routine guest of the late Wanuk and Bonoai and their family among whom I spent many happy hours sitting, eating and talking beneath the shade of the Starfruit tree in their yard. There, and elsewhere in town, I also had conversations with Maia, Nelson Kaiango, Sailas, whom I mentioned above, Jacob Ginau, Makus Murakau, Tom Sauma, Wangi and Nick Matui, among others. In the sister Murik villages of Darapap and Karau, I benefitted from dialogue with Andrew Komsing, Jamero, Yaase, James Kaparo and his wife, Regina, Joshua Sivik, Wapo, John Jawa, Smith Jakai, Mata and Errol, Frankie and Tabanus Wambu, Johnny Sakara and Evelyn, Noah Pame, Reuben Wapo, the late Luke Manambot and his second wife, Tekla, the late Joe Kabong and his two wives, Paulina and Du, Simon Baik, the late Willie Koki, his wife, Samoya, and their daughter, Aggie and her two sons, among many others.

I have been a faculty member of the Anthropology Department at the University of Minnesota during the entire time I did the research for, and wrote, this book. It has been a supportive intellectual and social environment. I thank the following colleagues at Minnesota: Mischa Penn, Timothy Dunnigan, William Beeman, John Ingham, Hoon Song and Steven Gudeman.

Of my little stream of Minnesota students and former students who contributed to this project, whether or not they knew they were doing so, I want to acknowledge Katherine Boris Dernbach, Joseph Esser, Jamon Halvaksz, Bridget Henning, Steve Kensinger, Eric K. Silverman, Amir Pouyan Shiva and Jolene Stritecky-Braun.

I should also express thanks for critical input from colleagues and friends in universities in the USA, Australia and elsewhere, a few of whom have unfortunately passed away. These people are George and the late

Laura Appell, F.G. Bailey, the late Gregory Bateson, Joshua Bell, Donald Brenneis, Kathryn Creely, Douglas Dalton, Virginia Dominguez, the late Anthony Forge, the late William Goode, Ilana Gershon, Michael Goddard, Richard Handler, Dan Jorgensen, my father, the late Seymour Martin Lipset, Nancy Lutkehaus, Alex Mawyer, the late Margaret Mead, Michael Meeker, the late Robert Merton, Anthony Oliver-Smith, Paul Roscoe, the late Melford Spiro, Marilyn Strathern and the late Don Tuzin.

While the Introduction and the Afterword were written specifically for this volume, each of its ethnographic chapters first appeared as journal articles between 2004 and 2011. I thank the editors and anonymous reviewers for their support but more importantly for their criticism. And I strongly dispel any suspicion that what have now become chapters in this book are merely republications of these earlier pieces. Not only have they been thoroughly revised in terms of a new theoretical argument which each serves to illustrate, they have also been updated where relevant.

Chapter 2 draws from two articles: "Modernity Without Romance: Masculinity and Desire in Courtship Stories Told by Young Papua New Guinean Men," *American Ethnologist* 31(2): 205–224 (2004), and "Women Without Qualities: Further Courtship Stories Told by Young Papua New Guinean Men," *Ethnology* 46(2): 93–111 (2007). Chapter 3 was partly published as "Tobacco, Good and Bad: Prosaics of Marijuana in a Sepik Society," *Oceania* 76: 245–257 (2006). Chapter 4 draws from "Mobail: Moral Ambivalence and the Domestication of Mobile Telephones in Peri-Urban Papua New Guinea," *Culture, Theory and Critique* 54(3): 335–354. Chapter 5 draws from "A Melanesian Pygmalion: Masculine Creativity and Symbolic Castration in a Postcolonial Backwater," *Ethos* 37(1): 50–78. Chapter 6 draws from "'Skirts-Money-Masks,' and other Chains of Signification in Post-Colonial Papua New Guinea," in D. Lipset and P. Roscoe (eds.) *Echoes of the Tambaran: Masculinity, History and the Subject* (Canberra: ANU E Press). Chapter 7 is based on "The Tides: Masculinity and Climate Change in Coastal Papua New Guinea," *Journal of the Royal Anthropological Institute* (NS) 17: 20–43.

Contents

1 Introduction: Masculinity, Modernity, Papua New Guinea   1

Part I   Dialogics of Masculine Alienation   27

2 Desire in Young Men's Courtship Stories   29

3 Marijuana, Youth and Society   57

4 Mobile Telephony in a Peri-urban Setting   79

Part II   In the Time and Space of the Other   99

5 Folk Theater and the Signifier   101

6 Money and Other Signifiers   135

7 In the Anthropocene   165

Afterword: Men's Dual Alienation in Other Pacific Modernities   193

Bibliography   209

Index   241

List of Figures

Fig. 1.1	The Murik Lakes and the Lower Sepik River	15
Fig. 1.2	Darapap village in 1981	17
Fig. 1.3	Darapap village in 2014	17
Fig. 1.4	Mobile phone dangling in the doorway of a house where a signal is available	18
Fig. 1.5	New Male Cult House in Karau village	20
Fig. 1.6	Kreer Camp, a peri-urban Murik settlement in Wewak town	22
Fig. 3.1	Rural fish and garden produce market	58
Fig. 3.2	Cigarettes for sale in a jar alongside a card game	61
Fig. 3.3	Tobacco and marijuana flows to the Murik lakes, 2001	63
Fig. 3.4	Murik woman smoking a pipe	66
Fig. 3.5	Tobacco leaves, newspaper and other foods hanging from a mortuary cape	67
Fig. 4.1	Street scene in Wewak	80
Fig. 4.2	Jakai Smith (*left*) and Jacob Sandar	86
Fig. 4.3	Two sisters with mobile phones	93
Fig. 5.1	Yanda, "the author" of *Woyon's Mother*, sitting with the mask and headdresses of his show	103
Fig. 5.2	A senior man at his retirement, decorated in the insignia of his lineage and the Male Cult. Note the snake's head motif on the apron of his loincloth	112
Fig. 5.3	At a Washing Feast, mourners squeeze inside a spirit effigy as they cleanse themselves of death pollution	117
Fig. 5.4	*Woyon's Mother* being readied inside the Male Cult House, Darapap village	128
Fig. 5.5	*Woyon's Mother* performed in Darapap village	129

Fig. 5.6   *Woyon's Mother* performed in honor of Sir Michael
            Somare's 40 years of service to the nation   130
Fig. 5.7   *Woyon's Mother* masks hang in the Male Cult House in
            Darapap village along with props from other shows   133
Fig. 6.1   Middle-class man decorated in lineage insignia for his initiation 138
Fig. 6.2   The Fog Man canoe prow   139
Fig. 6.3   A newly initiated Gaingiin grade   141
Fig. 6.4   Bananain mask   143
Fig. 6.5   Dimbwan mask   144
Fig. 6.6   Yangoron (right) begging for food   147
Fig. 6.7   A junior grade of maskers is beaten during their initiation rite 153
Fig. 6.8   Man with lime gourd   156
Fig. 6.9   Man with glass jar, for lime powder   157
Fig. 6.10   Man steering an outboard in a fiberglass boat   160
Fig. 6.11   Young man with steering paddle   161
Fig. 6.12   The outrigger canoe, Diskum   162
Fig. 6.13   The bus, Diskum   162
Fig. 7.1   Stands of dead trees along the Murik coast   166
Fig. 7.2   Big Murik village   187

CHAPTER 1

Introduction: Masculinity, Modernity, Papua New Guinea

This book focuses on dimensions of alienation among Murik men who live in rural and peri-urban communities in a new postcolonial state, Papua New Guinea (PNG). By "alienation of men," I refer to aspects of ungratified desire that are implicit and explicit in how they size up and act in characteristic circumstances in which they live. Analyses of several contexts reveal alienation not only in and from modernity in PNG but also in and from what I shall call "archaic" Murik culture. Moreover, I argue that dialogue between these two alienations is audible. Before introducing Murik society and PNG, I must start this introduction by enlarging on the four cardinal terms of my project: masculinity, modernity, alienation and dialogue.

MASCULINITIES

A major theoretical view of gender, to which I subscribe, holds that difference consists of a set of culturally constructed ideologies, statuses and practices as well as a biological form of embodiment (Mead 1963; Foucault 1978; Strathern 1988; Ortner 1996; Butler 2006). My interest here lies in the former, particularly because along the peripheries of modernity, where this ethnography is set, masculine subject-positions take composite and unpredictable forms that are not reducible to any physical attribute, much less to a single modern value. While acknowledging her great contribution to masculinity studies, I must therefore take exception to R.W. Connell's well-known "hegemonic models" framework. Connell recognized that

© The Author(s) 2017
D. Lipset, *Yabar*, Culture, Mind, and Society,
DOI 10.1007/978-3-319-51076-7_1

masculine discourse and practices—old and new, local and metropolitan, dominant and subordinate, unofficial and authorized, centripetal and centrifugal—may be plural on the global margins of modernity. But at the same time, she has tended to insist that power and esteem adhere to elites, e.g., to businessmen, politicians, soldiers, and celebrities, who possess "hegemonic masculinity" (Carrigan et al. 1985). For Connell, the "world gender order" is a system of power that such men embody and deploy (2005: 72, 1987, 1990, 1993, 2014). In other words, masculinity is an object of global discourse, but not a subject of its own signification. In an era of terrorism and fundamentalisms, such a position sounds less and less persuasive, much less comprehensive.

Theoretically, the anthropology of masculinities has adopted more of a bottom-up, contextualist perspective. Inequality, although obviously important in Latin America and elsewhere (Gutmann 2003), does not exhaust what it means to be a man. Masculinity is not only about dominance and subordination, it is rather historically dynamic and complicated. The diversity of masculinity in Japanese state-capitalism comes to mind (Roberson and Suzuki 2002). The varieties of machismo among working-class Mexican men, varieties that relate to other divisions in everyday life, would be another example (Gutmann 1996). Indigenous forms of gender identity and prestige coexist in differing ways with modernity but without being erased by the power of and models from the West. Heald (1999) traced the ambivalence with which Gisu people of Uganda judge male violence to moral contradictions in the culture. And Hodgson (2001) referred the stigma assigned to men who would abandon warrior, pastoral identities in favor of becoming modern to a local category. Normative roles and capacities of men thus become more complicated than perhaps Connell understood them. They may be and are crosscut, or "dislocated" by other forms of inequality, such as class and generation, and may even be adopted and enacted by both sexes (Cornwall and Lindisfarne 1994:3). As such, the anthropology of postcolonial masculinities has had the goal of collating comparative and/or regionally based ethnography whose case studies stick to analyses of closely observed events, emotions and practices.[1]

MODERNITIES

I take a similar approach to the ethnography of modernity, or more specifically of postcolonial modernities (Miller 1997).[2] I see them as historically situated and saturated in local values, perspectives and practices which do not necessarily originate in capitalism or the Enlightenment, much less the Global North. Modernity, in other words, is parochial, diverse and shifting as well as universalizing. But simultaneously, I acknowledge that local values, perspectives and practices inevitably encounter a subject position that is informed by several modernist orientations that I would briefly characterize as follows (Hallowell 1955).

Exceptionalism pervades the modern subject. The modern subject has a sense of being unprecedented; it possesses extraordinary moral agency in time and space. That is, the past is assumed to be illegitimate while "all ... normativity" of the present must be recreated from the "authority" of reason (Habermas 2001: 132–3). The institution that epitomizes modern exceptionalism, and the modern subject, is the sovereign state which monopolizes the distribution of universal rights to its citizenry on a bureaucratic rather than a social basis. In an oddly related vein, the modern subject is itself a kind of sovereign state, in that it also assumes that its desire is to be independent of the social. As such, it is self-aware, or reflexive. It is able to compose a self-narrative in response to its own questions about how to act, distinguish right from wrong and so forth. Not least, perhaps the key value of modern identity, objects and space is their alienability as capital rather than as fetishes or personified things. If a theme in all these elements of the modern subject is separation from moral community, from time and from space, perhaps it should not be surprising to view the definitive quality of that subject as an alienated ethos of uncertainty, loss of moral agency and estrangement.

Alienation

Accounts of alienation in early modern social theory not only took differing views of its characteristic qualities and causes; they evaluated it differently. Being critical of modernity, Karl Marx, Max Weber and Emile Durkheim, of course, condemned alienation as a symptom of the moral damage modern society and economy were doing to community and subject. For Marx, capital disempowered both the proletariat and the bourgeoisie from moral identity, their "species-being" (1990: 708, 1963: 191; see also Kim 2003). For Durkheim, the loss of collective forms of solidarity deprived people of legitimate means to achieve legitimate ends and made them prey to their worst inclinations (1995; Horton 1964). For Weber, formal rationality eventually left men imprisoned in the meaningless pursuit of empty material and instrument purposes, emptied, that is to say, of sacred value (Weber 1958b).

Perhaps Simmel appreciated the Janus-faced qualities of modern alienation most clearly. For him, modern society made man aware of his moral distance from the other but it also brought about or constituted an inner boundary that made an autonomous self possible. However the "unavoidable corollary" of a subjective sense of freedom (Simmel 1950: 338) was a sense of "homelessness" (Berger et al. 1973: 82). In other words, for Simmel, the subject position of modern man was estranged but generative.

For reasons that should quickly become evident, I shall now shift from these preliminary notes on alienation in early modern social theory to a psychoanalytic view of alienation in the work of Jacques Lacan, the well-known French neo-Freudian. For Lacan, alienation is not distinctive of modernity. Rather, alienation constitutes the subject in all societies whatever their relationship to capital and the state might be (Morris-Reich 2005). Paradoxically, he sees the subject as deprived of desire in return for the capacity to symbolically express and fulfill itself. All persons living in the world of language and sociopolitical order, the world of signification, must implicitly "endure" a kind of moral void at the center of their being.

In this cultural world, which Lacan calls "the Symbolic," signifiers stand for themselves as well as for what he calls an archaic, prediscursive "lack." This absence refers to the loss of the desire of the other, the other being nothing less than "the locus in which is situated the chain of the signifier that governs whatever may be made of the subject—it is the field of that living being in which the subject has to appear" (Lacan 1977b: 205). The features of this lack are of course difficult to imagine since they don't exist. However at the very least they imply an amoral isolation, a kind of collective and individual emptiness in the center of subject and collective order. Thus the predicament of the Lacanian concept of identity is that to the extent persons try to find fulfillment and satisfaction in other subjects and objects in society, they recreate rather than overcome the fundamental condition that has constituted their pursuit: the loss of the desire of the other.

Except for Simmel, social theorists envisioned nineteenth- and twentieth-century modernity as an era of great wounds in which the autonomous subject was diminished by a loss of legitimate agency. Now, the Lacanian view of alienation offers two interrelated insights into this problematic. The first is that alienation is both generative as well as debilitating, and this quality is represented by a masculine trope. Lacan associated acts of signification, which is to say, communication, with a strikingly human image—a phallus, a phallus which is *not* to be confused with the organ. The Lacanian phallus is rather a signifier of presence as well as absence. It signifies "dependence with respect to the desire of the Other" (Lacan 1977a: 17).

Its irretrievable dispossession from desire and its absent center associate the phallus with the loss of pleasure. But the register in which Lacan casts its alienation is equivocal rather than single-toned. The phallus is signified in people and things that represent both presence and absence at once. The phallus is an emptiness that appears as a force in society, thus to divide, or subtract, women from men by virtue of its illusions. Its modality is one of combination, mixture and incongruity that consists of rupture and continuity, melancholy and optimism. "The phallic signifier," as Žižek phrased this contradictory quality, "is ... an index of its own impossibility. In its very positivity, it is the signifier of 'castration'—that is, of its own lack… In the phallus, loss as such attains a positive existence" (1989: 157).

In my view, as a symbol of desire, gender and moral ambiguity, the Lacanian phallus offers a useful template for a reconsideration of the alienation of masculinity in PNG.[3] However, amid postcolonial modernity, everything—every signifier of legitimacy and agency—is multiplied. That is to say, moral order is plural. Instead of a single Symbolic, multiple languages, names, cosmologies, laws, medical systems, currencies and so forth coexist, sometimes in competition with each other, as rival signs of order, and at other times in combination with each other. So instead of one Symbolic into which the phallus is exiled, I am suggesting that there may be two, both of which take their cut from the "very life" of the subject, thus to "bind him to the signifier" (Lacan 1977a: 28). Together, the two Symbolics—the archaic one and that of postcolonial modernity—give rise to unpredictable, complicated chains of masculine signification. In PNG, and this is the point that makes PNG both fascinating and analytically challenging, the former has not been eliminated or completely transformed by the latter. However inaccessible they may be elsewhere in the Pacific, modern PNG is full of archaic signifiers that continue to be both productive and empty.

Dialogism

If the Lacanian phallus suggests directions for an analysis of masculine alienation in PNG, I find the concept of "dialogue" in the work of the Russian literary critic and semiotician, Mikhail Bakhtin, useful for thinking about relationships between its archaic and modern forms (1984a). In his view, the voice is indivisibly social, or dialogical. The voice in dialogue is made up of a shifting relationship between official, or centripetal, voices and unofficial, or centrifugal, ones. In particular, Bakhtin focused on dialogue in which non-state modes of expression challenged the power and values of authority, and were distinctively egalitarian. Though voices on the margins might be politically subordinate to official institutions in their various guises, Bakhtin insisted that they retained their own autonomous character as "unmerged" (1984a: 6). Implicit in his concept of dialogue is a notion of discourse and agency, or discursive agency, in society that emphasizes the extent to which voices contest each other in inconclusive, or what he called "unfinalized," ways (1984a: 32). Comedy, carnivalesque parody, puns and metaphor typify the egalitarian and unfixed register of the dialogical voice. Suffice it to say, it is not single-toned but composite.

For my purposes, it is impossible to overstate the point that the Bakhtinian notion of dialogue is not literal. That is to say, it is not limited to actual voices. Dialogue does or does not require speech, the utterances of actual, living persons. It is not just made up of voices talking back and forth. Voices in and of themselves, he argues, are saturated with the words of others, whether or not dialogue is actually taking place. Dialogism therefore refers both to present and absent interlocutors. It refers not only to how language may be used socially but also to how metaphor, style, intonation and so forth may themselves be understood as "answers," typically between opposing regimes of authority, that struggle with and against each other to compose a fluid discursive field. In parody, for example, the voice stylization of the other is incorporated for the purposes of ridicule. In "hidden polemic," the object of derision is implied but unacknowledged. In the novels of Dostoevsky, characters are "full of other people's words" (Bakhtin 1984a: 201). The medieval carnivalesque voice fascinated the exiled Bakhtin the most (Bakhtin 1984b). This was the voice that answered the dogmas of the state and the church in comic registers that were, in his view, open ended and transgressive, but together with the legitimate institutions they defied, constituted a coordinate, yet contrary, dialogue. And this pretty well synthesizes how I view the alienation of modernity and the archaic in PNG.

Masculine Alienation in Papua New Guinea

Having suggested a general view of men's dual alienation in which dialogue takes place between modern and archaic voices, a brief overview of some important expressions of that dual alienation is next in order. Prior to such an overview, I should mention that the pace (and quality) of contributions to the literature on modernity in PNG has held steady since the late 1980s.[4] However, at the same time, while men have been featured, as if hidden in plain sight, masculine alienation has not been a center of analysis (with one magnificent exception, see Tuzin 1997).[5]

Under the democratic rule of an ineffective Westminster-style government, PNG is a *rentier* state (Barma 2014), or perhaps one could call it an alienated state. The economy largely depends on Asian and Western extraction industries exploiting enormous tracts of old growth forest and huge deposits of minerals and natural gas. The state is enclaved: each of its 22 provinces has a municipal center and perhaps one or two other administrative outposts that vary in size. But less than 15% of the country lives in cities and towns, and a significant proportion of the urban population are migrant villagers who inhabit squatter settlements, where they do not own the land on which they live, and whose employment status is often uncertain. Jobs in town, as I indicate in Chap. 4, are few and far between. There is an urban middle class, to be sure; but no less than in the villages, solidarity among elites, peri-urbanites and rural kin remains "mechanical" in the Durkheimian sense of being based in egalitarian resemblance rather than difference. However, today this kind of unity has become tinged with estrangement. Semi-autonomous, kinship-based obligations and relationships continue to rule the day ethically. Indeed, even the state is decidedly regional in makeup, comprised as it is of autonomous tribal economies led by local-level authorities of one sort or another who own the means of production, for example, lineage land. National elections, held since 1975, thus take an intensely parochial cast, and political coalitions conventionally distribute ministerial positions so as to reflect this kind of regionalism and have repeatedly found their hold on the reigns of power vulnerable to successful no-confidence motions (Lipset 1989).

During the first 40 years of independence, regional isolation was also sustained by lack of infrastructure. Radio and travel were the main media linking urban and rural communities. Infrastructure was absent, deficient and/or deteriorating. Roads were either nonexistent, poorly maintained, or opportunities for crime, but travel, via air, boat and various kinds of automobile, was nonetheless possible. One more, albeit clichéd, datum about communication is perhaps a significant symptom of national alienation: PNG is known for extreme linguistic diversity (over 800 vernaculars) that is cross-cut by two market languages, *Tokpisin* and Motu, as well as by English. That is to say, PNG is a deeply polyglot modernity that was and remains nothing if not exceedingly fragmented.

Perhaps another indication of the recalcitrance of tribal constituencies from the modern state is how narrow civil society is in PNG. The existence of a separate, extra-state system of practices and values associated with public virtue and voluntary forms of trust is limited and is only starting to emerge. Although there is indeed a growing NGO culture, the "Melanesian street," as public space, is perceived as dangerous to pickpockets, holdups or drunk young men. Still, urban folk market, meet and talk to kin and "mates" on sidewalks, ride buses and so forth. However, the preference of urban elites to remote villagers is to conduct as much of day-to-day life among kin, or among kin-like relations, where moral accountability is predictable, if not altogether reliable.

A few general remarks about the contradictory nature of men's interests and values amid this state of alienation. At all ranks in society, modernity offers them and they take advantage of opportunities. Men in PNG are deeply engaged in national politics and government. They read and listen to the news. While they criticize the misdeeds and corruption of politicians, middle-class men stand in huge numbers for election. In the cities, young men seek employment in the ubiquitous private security companies (Lusby 2014). Elsewhere in the country, they work in various capacities for the extraction industries, principally, mining, oil and industrial logging.[6]

Simultaneously, in the rural villages, men work in small-holder agriculture, cash cropping foods and commodities (Allen et al. 2005).[7] Rural men are also entrepreneurial. They start small businesses and seek a variety of other modes of development (Sharp 2016), as well as conservation projects (West 2006) and informal opportunities to make money with and/ or from kin and other community members (McCormack and Barclay 2013; Bourke and Harwood 2009; Sharp et al. 2015). Rural men go to town for various reasons, to access healthcare, prepare for a funeral, enroll children in school or receive government pension checks. And when they do, they stay with kin (Tokpisin: *wantoks*) in squatters' camps during visits of temporary or longer duration (Koczberski and Curry 2004; Numbasa and Koczberski 2012). Men also stand for and hold local-level offices in their communities and worship in various denominations of missionary Christianity they themselves have come to lead (Robbins 2004). From Christianity, they also adopt new ideas of personal responsibility and moral obligation that emphasize gender equity (Cox and Macintyre 2014), the mutuality of companionate marriage (Wardlow 2006: 73) as well as new ways of raising children (Silverman 2016: 198–199).

At the same time they are duped by the fantasy of suddenly attaining modern prosperity through fast money schemes. John Cox reported a Ponzi scam called U-Vistract that promised 100% monthly returns and drew "as many as 200,000 investors" in the national capital and elsewhere in PNG in 1999 (2013: 176; see also Cox and Macintyre 2014: 141). Elite politicians, high-level public servants, leaders of Pentecostal churches, pastors and other "big shots" as well as the lower classes, men who were otherwise the objects of criticism as financially irresponsible, wasteful and careless with money, spending wages on beer and male sociality, sought to forego their irresponsible masculine natures by investing in fast money schemes that not only claimed to reward male virtue but also as a kind of moral proxy for the postcolonial state that would provide people the tangible benefits—roads, schools, business skills—that it was failing to do.[8]

While modernity in PNG has certainly offered men many opportunities, there can be little doubt that for many, it is very much a time and space of the other (Luker and Dinnen 2010; Zimmer-Tamakoshi 2012).[9] In addition to "nostalgia ... deep enough to serve as an emotional touchstone for a distinction between *kastam* and modernity" (LiPuma 1999: 201), violence, both in practice and as an attitude, is a prominent feature of their gender (Wardlow 2006; Dinnen and Ley 2000; Jolly 2012). Seeing it as resonating with the globalized culture of hypermasculine, working-class men, Martha Macintyre (2008) traced the prevalence of violence back to rural norms in which men were forceful, wealthy and dominant. In a context of increasing mobility, and the contemporary weaknesses of the postcolonial state in PNG, she observed that male youth, armed with weapons, worked in uniform as "security" guards. At the same time, other youth were adopting dress and comportment that included dreadlocks, rowdiness, drinking, combativeness, mock fights, risk-taking and so forth. Police, moreover, were difficult to distinguish from the latter youth. Both possessed identical levels of education, sense of style and aggressive temper.

Male violence in PNG evokes the Lacanian signifier, women being its inevitable target. Young women reported attacks both in towns and villages. Sexual assaults, gang rapes (Tokpisin: *lainap*), with the consequence of accelerating rates of HIV+ infection, were associated with the increased movement of men, the so-called MMMs, or mobile men with money, roaming about cities and the country (Lepani 2008). Bridewealth, now paid in money and used to legitimize a husband's authority and entitlement to a wife's labor, sexuality and obedience, had been dehumanized. Now the idea was that marital obligation was merely a property right.

A man "owned" his wife, having "purchased" her. Violence was a legitimate punishment should a woman fail to live up to conjugal duties. "By far, the commonest 'mistake' ... found ... in Chimbu was for a wife to refuse her husband sex" (Eves 2010: 57). Or, to put it more generally, violence had become a male "objection ... to any exercise of agency" on the part of wives (Eves 2010: 58). With apologies to Lacan, but in Hagen, violence was at once a tropic and physical answer to the phallus.

Criminal gangs of urban youth (Tokpisin: *raskol*) imperiled the postcolonial scene in the 1990s. Writing in 2010, Luker and Monsell-Davis were of the opinion that *raskols* "remain[ed] ... the symbol of PNG's 'law and order' problems" (2010: 81). What was the nature of their alienation from the archaic and modernity? Were they comparable to Sicilian bandits (Hobsbawm 1969)? Were they an undereducated *lumpenproletariate* driven by outrage against corrupt politicians, greedy businessmen and disrespectful missionaries (Morauta 1987; Hart Nibbrig 1992; Kulick 1993)? Or, were they neo-*bigmen*, seeking to create power and maintain loyalties through strategic acts of generosity, à la Melanesian leaders of yore (Harris 1988; Dinnen 1995, 2001)? Did *raskol* gangs parallel archaic forms of social organization, replacing the shifting alliances of Highlands clanship? Were they urban warriors, reinstituting the misogyny of male cults (Luker and Monsell-Davis 2010: 87–88)? Were they just lost souls, educated but unemployed, deadened by the detribalized, moral chaos left by face-to-face societies in decline? Or, were they just burglars, muggers and rapists, that is, small-time crooks and street corner thugs? What was their dialogue with pre-state, Melanesian institutions and modernity in PNG?

Unemployment, Michael Goddard argued, did not cause *raskolism*, but rather *raskolism* caused unemployment (2001: 21). Rather than a single-toned rejection of the state, the culture of *raskolism* resulted from "an integration of pre-capitalist ... behavior into a cash-economic environment" (Goddard 1992: 20, see also Goddard 1995: 73). That is, *raskol* leadership was not estranged from urban communities. Stolen money or goods were used for instant gratification or in ostentatious celebrations. "The most common way to spend money" in 1991 was "to buy huge supplies of beer which [were] ... consumed immediately and orgiastically" (Goddard 1992: 29). Money was not saved but shared. Wealth obtained through crime was consumed in binges (see also Dinnen 2001). "The dispersal of gains ... [was] a process which involves ... a ... Melanesian pattern of distribution and consumption" (Goddard 1992: 29) in return for which leaders received loyalty and support, or at least acquiescence, particularly in relation to police investigations. As their redistributive activities resembled those seen in rural contexts, Goddard dubbed *raskol* leaders "big men of crime" (1995: 65, see also Schiltz 1985: 158). In other words, signifiers of *raskol* masculinity expressed alienation from modernity in PNG in an archaic register.

But rural men were no less alienated from the archaic signifier.[10] In the Southern Highlands, for example, Wiru men feared that they were literally "shrinking in size" (Clark 1989: 120). The state, missionary Christianity and development projects had led to the cessation of ceremonial exchange as well as their Male Cult. And the Wiru verb associated with "shrinking ... is used in reference to the cordyline plant, the white growing tip of which has the same name as the penis" (Clark 1989: 136–7). Cordyline plants, so their ethnographer explained, honor "male achievements and ... are boundary markers" (Clark 1989: 137).

Among the nearby Duna, the masculine signifier was no less flagging. The traditional separation of young men from women in bachelor huts and domestic houses had been abandoned. Fathers had lost control of sons. Courting songs about virility and power that men used to sing to immobilize women with desire had given way to laments about unfaithful girls. "The 'woe-is-me' and the 'one that got away' theme appears over and over again" (Haley 2008: 225). Duna men had come to see themselves as having nothing to offer. The young men of the bachelor cult, the "beautiful shining men of the pre-colonial period," were now in hiding from modernity in PNG. Taking up "guns, marijuana, discos, pornographic movies and violence" (Haley 2008: 226), their anomie, that is, their loss of, or fall from, archaic agency, answered a no less empty postcolonial state whose promises of development had failed to materialize, whose schools had shut down and whose healthcare services had ended.

I see this kind of dual alienation exemplified in the sad case of Urapmin men (Robbins 1998, 2004, 2005). In their archaic Symbolic, these remote West Sepik horticulturalists held that persons balanced willfulness with concern for the needs of the other; and the good apparently combined with the bad to reproduce moral community. Oddly, however, the willfulness of Urapmin men did not extend to marriage. Leaders might assert their interests in the community, but in matrimonial matters, men faced a taboo and, like the Lacanian signifier, had to depend upon the desire of the other. After adopting Baptist Christianity in the late 1970s, they abandoned traditional prohibitions, thus entering into what they call "free time" (Robbins 2004: 220). Although they substituted a general notion of

"God's will" that enjoined them to look after one another, Christianity left them alienated from modernity; it made "sinners of all Urapmin" (Robbins 1998: 310). As a replacement for reconciliation rites, a new form of possession-dancing they called "spirit-discos" was invented. These celebrations would go on until dancers, no longer possessed by the Holy Spirit, crumpled to the floor. On the one hand, Robbins saw in this outcome "a paradigmatic image of the person beyond desire and … sinful willfulness." But on the other, he added an intriguing observation. "Both the physical ecstasy" of the dance and the "collapse of the possessed look … sexual." If so, was this a Lacanian image of the loss of the desire of the other rather than its fulfillment? Was it rather an image of being "stripped" of "potency and equivalence" by life on the margins of the global world (Robbins 1998: 311–13)? One could hardly ask for a more poignant example of Lacanian alienation in dialogue with modernity and the archaic.

But I want to insist that the invention of political involvement, employment of various kinds, local-level leadership, fathering, even *raskol* feasting as well as "spirit-discos" are generative answers to the archaic and to modernity (Hermann et al. 2014; Rollason 2014). Let me cite a last example of this Janus-faced kind of alienation among rural men. In the Western Province, Gogodala men competed in canoe races and rugby league matches. Being a deltaic "canoe people" who held a canoe-based worldview, the canoe was a metaphor of masculine embodiment and agency that answered moral challenges posed by both Gogodala society and modernity.

Having decorated their boats with emblems of ancestors and the land, rowers observed taboos to make them strong, taboos that separated them from the desire of young women. Senior men also bespelled them. Then, upon "the completion of a … race, the decorated paddlers and supporters move in a clan huddle … to the football field, singing canoe songs and carrying powerful clan paraphernalia as they prepare for rugby league matches later in the day" (Wilde 2004a: 287). Rugby was no less enhanced by magical spells and the athletes went on observing sexual taboos and other moral injunctions that were meant to serve or preserve the collective agency of the team. At the league final, the opposing rugby teams gathered at the Gogodala Council Chambers and from there walked to the pitch singing canoe victory songs and in the case of one team which caught the attention of Charles Wilde, their ethnographer, they stroked paddles as if racing in a canoe (2004a: 295). In other words, sports were not a tepid post-contact substitute for warfare à la Kwakiutl *potlatch* (Codere 1950) but had rather come to have a double-voiced meaning for men. They asserted the agency of their archaic signifier, that is, its autonomy from the desire of the other, in response to the modern context. There is one Lacanian detail to add: the signal to start a canoe race is *Sawiya*, *Sawiya* being the name of "the mother" of all Gogodala people (Wilde 2004a). That is, Gogodala canoes remained a signifier, not of masculine alienation in a tragic register of isolation, estrangement and violence but of masculine alienation in the contradictory register of the Lacanian signifier.

Modernity in PNG has also begun to bring about an awkward dialogue between haves and have-nots (Gewertz and Errington 1999). Urban and rural elites referred to, somewhat equivocally, as *bigshots* in Tokpisin (rather than *bigmen*) by village kin, both seek to detach themselves from local-level duties and disregard petitions at the same time as they try to fulfill ritual obligations. On Lihir Island, using royalty payments from a big gold mine, hereditary landowners pour money into purchases of pigs and store-bought goods they used to obtain through affinal exchange networks. They have even begun to stage *premortem* funerals which celebrate the prestige of their (ongoing) lives rather than the passage of their souls to the afterlife (Bainton and Macintyre 2016). Of course, less fortunate rivals complain that such ritual innovations are bogus. In a similar argument taking place in New Britain, well-to-do Tolai men, who live in the national capital, prefer to see themselves as men who do not owe anything to backward village relatives. They thus buy nonclan land, hire nonkin and hope to retire in Australia. But, like Lihir men, they still insist upon hosting mortuary rites replete with *tubuan* mask-spirits and the ceremonial exchange of (purchased) shell valuables. Doing so, they subject themselves to criticism in terms of the very values they would disavow. Accused of commercializing custom, villagers distrust and scorn them for being greedy and disrespecting reciprocity, and its alternating equivalencies (Martin 2013). The substitution of commodities has effected masculinity as well. It has reduced the value of women's labor (in raising pigs and gardening) from the process of ritual performance, thus making men seem less dependent on them and on society, more generally.

This is my point about the alienation of masculinity: it is incongruous. Men's voices and practices are not reducible to a common, hegemonic denominator of superior status/power/knowledge. In their dialogue with the empty signifiers of modernity in PNG, they answer in the voice of an archaic but no less empty signifier. And in their dialogue with the archaic, they answer in the empty signifiers of modernity. What do they say? Their answer is contradictory.

Masculine Alienation Among the Murik

As a whole, this book may be viewed as a case study of men's dual alienation from, and in dialogue with, modernity and their particular archaic, whose theoretical and regional features I began to work out above. Specifically, it focuses on the men of the Murik Lakes in PNG, more or less during a 25-year period ending in 2014. Let me therefore sketch out some features of the setting in which these men (and women) lived during this time and in so doing explain what they illustrate so clearly.

The Murik Lakes are part of the coastal estuary of the Sepik River (Fig. 1.1). The five Murik villages are built along a large ecosystem of interconnected mangrove lagoons that are separated from the Pacific by narrow barrier beaches that have been eroded by rising sea levels since 2007 (see Chap. 7). By contrast to the rich variety and quantity of marine fish and shellfish that make their nursery in its vast, becalmed habitat, and again, by contrast to its extensive mangrove cover, what is distinctive of this environment is a material lack, which is a lack of arable land. The environment has given rise to a cultural adaptation: reproduction of the moral community constantly involves Murik men and women in intertribal exchange that is supplemented by the market. Travel in boats—dugout canoes and small fiberglass boats—therefore constitutes a significant dimension of the means of production and communication in the society.

The Murik fish and exploit their vast commons with its complicated system of marine tenure (Lipset 2014a). But modernity has made their rich resource into a kind of poverty. For reasons I shall explain, their fishery is small-scale. And its relations of production remain based in a sexual division of labor and the domestic group. Men fish with drift nets and spear guns while women fish with drop lines and gather shellfish by hand. Their main resource, the Murik Lakes, remains a rich commons. However, they have lost access to their main market located in Wewak, the provincial capital about 40 miles up the coast to the west. First, their large, 50–65-foot outrigger canoes were replaced by small fiberglass, 19–23-foot boats, which cut space for passengers more or less in half. Second, gasoline costs forced boat owners to increase fares to town to such an extent that travel to market has become too expensive for most villagers. Murik fishwives, whose smoked fish and fresh shellfish used to fill stall after stall in the fish section of the provincial market of the 1980s, today man just a few tables at the end of a long row that is now dominated by riverine fish. As a result, the first years of the twenty-first century witnessed the revival of biweekly,

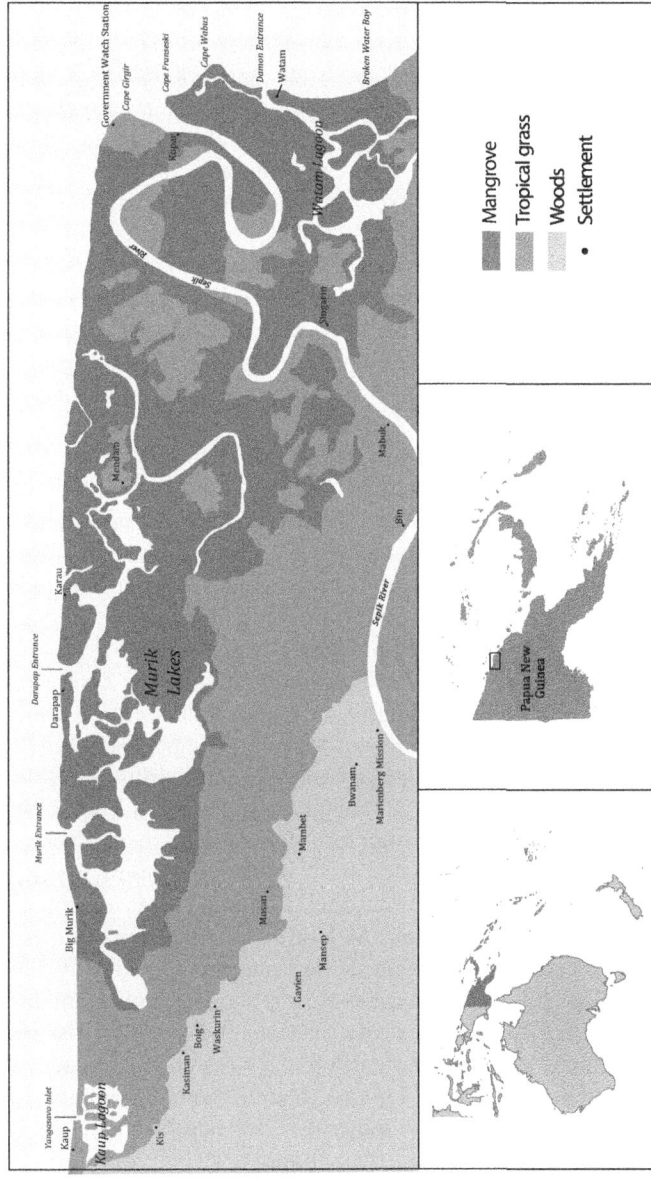

Fig. 1.1 The Murik Lakes and the Lower Sepik River

regional markets with their inland trading partners that begin as cash markets and end in barter.

Formerly, the Murik bartered for the garden produce and sago flour they lack through an intertribal exchange network inland and upriver (see Chap. 3). In addition to foodstuffs, Murik men achieved renown along the coast and among the offshore islanders as middlemen and impresarios who exported Sepik foods, shell and teeth valuables, as well as folk theater (see Chap. 5). As money and market integration increased during the twentieth century, Murik men and goods were largely dispossessed of value.

There is a sandbar in the lakes called "Valuables Ground" (*mwara'ajiin*) where women gather cowrie shells (*mungatek*) that are used to decorate ornaments that are either worn in rarely celebrated rites of passage or sold to upriver trading partners. Today, of course, this kind of value is mediated by the state rather than produced autonomously in the locality. Money and commodities cost men their advantage in intertribal barter relations. With the availability of tinned fish, the demand for and value of Murik fish declined. Meanwhile, demand for sago flour and vegetables produced by inland trading partners persisted unabated. Murik seafood and crafts, woven Murik baskets, shell ornaments and carvings still find their way to regional trading partners as gifts. But the pace of overseas trade, and the renown it afforded Murik men, has slowed and contracted in scale (see Tiesler 1969/70, see also Munn 1986).

As rural society became increasingly integrated in the cash economy, fish began to be sold to kin in neighboring households. At the same time, exchange remained embedded in an archaic, precapitalist ethos, whose spirit of generosity and hospitality to junior kin and visiting trading partners remained modeled upon a "maternal schema" (Lipset 1997: 3). Today, however, Murik men cannot and do not view themselves as great and good mothers but as alienated from modern economy which forces them to work rather harder than did their forefathers just to subsist much less to save anything in the bank. As I say, what their environment possesses, namely, seafood, or protein, is no longer as prized as it once was before it could be purchased in cans. Now what their environment lacks, as they themselves observe, is exactly that which is plentiful elsewhere in the region, namely, land, land to garden and raise coffee, cocoa or other cash crops, land to raise cattle, land to clearcut timber from and land to make money from. Today, although empty rice bags litter the Murik villages, they suggest scarcity rather than abundance.

Fig. 1.2 Darapap village in 1981. Photo: David Lipset

Fig. 1.3 Darapap village in 2014. Photo: David Lipset

In addition to economic decline, the material condition of rural communities presents a similar picture of stagnation. Outwardly, Murik villages in 2014 looked much the same as they did in 1981, when I first saw them (Figs. 1.2 and 1.3). Murik people continue to live in the kind of buildings their ancestors used to construct. Men still build pile-and-thatch houses from "bush" materials. Groups of young men go out in the little, motorized boats mentioned above and collect the leaves of wild sago palms for wall and roof thatch from shallow canals or cut the hardest mangrove wood for the frame. Wooden dugout canoes are everywhere. When dilapidated, some are used as planters, or they are overturned and become benches or are chopped up, and their sidings serve as bridge planks set on top of scaffolds over the lake tides that have begun to inundate the villages at higher levels than in the 1980s and 1990s. There is still no running water, and rainwater is still collected in rusting 44 gallon drums, old canoes, aluminum water tanks or from a handful of freshwater springs that are dispersed at varying distances from the villages throughout the lakes.

Lacking development projects, evidence of modern opportunity is visible in the white fiberglass boats, new outboard motors hanging up beneath houses, the Catholic and Seventh Day Adventist churches and the government schools. A few villagers have begun to make use of solar panels to power radios, over which they keep up with the news. One has also started to hear the muffled rumble of generators at night powering up DVD players. But the overall picture, as I say, could hardly be characterized as one of progress. While there are mobile phones aplenty, no signal reaches the Murik Lakes except in a few serendipitous spots, at certain times of the day, where and when a weak, unreliable signal may be received on a handset (Fig. 1.4).

Fig. 1.4 Mobile phone dangling in the doorway of a house where a signal is available. Photo: David Lipset (2014)

Village society consists of ubiquitous kinship. Broadly speaking, it offers no anonymity. Some people even claim that everybody's footprints are unique and recognizably so. Model Murik communities are divided up into named hamlets made up of a cluster of households, which domicile extended families related through siblingship. Largely in the aftermath of storms, however, this kind of order has given way to more random settlements in three of the five villages–and property disputes. Households are also related to named, cognatic lineages whose dispersed members live elsewhere in the Murik Lakes as well as in non-Murik communities, such as Kopar on the Sepik River and Kayan in the Lower Ramu. These descent groups, which are led by senior, firstborn men and women, are differentiated by named heirlooms, the most notable of which is a woven basket that is decorated by a distinctive tartan. They occasionally assemble for mortuary rites and such. Lineage membership used to be associated with incest prohibitions but today youth marry without concern or regard for common descent or the concerns of elders. Bridewealth was not exchanged in the past. Nor is it today. Sister-exchange is also little more than a cultural memory (see Chap. 2). Affinal avoidances do remain carefully observed, I should add. They involve name taboos and keeping spatial distances, particularly from cross-sex in-laws. All of which is to say this: in daily life men's voices are immersed in their domestic statuses. Houses they build for their families and canoes they carve for their wives, daughters and sisters.

In most Murik communities, the Male Cult, a matrilateral dual organization, does preserve its single-sex sanctum. In its pile-and-thatch buildings decorated with short, overhanging roof gables, men still gather informally on the weekend or hold occasional meetings. But men do not play bamboo flute-spirits there anymore. And today, only two of them still house the spear spirits, the Kakar, which women must avoid at all costs. However, the power and frequency of ritual activity in the Murik Male Cult has been curtailed. Rarely do moieties compete for cultic authority. Rarely are young men initiated. And no longer does the Cult bestow the privilege of marrying upon them or send youth off to fight either for ritual purposes or to defend the community. However, new Men's Houses are still constructed by rival moieties and when men assemble, they do seat themselves according to their cultic rank (Fig. 1.5).

The Male Cult has two institutional allies that reflect its contemporary emasculation. One is the patrilateral Female Cult which is in much stronger shape in the sense that the rate at which it goes on initiating girls and

Fig. 1.5 New Male Cult House in Karau village. Photo: David Lipset (2012)

women is certainly much more frequent than the Male Cult.[11] The other is the "Gaingiin Society," the public masquerade made up of seven initiatory age-classes that once provided a training ground for the Male Cult (see Chap. 6). The full range of its age-class system remains active only in one of five villages. Until 2007 or so, when rising sea levels made the ground simply too slippery there, the most junior grade of spirit-maskers donned costumes and sprinted about the plazas, avenues and walking paths of that village as they pleased, chasing and threatening to spear anyone junior to themselves with great impunity. In 2014, these maskers had vanished, although senior grades continued to taboo harvesting coconuts for one reason or another usually having to do with preparations for mortuary rites.

If modernity has shrunk the regional and ritual status of Murik men, they do go on being active in local-level governance, which is conducted by democratically elected councilors and magistrates. Monday morning meetings used to be held under the village councilor's auspices for the purposes of organizing community work projects, on the government school buildings or church maintenance. Today, these are irregular. Although village courts are not convened, moots are assembled wherein parties and onlookers gather in public space otherwise used for regular village-wide meetings or in a house. In addition, every few years, on secondment from the district seat or the provincial capital, police make an appearance in the villages, in response to one kind of crime or another, and either drag an individual or a handful of people off to face a regional court, or else they engage in some other dramatic, sometimes rather brutal, show of force (see Chap. 3).

Now it is true that Murik youth volunteered in the colonial police forces prior to World War I, and a steady trickle of men have since served as policemen, prison warders and so forth, not only for the Australian and the postcolonial administrations but also for the Japanese military during their three or so years occupation of the Murik coast. And, it is no less true that Sir Michael Somare, the first prime minister of the postcolonial state of PNG (1975–81), and native son of the Murik Lakes, has loomed over the somewhat distant but persistent relationship of Murik society to the state (Somare 1975). Sir Michael has affected Murik identity in, and orientation toward, the state in a culturally distinctive way. But concretely, he has added nothing to any aspect of village life. Like rural modernity in PNG more generally, moral imagination consists of a dialogue between local concepts of the person and a lame and ill-equipped state.

A sizable number of Murik families have left the Murik Lakes to resettle in town. A large Murik diaspora lives in Wewak, the capital of the East Sepik Province, but smaller groups can be found in other cities in PNG (and on Facebook). They are somewhat stratified as employed middle-class and peri-urban townspeople. In Wewak, most of the latter live in one of three beachfront settlements that have reassembled the boundaries of village society no less than they have recreated the distinctive intertidal environment of the Murik Lakes (Fig. 1.6).[12] In these camps, houses are packed tight in tiny spaces. Cobbled together from bush materials, salvaged cardboard, wooden planks and plastic tarpaulins, they domicile large, extended families, with lots of young children. Dugout canoes and fiberglass boats line the beaches. There is running water, but they lack electricity and other utilities, such as garbage collection or toilets. Children leave in the mornings and go to school. People worship on a weekly basis. A few family members hold down working-class jobs and receive a regular paycheck. Kinswomen often work in the informal economy and man little stalls vending phonecards, cigarettes, betel nuts, batteries and the like. Young men may sell newspapers or do piece-work around town. Middle-aged and senior men and women take out small outrigger canoes into the harbor and fish in the early mornings. Everybody goes to the big, town markets, trade stores and banks. They buy and read daily newspapers. And, of course, they make constant use of mobile phones to coordinate their comings and goings in town (see Chap. 4).

Fig. 1.6 Kreer Camp, a peri-urban Murik settlement in Wewak town. Photo: David Lipset (2014)

The point I cannot make strongly enough, however, is that peri-urban folk are deeply suspicious of the "public sphere" (Habermas 2001: 3). Instead, their moral compass remains largely (but of course not entirely) oriented by the rural habitus they left behind. Even the middle classes return "home," either to Wewak town or the villages, as often as they can. In other words, their relationship to modernity is contradictory rather than consistent. For example, the Murik are, like the Gogodala, a "canoe people." Not only do canoes and boats transport fishermen throughout the Murik Lakes and about the region, the "canoe" is understood as a form of embodiment and personhood (Lipset 2014b). The body is a "canoe" for its passenger the spirit. It is therefore interesting that airplanes, buses and even grocery carts are all called "canoes" today. These vehicles do not refer to units constituent of Murik personhood in society however. They are not human or collective bodies. They are only said to be "canoes" because of their vehicle-like capacity to facilitate the movement of alienated people and goods through a space and time of the other. Understanding the extension of this quintessential metaphor of Murik identity—minus its reference to Murik identity—amid the ambient context of modernity in PNG expresses the central problem with which this book is concerned.

The Chapters

The book is divided into two parts. Largely relying on Bakhtin's concept of dialogism, the first part consists of chapters on courtship, marijuana and mobile phones. My argument is that men voice their alienation from modern institutions in contemporary PNG in terms of their archaic, but abiding, values. The decline of the Male Cult juxtaposed with continuities in marriage and kinship has turned courtship into an exquisite expression of young men's alienation. They assert moral agency but in subject positions that do not idealize the other the way modern romance encourages them to do. They also smoke marijuana. In dialogue with senior men, youth avow that small-scale traffic is profitable and consuming the drug is enjoyable, adopting a voice of modern rationality and reflexivity as they do. In response, their elders not only condemn them and the drug as a source of disorder in the community, they also accuse the postcolonial state of corrupt regulatory practices. In town, meanwhile, we hear of men's alienation in their uses of and attitudes about mobile phones. The new social media are applauded for permitting men to maintain contact with kin and overseas trading partners across space and time but they are also criticized for enabling youth and the criminal element in modern society to make trouble.

In the second half of the book, I adopt the Lacanian trope of the empty signifier to argue that not only are men alienated from modernity but they are also alienated from archaic Murik culture. Specifically, its first chapter analyzes a new piece of Murik folk theater that was created during the early 1990s and was then repeatedly performed in a variety of contexts. The show, as I argue, answered the desire of which modernity had deprived its author, the Male Cult. Its centerpiece, the masked figure of a beautiful woman, expressed men's collective disconnection from the desire of the archaic and the modern other as well as the pleasure they took from the recognition that the show created. In the archaic context, this alienation from "her" desire had a literal meaning. As I go on to point out in the next chapter, men substituted money for sexual intercourse in compensation for grade-taking in their masking society. This substitution took place amid a broader context in which the archaic signifier of the Male Cult was being symbolically dismembered by the empty signifiers of the state. The last chapter then turns to men's dialogue about the tides that began to break through Murik beaches and flood Murik villages in 2007. Rival concepts of magical and modern agency revealed yet another dimension of masculine alienation and symbolic emasculation. But, again, my view is that climate change, and the new modernity that it foretells, was not a context of a new alienation from the other. Rather, masculine desire was already estranged from the signifier prior to the annual tides that have now begun to erode Murik beaches.

In a comparative Afterword, I briefly discuss men in Hawaii, the Federated States of Micronesia, the Kingdom of Tonga and New Zealand/Aotearoa by way of suggesting why men's dual alienation is so clear in the case of the Murik in PNG. The emptiness of their archaic signifier had not been transformed beyond recognition in the course of its brief colonial and postcolonial history. Paradoxically enough, while Murik men are acutely aware of modernity's signifiers, the qualities of their archaic voices had remained relatively independent and unmerged, at least for the time being.

Notes

1. See several recent, regionally based, edited collections on postcolonial masculinities by Lindsay and Miescher (2003), Ouzgane and Morrell (2005) on African men, Gutmann on Latin America (2003), Taga (2005) on East Asian men, Roberson and Suzuki (2003) on Japanese men and Ouzgane (2006) on Islamic masculinities. On modernity and gender cross-culturally, see Hodgson (2001). For a general discussion of postcolonial masculinity, see Morell and Swart (2005).
2. The ethnographic literature on and more general anthropological accounts of modernity are extensive. See Ong on women factory workers in Malaysia (1987), Taussig on capitalism in Bolivia and Columbia (1980), Geshiere on witchcraft in Cameroon (1997), Miller on Trinidad (1997), Barker, Harms and Lindquist on Southeast Asia (2014), among many others. For broader discussions of modernity, see Asad (2003), Appadurai (1996) and Trouillot (2002).
3. For another Lacanian account of a Melanesian society, see Weiner 1995.
4. On various dimensions of modernity in PNG and elsewhere in the Pacific, see Epstein (1968), Salisbury (1970), Finney (1973), Grossman (1984), Sexton (1982), Carrier and Carrier (1989), Bergendorff (1996), Zimmer-Tamakoshi (1998), Akin and Robbins (1999), LiPuma (2000), Robbins

and Wardlow (2006), Goddard (2005), Bamford (2007), Patterson and Macintyre (2011), West (2012) and Rollason (2014).
5. See, for example, Knauft (2002), Reed (2003), Robbins (2004), Bashkow (2006), Kirsch (2006) and Martin (2013).
6. On mining, see Kirsch (2006), Rumsey and Weiner (2001), Filer (2012), Golub (2015) and Jacka (2015). On oil, see Gilberthorpe (2013). And on industrial logging, see Lea (2005), Barker (2008), Halvaksz (2013), Sillitoe and Filer (2014) and Sillitoe (2014).
7. They raise three export crops, coffee, oil palm and cocoa (Koczberski and Curry 2005; Curry et al. 2012; West 2012).
8. They also gamble in the more conventional sense of betting on cards, slot machines, sports and online gaming (Zimmer 1987; Pickles 2014).
9. Young men commit crime (Harris 1988; Dinnen 1995, 2001; Goddard 2001; Luker and Monsell-Davis 2010; Lakhani and Willman 2014), beat their wives (Wardlow 2006; Jolly et al. 2012), spread STDs (Eves 2003; Hammar 2010; Wardlow 2008; Butt and Eves 2008), consume marijuana (Halvaksz 2006; Bell 2006) and abuse South Pacific Lager and home brew (Dernbach and Marshall 2001).
10. These were manifest in weakened political systems (Zimmer-Tamakoshi 1997), generational conflict (Haley 2008), atrophied forms of ceremonial exchange (Clark 1989), lost magical power (see Chap. 7), abandoned or betrayed Male Cults (Tuzin 1997) and, not least, by their own conversion to Christianity and its concepts of the intrinsic sinfulness of human beings (Robbins 2004).
11. Murik men blame "mothers" for being "weak," unlike them, for this ritual imbalance. Custom dictates that fathers sponsor daughters' initiations into the Female Cult while mothers sponsor sons' entry into the Male Cult. The "cost," they add, "for women" also enters into the imbalance. Daughters "only" require a single pig while sons' initiations involve several.
12. Heads of peri-urban and middle-class households seek to fulfill ritual obligations to village kin. At the same time, intermarriage with non-Murik spouses takes place among generations who have been raised in cities (see Chap. 2). Fluency among them in the Murik vernacular is only passive at best, having been replaced by Tokpisin and English.

PART I

Dialogics of Masculine Alienation

At some earlier time those worlds were self-sufficient, organically sealed, and stable; each made sense as an isolated unit. Capitalism destroyed the isolation of these worlds, broke down the seclusion and ideological self-sufficiency of these social spheres. In its tendency to level everything, to leave intact no divisions except the division between proletariat and capitalist, capitalism jolted these worlds and wove them into its own contradictory evolving unity. These worlds had not yet lost their own individual profile, worked out over centuries, but they had ceased to be self-sufficient. Every atom of life trembled with this contradictory unity of the capitalist world and capitalist consciousness, permitting nothing to rest easily in isolation, but at the same time resolving nothing. The spirit of this world-in-the-state-of-becoming found its fullest expression in the works of Dostoevsky (Bakhtin 1984b: 19–20).

CHAPTER 2

Desire in Young Men's Courtship Stories

The self that is characteristically associated with modernity is entangled in a moral contradiction. The abstract qualities of modernity—the "emptying of time and space" (Giddens 1990: 18)—or, the replacement of face-to-face relations by anonymous relations between strangers, the compression of time and space, the use of money, the impermanence and disposability of objects, have all called personal uniqueness into question. But while abstraction gives rise to social distance, not to mention anxiety, mistrust and suspicion, it also creates what Anthony Giddens called the "reflexive project" of the self (1991: 32f). Modern alienation, in other words, is bound up with individualism whose "essence is psychologism, the experience and interpretation of the world according to our internal reactions" (Simmel 2007: 20), an interiority that provides comfort in the midst of modern uncertainties (Simmel 1978: 477).

Now, if one of the primary goals of the reflexive project, for which the self is responsible, must be to "keep a ... narrative going" over the course of time (Giddens 1991: 54), a key moment in that narrative must surely involve romantic love. By posing the question of how I feel about the other—the other to whom I am attracted or infatuated, or by whom I am aroused—romance provokes and inspires a modern voice. "The telling of a story is one of the meanings of a 'romance,' but this story ... became individualized, inserting self and other into a personal narrative which had no particular reference to wider social processes" (Giddens 1992: 39–40).

© The Author(s) 2017
D. Lipset, *Yabar*, Culture, Mind, and Society,
DOI 10.1007/978-3-319-51076-7_2

In the midst of all its abstractness, romantic love provokes an urgent need for a kind of storytelling in which the subject-centered voice must prevail.[1]

The sociological literature on romantic love has largely sought to explain its *presence*, by reference to historical causes, social structure, socioeconomic functions or charismatic appeal. But what I intend to do in this second chapter, more or less, reverses this question: that is, I ask how, in the *absence* of romance discourse, do Murik young men talk about how they court and marry? And then, having interpreted the imagery of the other and concepts of agency that they do use in their courtship discourse, I return to the issue of what light their representations of desire may shed on modernity in PNG and their alienation from it.

LOVE AND MODERNITY?

Jack Goody dismissed Giddens' claim that romantic love introduced a new narrative form of introspection. "Life histories," he declared, "were certainly individualized from the beginning of time, with notions of self … being universal but taking different forms" (1998: 103). This kind of reflexivity was not promoted by romantic love for Goody but was rather encouraged by reading and writing. While reading is a contemplative mode of understanding, writing permits expressions of longing for an absent other. Writing "creates an object outside oneself in a way speech cannot do, at least [not] in the same clear-cut fashion" (Goody 1998: 109–110). Writing, in short, makes the heart grow fond: the idealization it permits may flourish at a distance. Thus, the spread of romantic love "can [be] link[ed] … with changes in communication techniques and practices, changes that differentially affect … groups at different times and places" (Goody 1998: 106–107). Romantic love is therefore found in cultures with developed literary traditions. Romantic love is evident in Chinese love poetry as well as in Arabic tales. "Literacy is the key to the mode of representation of love" (Goody 1998: 123). Thus, love is not exclusively European, nor exclusively modern, but it is rather a discourse that has been promoted by the ability to read and write.

I sympathize with Goody's critique of Giddens' view of romantic love as Eurocentric. I also join him in holding the view that romantic love is not a distinctively Western phenomenon.[2] It is not the invention of a modern economy, modern individualism or the atomism of modern society. It is not "the Siamese twin of modernity" as Howard Gadlin concluded (1977: 34). But literacy? Although the theoretical relationship of literacy to culture has been the object of ongoing, and important, debate in the social sciences, I think it is clear from the ethnography of literacy that there is nothing intrinsic about literacy that causes or imposes an invariable set of changes upon all cultures (see Besnier 1995). For my purposes, one need look no further than *The Sexual Life of Savages* (Malinowski 1987: 264) to learn that at least some imagery of romantic love—such as the use of imagination to win the heart of the other, steadfast preference, an appreciation of the personality of the beloved and feelings of loss—were experienced by pre-literate Trobriand Islanders.[3] Moreover, although the data are somewhat ambiguous, and depend upon the criteria of definition (Lindholm 2001: 353), it would seem that elements of romantic love, clustered in different configurations, are experienced in various cultures, be they minimally or thoroughly literate (Jankowiak and Fischer 1992).[4]

If romantic love is neither a by-product nor a symptom of European modernity, and if it cannot be associated with literacy, then what, if anything at all, is distinctive about it? Two things, I think. First, whatever its theoretical relationship to modernity, outside of Euro-America, young people do *perceive* romantic love as a distinctively modern relationship discourse, particularly when they view it as the exclusive motivational basis for courtship leading to marriage which is completely *separate from the collective concerns of kinship or economy*. And second, representations of romantic love proliferate all over the postcolonial world. Missionaries, the mass media and advertising all proclaim and endorse it as modern and Western. Meanwhile, ethnographic research into the relationship between romantic love and modernity has tended to focus on how romance may become a tactic in an inter-generational politics (asserted by youth) for independence from parents or lineage elders and/or in a cross-gender politics (asserted by women) for power vis à vis a patriarchy (Collier 1974; Wolf 1982).[5]

In the contemporary Pacific, courtship has been seen to contribute to generational conflict (Marksbury 1995).[6] Under the influence of Hollywood movies, ideas about love held by young, village-based Aboriginal Australians in Arnhem Land have become part of their "paradigm of adolescent resistance" against adult authority (Burbank 1995: 193).[7] Young Chambri men and women from the middle Sepik River challenged elders over the right to choose their own spouses (Gewertz and Errington 1992). The youth did not want to marry exogamously, however, nor did they even wish to live apart from kin. They fled to town because they wanted the freedom to pursue desire and romance, as well as other aspects of modernity, with fellow urban Chambri, without worrying about sorcery retaliation by angry parents. Not surprisingly, Rosi and Zimmer-Tamakoshi (1995) found no generational conflict associated with romantic love among young elites enrolled in art school in the national capital of Papua New Guinea. These young people expressed no intention or wish ever to return home to live with kin again.

In Murik Lakes, while courtship and marriage do cause generational conflict from time to time, they do not seem to pit individualism against collectivist values. Youth sometimes try to press things by defying the wishes of parents. Or, they try to defeat coeval rivals. That is to say, they make claims and counterclaims to marry but they did not and today do not represent them in terms of modernist reasons. They do not do so for love.

In order to begin to explain how and why they tell courtship stories in what I want to call Homeric rather than romantic terms, I must briefly introduce Bakhtin's notion of chronotope (1981) which I find useful because of its focus on how human agency may be integrated in time and space in narratives (see Chap. 7).

Two Chronotopes of Love

A chronotope, according to Bakhtin, shapes the ways in which time and space are fixed and interwoven in literary narrative.[8] A chronotope, in brief, is a fictional setting. For example, in "ancient Greek romance" actors "enter ... adventuristic time as ... person[s] to whom something happens" (Bakhtin 1981: 95). Initiative in this chronotope is tempered by fortune, good and bad. Fortune, not agency, controls meetings and failures to meet. A sequence of unexpected events and chance encounters take place "that is entirely composed of contingency" (1981: 89ff). In other words, chronotopes orient time and space with particular reference to the degree and kind of agency its heroes do or do not possess.[9]

In what I call the chronotope of modern romance, a kind of metamorphosis of a discrete and isolated self takes place. The subject turns into something other than what he or she once thought they were; that is, the person becomes a combination of self and other. And this transformation may take place, not through slow developing moments but instantaneously, via a crisis, as it were. In the chronotope of modern romance, a merger with an etherealized beloved may occur, a merger during which ordinary time becomes obliterated, and intimate spaces, during dates, rituals, honeymoons and so forth, are privileged. The settings of the world, subjectively opposed to the broad expanses of everyday life, are reduced to microcosms, small but utterly significant times and spaces in which persons act in small but utterly significant ways. They speak their inner voices and they feel and act in ways that express desire, an impassioned and embodied agency that exudes, if nothing else, moral longing. The center of the chronotope of modern romance is desire, of course, but no less central is an image of extraordinary process in which agency is called into question by the transformation of the self's merger with the other (Lipset 2015).

In a contrasting chronotope of courtship that I want to introduce now, agency is less differentiated from, or perhaps it would be better to say that it is more closely identified with, the wider locales in which people play out their pending attachments. Now, for reasons that will become apparent, I will call this second one a chronotope of Homeric courtship. I liken the agency of its heroes in time and space not to Homer *per se* but to Eric Auerbach's portrayal of Homer's *Odysseus* in the famous first chapter of his masterwork, *Mimesis: The Representation of Reality in Western Literature* (1957; see also Bakker 1999).[10]

Homer casts Odysseus abroad, Auerbach observes, into a geography that receives a more elaborate portrayal than the subjectivity of the hero. Events occur in the foreground, and they are uninterrupted in their interconnections. Their meanings are unmistakable. This is "the basic impulse of the Homeric style: to represent phenomena in a fully externalized form, visible and palpable in all their parts, and completely fixed in their spatial and temporal relations" (Auerbach 1957: 4).[11] History, events and experience, although vividly described, have little or no effect upon Odysseus. The hero's character does not change in the course of the narrative. He is not subject to psychological development. He is not subject to the passage of time or through space. Rather than speaking from their souls, in the chronotope of Homeric courtship actors appear in clearly circumscribed, wholly realistic and perceptible, yet temporally and spatially static, terms. "Never is there a form left fragmentary or half-illuminated, never a lacuna, never a gap, never a glimpse of unplumbed depths" (Auerbach 1957: 4).[12]

In this chapter, I make use of these two chronotopes to analyze a small sample of courtship narratives that I collected from young Murik men in 2001. My argument will be that they told their stories in a Homeric chronotope rather than a chronotope of modern romance. Amid modernity in PNG, involving all the abstraction and subjectivity to which I alluded at the outset of this chapter, as well as the atrophy of the Male Cult, the continuity of marriage norms and kinship had made courtship a highly significant context. Young men might assert moral agency in courtship, but in a way that voiced a dimension of their alienation from modernity, namely, in terms of contrasting assumptions about the difference between self and other.

Before turning to the courtship narratives, I must briefly outline how Murik courtship and marriage changed during the twentieth century and then introduce several turning points in the relationship of Murik masculinity to modernity in PNG.

Marriage in Murik Society

In the pre-colonial era, the Male and Female Cults organized Murik marriage although I am not entirely sure how. It seems that young men and women belonging to exogamous matri-moieties were selected (by parents?) in order to fulfill sister-exchange obligations (see Levi-Strauss 1969).[13] Initiation rites bestowed the right to marry and endowed *both* sexes with charisma, in its classic meaning of spiritually endowed agency, or, in this case, magical charms (*numaruk* or *pueduk moan*). This charisma exposed a problem of authority between the Male Cult and domestic society which I think predated the interventions of the colonial state. The wishes of cult elders aside, and regardless of their marital status, young men sought magically to seduce women, women by whom they were magically attracted. However potent their charms, their secret intentions were inevitably countered by those of rival lovers, which led to intra-generational conflicts, fistfights, brawling and sorcery accusations. The authority structure of Murik marriage offered no ready solution to the steady cackle of gossip and violent outbursts that preoccupied the society with the intrigues of youth.

Today, as in times past, first marriages remain volatile and are typically broken up by extra-marital affairs, which lead to conflict between rivals. Unencumbered as it is by having to return bridewealth, divorce simply involves going back home. Youthful marriages amount to little more than a series of temporary, trial relationships. Father Joseph Schmidt, the Society of the Divine Word missionary who lived on the Murik coast for the greater part of the first half of the twentieth century, took avid interest in the affairs of the young, kept a diary about them and included the following excerpt from it in one of the three articles he published in *Anthropos*, the church's anthropology journal:

> The young woman, X, married Y, on November 19, 1919, and by April 1920, she had married three others; the fourth was the brother of the third, with whom she is still married. The young man A married B in 1918 (probably in response to pressure from the adults), a little later he also [married] C. B was with him three times and backed out. Then she ... married another. She ran away to a youth in another village; there, a big fight ensued. A was hit by a blow on the head with an axe which went down to the skull. It was thought he would die. I bandaged him at once. (Schmidt 1926: 48)

Now I concede that Father Schmidt's notes may have been a little biased by a missionary's zeal to condemn the rivalries and fissile ethos of Murik marriage in favor of the sacramental marriage he was proselytizing.[14] But my point here is only that his picture of the cycle of optative marriage, affairs, divorce and conflict (all apparently independent of the Male and Female Cults) matches the process that I came to know in the late twentieth and early twenty-first centuries.

The absence in Schmidt's account of any direct reference to sentiments of desire and passion, apart from fighting, also coincides with my own observations of Murik courtship. A male youth might offer a gift to a girl as a gesture of his attraction to her. He might also perform some service for her parents by way of requesting their permission to marry her by signaling his willingness to begin to do brideservice for them. In 1981, for example, Murakau Wino told me a story about marrying Minjamok sometime in the late 1940s. Notice how, at the start of his narrative, he depicted his desire to do so.

> I erected houseposts for Minjamok's parents... I [then] brought the roof leaves and finished assembling the house... I told Yame, my [classificatory] mother's brother, to send for her. He was the middleman... He brought Minjamok to his mother's house at night. My father, Wino, was angry. It appeared to him that my work [on the house] was going for naught since he thought that Yame was going to marry Minjamok... Minjamok had been betrothed to Yame. But Basa, her mother, did not want him to marry her [daughter]. Minjamok could not be found in any event. She had spent the night with me and [was] hiding in a mosquito basket... Yarong [her mother's brother] went to her family and told them that their daughter was already married to me. Basa [her mother] said to ... Yarong, "Well, he built the house without the help of Yame"... The [rest of the family] ... had no answer ... Minjamok's things were brought to ... my mother's house.[15]

Here is a clear glimpse of the Homeric chronotope in male courtship discourse. The hero, his passion, initiative in the face of an obstacle, the moment of ambiguity and its resolution are all set in discrete and precise spatial and temporal terms, rather than in terms of the mysteries of and the ecstatic metamorphoses caused by the heart. Murakau builds a house for the parents of Minjamok, his intended. He sends for her, via an intermediary (see Chap. 4, wherein this is contrasted with the use of mobile phones) and she is brought to the house of his mother's brother "at night," a move that upsets Murakau's father. Some sort of a misunderstanding that may have to do with moiety exchange in the Male Cult occurs. Minjamok hides (her desire) as a result. She has already been betrothed to another boy, an arrangement to which her mother objects, but ends up marrying her "beloved," the narrator, with whom she is already sexually involved. Although metaphors of desire are unvoiced, or at least indirectly voiced, the intermediaries, the nighttime, the mosquito basket, they are not mistakable. Desire appears in scrupulously externalized imagery; the narrator initially tells about it through the construction of buildings and locations. Desire gives rise to conflict between kin, rather than to subjective turmoil, and when the wrangle between the parents is sorted out, the result favors the desire of the young lovers, which conclusion is represented by muted assent and by Minjamok moving in with her new husband's kin.

What is also missing from the story is not just sentiment but any reference to the sway of magic over desire. As I say, onward from initiation, love was charismatic, enchanted labor. For an excellent depiction of the agency of love magic as a metaphor of secret desire, I now turn to an episode in the tale of Kumbun, an ancestor-spirit man, who elopes with a girl called Darua. Father Schmidt collected the story in the 1920s.

> Darua was [secluded] in the Female Cult House [during her initiation] when her father picked a man for her [to marry]. The people in this man's lineage helped process sago flour for Darua's end-of-initiation rite. The day of the celebration approached. Meantime, [the spirit-man] Kumbun hid in his house. When he came down, he had adorned himself with red tree sap and limped... He took betel nuts, made magic over them, and then gave them to his sister, Kanis. She brought them to Darua to chew. Kumbun told his mother, "Go and get all of Darua's ornaments from her." She did so. He bespelled them and had them returned. Kumbun also

prepared [e.g., bespelled] scented things for Darua, and his sister took them to her. On the day when her seclusion ended, the women brought her to the sea, so that she could bathe… In the afternoon, Darua came out of the [Women's Cult] House beautifully ornamented and sat down below on the platform. The men danced before her then. Darua looked at no one except Kumbun, who was the last to dance… As evening came, Kumbun took Darua and they both went away [eloped].

Next day, the people sought Darua and asked each other: "Where is Darua?" "She left last night."

Consequently, the [young] man whom her father had chosen for her did not get [to marry] her. The people scolded Kumbun who had carried [Darua] off (Schmidt 1933: 675).

The story of the courtship and marriage of Kumbun and Darua is fixed in space and time. While secluded inside the Women's Cult House, Darua has been betrothed in the old way. Kinspeople of her fiancé work on behalf of the marriage. Due to his desire to marry Darua, the hero is to be found in hiding, only to emerge in disguise as beautiful cripple. What does Kumbun do? Kumbun casts love spells to enchant Darua. Thus: "Darua looked at no one except" him. On the morning of the day of her discharge from initiatory seclusion, she goes to bathe in the sea, that is, to cleanse herself of ritual pollution. Later that afternoon, seated on a platform together with the other initiates, she watches dancers perform. Darua has also been anointed by Women's Cult elders with great doses of love magic that are meant to reduce Kumbun to a state of helpless desire for her (Barlow 1995). That evening, she "elopes" with him. On the following day, the departure of the couple is said to be a mystery. Where did she go, onlookers wonder? But the answer is instantly revealed, "She left last night." Desire is located in space, "she left," and time, "last night," rather than in sentiment. And, it is again depicted as a process of sorting out divided social claims rather than emotional ones. In other words, attraction is represented in terms of parental obstacles, as well as in terms of definite times and specific spaces, and the power of desire is lastly hidden in men's and women's secret charisma.

The concealed representation of desire was also institutionalized in the Male Cult (see Chaps. 5 and 6). In its sanctum, the very act of sexual intercourse, and the possessive jealousy it was culturally expected to arouse, was subjected to a course in sublimation. Murik husbands did not monopolize rights to their sexual relationship with wives. They were rewarded for relinquishing these rights to cult partners as part of a moiety competition for authority over the most powerful and prestigious spirit-men in Murik cosmology, the Kakar (cf. Thurnwald 1916). One of the avowed purposes of this competition was to instill the men with sacred invulnerabilities and military power by training them to repress sexual jealousy, that is, to be stoic and control their rage (see Lipset 1997: 177–215). The Homeric heroes of the Male Cult were thus removed from an emotionally entangled world. But the story they told about what they were required to do in exchange for masculine agency was symptomatic of the turbulence that their archaic desire nevertheless created within the domestic community.

Military excursions with the support of the Male Cult had more or less ceased by the 1960s, as did the exchange of wives' sexual services (see Chap. 6). But my argument is that the archaic, or pre-modern, construction of courtship—without direct expressions of desire—largely persisted in form and meaning. The gesture of gift-giving and the efficacy of love magic, the volatility of first marriages, a flexible concept of sister-exchange and the impunity with which the young choose their own partners would be instantly recognizable, I have no doubt, as distinctively "Murik" to any early twentieth century man or woman, should such a person return to the villages in the early twenty-first century. This is *not* to assert that social change has not been going on. Not at all. It is rather to assert that kinship, courtship and marriage practices have remained insulated from what LiPuma (2001) has justly termed the "encompassment" of indigenous values by modernity in PNG. In this context, the absence of a subject-centered voice, while normative at the local level, reflects an important dimension of the estrangement of young Murik men from that encompassment.

In general, the inroads of modernity have alienated Murik men more than women, thereby raising the equality and interdependency of the sexes to an even greater level than during the early twentieth century. In particular, modernity had devastated opportunities for male youth to assume and assert some kind of customary, or neo-customary, gender identity, or at least one that combines the one with a form of modern masculinity, such as employment, in any effective way (see Chap. 4). This outcome is consistent with other data about how capitalist transformation has differentially affected men and women in this region of the Pacific (see, e.g., Knauft 2002: 27).

In Murik, however, despite changes that have damaged their role in the economy and erased important ritual distinctions in male life, adherence to local concepts of kinship seems to have remained undeterred by twentieth century events. The organization of courtship and marriage, as I have suggested, had shifted but little; young men and women go on possessing the same sort of choice and go on expressing choices in the idioms and imagery of desire that they did early in the twentieth century—minus the authority of the Male Cult. All appearances to the contrary, the narratives that follow are not set within a chronotope of modern romance, in which the male self expresses longing for the love of the other (see Lipset 2015).[16] They do not reveal the voice of a subject-centered, reflexive self in a society where it is assumed that individuals are "different from one another" (Durkheim 1995: 84). Instead, within the context of an emasculated secret society, Chinese fiberglass boats, market dispossession and failed fisheries development, all amid an independent PNG founded by no less than one of their own sons, young men's desire adds another element of estrangement from modernity. The following courtship narratives, which are drawn from a series of interviews I did with several young men (n = 8) in 2001, allow us to overhear one side of the dual alienation of contemporary manhood in modern PNG.[17]

Desire in the Chronotope of Homeric Courtship

While each story portrays a hero facing down a challenge to his masculinity, the order in which I have sorted them features the most direct expression of desire for the beloved, which is understated, to the least, in which desire is completely denied.

The first narrative opens with a kind of a Shavian scene of male desire aroused by a young woman selling her wares at an urban market (Shaw 2003). But in PNG, the woman does not stand for how the heart (and then education) may pierce class difference, as it did in Pygmalion (see Chap. 5). The scene rather brings to light some of the prevailing tropes of modernity in PNG. Here, time and space are quantified and abstract, as well as being administered by the state. Here, the informal economy meets the formal one. Here, men and women, speaking *Tokpisin*, often engage one another as intertribal strangers. And of course, here people shop—from vendors who for the most part are women.

"I Met Her Myself"

Makus Murakau was then about 30 years old (the son of the previous narrator). Raised in Darapap village by his parents, both of whom were lifelong villagers, at that time, he was employed in town. His story describes how he met and courted his first wife who hailed from a non-Murik village located about 100 miles up the coast to the west of the Murik Lakes.

> She was selling mangoes … at the Dagua market in Wewak. I bought one from her. I met her myself. She [then] sent me a letter through a mutual friend, a boy from the Sepik River. The letter said that "if I had my father's bones," I would come visit her in her village… My friend knew the village. I was working at that time at the Sepik Copra Marketing Board. It was Thursday. I got my little *toea* [i.e., received his pay]. I bought some beer. At that time, I was drinking beer [i.e., he did not then belong to the Seventh Day Adventist church]. I took my bush knife for protection. I bought a K3 [ticket for the] bus! It was far! I got to her village. No one there knew who I was. The village magistrate wanted to arrest me. But we sorted things out. They came to understand what I was doing in the village. I showed them the letter. Then, they started talking about custom. I got two bags of rice, one carton of tinned fish and put K100 on top of the gift.[18] They did not complain.

Makus asserted initiative. As he says, "I met her myself." It should be more than evident that agency in his courtship tale was not afforded the subjective excesses of the chronotope of modern romance. He did not seek to lose himself in a microcosm of the other. He did not idealize his beloved. And he was not overcome by euphoria. Set in the marketplace, the couple's first meeting, and his instigation of it, he represents offhandedly. It took place by means of a purchase.[19] Makus, as it were, bought one of the young woman's "fruits." In turn, he recalled that she wrote him a letter that was hand delivered by a mutual acquaintance (rather than by kin).

What sort of a "love letter" was it? How did its author contemplate her longing and her absent other? What kind of autobiographical skills did it reveal? In retrospect, the metaphor that stood out to Makus did not flatter his masculine qualities. It did not express the woman's romantic or erotic desire for him. Instead, she challenged his collective masculinity: Should he possess "his father's bones," which is to say, "should he be a man who was a true member of his father's lineage," and therefore possess the hereditary power of its patrimony, he would have the ability to overcome obstacles and come for her. Perhaps the woman did profess her love for him. Perhaps the letter did dwell upon how handsome he was. But he recounted none of it to me. Instead, he set events out in coordinate segments of abstract time and space. "It was Thursday," when he prepared to go to her village, not as a passenger on an outrigger canoe on which he would have held hereditary rights to voyage to engage in gift exchanges with hereditary trading partners (Lipset 1985), but on a bus full of strangers for which he had to pay a fare in the currency of the state. Upon arrival, Makus was anonymous. The mystery of his identity was not resolved either by disclosure of names of ancestors or by gestures such as laying out canoe rollers. Instead, a representative of the state, a village magistrate, threatened to jail him. It was a symbol of modern agency, education and communication; "a letter" quickly resolved who he was and turned him into a potential affine. Both customary and modern conjunctions—bridewealth, the bus and the letter—served to define the courtship through direct and uninterrupted declarations. Why? Because in this chronotope, the relationship of self and other is fundamentally one of resemblance. Relationship is taken for granted; it requires no bridge of passion or the travail of reflection. The passage through abstract time and space was merely a background as were commodities exchanged as gifts. Makus talked about courtship in the scrupulously externalized terms of the Homeric chronotope. No modern, reflexive self, questioning his feelings for the beloved, or withdrawing into a time and space of passion, was audible in his story.

"She Had Nothing"

In a second narrative, the courtship process does not start in the marketplace but amid gender-role reversals for which the Sepik region of PNG is, or at least was once, ethnographically famous.[20] Like Makus, the second narrator, called Beldon, had also left the Murik Lakes to work in town. Then in his late 30s, and just a few years older than Makus, Beldon was raised in the village and was not a Christian.

> I went to Wewak and had a job in a store for a time. I was still married to Yaki [my first wife] and our kids were going to school [in town]. I went to [to the Highlands] by boat via Madang and then by car. I worked for a [Murik tribesman] on a coffee plantation. Then, I got another job on a

cocoa plantation. [A woman] … sent me a letter to come back to Wewak quickly because Yaki was seeing someone else. I returned to Wewak. But the day before I arrived, Yaki left for [the town of] Lae [with her new husband]. I was in charge of the kids. I got another job supervising a trade store in Kreer market… I looked after the kids all by myself. It was very hard work… I cooked… On the weekends, I did the laundry. I saw a group of Darapap women on their way to … a meeting of the … [Seventh Day Adventist] Women's Federation. In that group was a cousin-sister of Yaki, Sarah. She had nothing, no food, no money. She was unmarried. She had no children… I took a loan from my boss at the trade store… I gave her a gift [of money]… Later, I … told … her that I wanted to marry her, but if she were … willing, she would have to be ready to get along with and look after my kids. She said she wanted to marry me and that she would be happy to take care of them. So we married and … moved back to the village.

In the world Beldon describes, time and space are divided by separations, disconnections and identity reversals, but these gaps do not interrupt or create uncertainties in the narrative. Beldon is not at all lost, a homeless, hovering stranger. He and Yaki go to town to enroll children in an urban school. Beldon then leaves Yaki in order to go work (for kin) in specific contexts elsewhere in PNG for reasons that are left unexplained but do not interfere with the sequence of events. In his absence, Yaki begins an affair with another man. The news reaches Beldon by letter, not by love letter, to be sure. A kinswoman informs him that he has been cuckolded. Time and space are specified: he attempts to intercede with his wife but misses meeting her not because of indecision but by being a day too late for reasons unspecified, or one could say, by chance, a modern notion of causation. She had already left with her new man to go live in another city where he is employed. In addition to his wife's betrayal, Beldon's masculinity is further called into question, as he becomes a man having to do what in the Murik sexual division of labor is ordinarily classified as women's work; he does childcare and domestic chores himself.

But this is only a temporary turnabout. An image of kinswomen then presents itself. Among them is Sarah, whom he instantly recognizes as an affine. Instead of desirable qualities, Beldon is attracted by her nullity: "she had nothing." She is poor, without children and food, lacking in feminine attributes. If Beldon, as a father, has become an incomplete, or perhaps androgynous, man who has lost or been dispossessed of his wife, and must therefore "mother" his children, then he has been drawn to Sarah because she too is a deficit-riddled and not then a full-fledged woman. She too is lacking. His desire thus seems represented more as pity than passion. That is, an image of dependency, of the self in need of the other, catches his eye, rather than positive qualities, such as the girl's beauty, personality or wealth.

Desire to begin a relationship with Sarah he expresses through a gift. But the gift requires money. Indeed, it is a sum of money. Beldon must go into debt with his employer in order to get and give it to her. Inevitably, the gift leads to a marriage proposal. What is Beldon's condition? That Sarah agree "to mother" his children. In other words, he predicates marriage not on his own, or their, mutual love but on her willingness to parent. In this narrative, Beldon's masculinity was tested by having been cheated on and tested again by having to do women's chores. But the solution he devises, to choose a new wife, not only revealed no basis of a subject in a chronotope of romance but also explicitly derived from an absence rather than from an idealization of a unique other or a wish to merge with her.[21] The actions of the Homeric hero know no backgrounds. They know of no reflexive narrative. Beldon does not long for love; neither does he brood or mope. Again, self and other appear in unambiguous terms that do not delineate personal qualities and subjective feeling-states. But as such, and this is my main point, when the chronotope of Homeric courtship is viewed as an answer in dialogue with modernity in which romance is idealized, it becomes an alienated answer, one that suggests that the kind of courtship its narrators practice belongs to an archaic life-world in which the formation of conjugal relationships does not presuppose the normative emotions that modernity would associate with it.

"I Didn't Know the Girl"

In the last story of this trio, desire completely drops out of the hero's motivations, which is to say, the woman becomes anonymous, although she is not a stranger. As in the account of the mango seller, the courtship process is advanced by the narrator's answer to a slight against his honor. But unlike either of the two preceding stories, this third one is set in a village rather than in town. Tabanus Wambu, the narrator, was then about 25 years old. He had been raised in Darapap by village parents. He belonged to no church. The woman in question was from one of the "bush Murik" villages, the horticultural trading partners who live just inland from the lakes.

DL:	You were staying with your elder brother in [the Highlands]?
Tabanus:	I was up there [in the Highlands]. I returned to [the village of] Darapap. I was here for one week when he came and attacked me, this relative of M.'s.
DL:	He came to the house, or?
T:	He attacked me outside—
DL:	He came and—
T:	He came and called me and we fought.
DL:	What are you saying?[22]
T:	He said, "You came back here to the village. You didn't come back to sit quietly and behave yourself. You came to make trouble and hit on our women again." I answered him, "I don't know what you are talking about." I fought back. I was angry. I fought for my rights.
DL:	What was this girl's name?
T:	Paula
DL:	OK, had she married him already?
T:	No. They weren't married. The two of them were just having an affair.
DL:	OK.
T:	After the fight, I didn't think about Paula, but then I thought to myself, "If I am my father's son, I better do something in front of everybody. After all, I fought for her."
DL:	So when you came back from [the Highlands], she was here in the village?
T:	She was here.
DL:	Before, before you fought, had you noticed her a little, or?
T:	No.
DL:	Did you know her at all?
T:	I didn't know her. I was in the Highlands. I came back to the village and I did not know of her.
DL:	Why did he attack you then?
T:	I would say this: the custom of young people in the village is to fight like that because 'eyes pop out.' Eyes pop out at other guys' girls.
DL:	He was jealous, eh?
T:	Yeah, he was jealous.
DL:	He thought you had designs on Paula?
T:	Yeah, but I didn't know her at all.

DL:	You hadn't even seen her?
T:	Yeah, I hadn't laid eyes on her.
DL:	OK
T:	After we finished fighting, I didn't know the girl. I didn't know where she lived, in which house. People told me where she was living. I went there—
DL:	OK, she said what?
T:	When I went to her, she said…
DL:	Paula?
T:	Yeah, Paula did not say anything. She did not object when I took her home with me. I was strong. According to our custom, if you fight for a woman, an unmarried woman, then you ought to go take the woman from her boyfriend in front of him. You should take the woman for whom you have shown your anger, shown your strength.
DL:	When you went to her, did you explain yourself like that? Or, what did you tell her?
T:	When I went to her, I said, "I am here to get you." She herself had seen the fight.
DL:	Ah.
T:	So when I came for her, she knew what to expect.
DL:	Where did you two go?
T:	Back home. I stayed here with her for four months and then for four more months. Then we had our first child… The two of us stayed here, then we went to Boig for seven months, after which I returned to Darapap.
DL:	With her?
T:	I left her there and I came back here.
DL:	Ah, she is staying up there.
T:	Yeah.
DL:	OK.
T:	I don't worry about women. I am a man who has to move around. I have to keep moving.[23]

Observe how precisely Tabanus establishes events in his narrative. "One week" after his return from visiting a specific foreign space to the familiar space of Darapap village, he is attacked "outside," that is, in the public eye. After establishing co-residence, the couple live together in Darapap for "four months." Evidently discovering that Paula has become pregnant, they go on for another "four months" and then, after the baby is born, they go to live bilocally for "seven months" in Boig village. By contrast to the detail of this itinerary, the elaboration of emotion-discourse in the story is rudimentary. Upon being confronted, Tabanus fights back "for my rights," but not because of a specific kind of sentiment, say, anger or honor, or even for Paula. He did not know, in other words, whose affections he was being accused of stealing. Paula's kin, it is true, were probably not "total strangers" to Tabanus since she came from a Bush Murik village.[24] But I do not doubt his claim that desire played no role whatsoever in his decision to propose to her. The marriage, as he recounted it, did not arise from romantic courtship but from collective and archaic norms about masculinity to which both he and Paula subscribed. Presumably, the "custom" Tabanus cited, that is, a man's right to start a relationship with a woman after fighting for her, might ordinarily have been motivated by knowing her and finding her attractive in some sense—as it did in the incident cited above recorded by Father Schmidt. However, in this instance, Tabanus professed no feeling at all for Paula when he fought over her. He did not even know, he declares, who she was, much less where she was living. Did that bother him? Not a great deal, it would seem. He goes on to talk about the birth of a child that, in Murik terms, is a claim to conjugal viability rather than the growth of mutual love.

The narrative thus describes a crisis in the biography of the gender of its hero that is resolved by deeds that have consequences on his subsequent life. But the feelings he attributes both to himself, as a man, and to the marriage are exquisitely represented in terms of a Homeric chronotope. That is, the reasons for courtship are cast externally, motivated by a challenge to his masculinity, and not cast in the subjective terms of romance. No contour of personhood is blurred. "Eyes," on the contrary, "pop out." Psychological process receives no attention: nothing is concealed. The beloved is not an object of contemplation. And lastly, the identity of the hero is firm, unchanged by the passage of chronological time and the turn of events. "I don't worry about women," Tabanus declares, "I am a man who has to move around. I have to keep moving."

Modernity Without Romance

These three stories show that, despite a century of modern influence, young Murik men phrase courtship in terms of a Homeric rather than a romantic chronotope. That is, they court in voices that are not subject-centered.

Why? Why are their voices so engrossed in gift-giving and the details of travel but so muted about qualities of the other? Why do these courtship tales imagine the self moving through abstract times and spaces without the least fear of anonymity, much less the pleasure of the freedom it is supposed to bestow?

Of the multiple, contradictory values that appeal to young men in contemporary PNG, courtship is not, it should be admitted, the only crossroads in the formation of their identities. It does not comprehensively define who they are. It is just one pivotal decision among many others. But courtship does mark a significant moment in their negotiation of gender identity in Murik society and modernity in PNG. No doubt, it is possible to argue that romance discourse may be viewed as independent of history and the changing structure of society, in other words, purely as a poetics. And, no doubt, other institutions, like popular media, exert important influence on the meaning and practice of desire (Appadurai 1996). My view, however, is that the images and metaphors of courtship in these narratives reflect—at least, in part—the extent to which these young men, and the segment of the society for which they stand, are alienated from modernity. Moreover, they reflect the extent to which their agency has not become disembedded from local, archaic processes and values. Makus dutifully sought parental permission and willingly paid bridewealth. Beldon offered Sarah a gift. And Tabanus fought for his honor. Apart from Makus' terse admission that he had "met her myself," these stories represent little by way of a modern, individuated subjectivity in which the beloved is idealized without reference to sociocultural process. Instead, they attend more closely to the hero's adventures in and travel through everyday life in modern contexts within the postcolonial state.

What then does travel and adventure mean in these stories? How are they represented? First of all, in Murik culture, while maritime trade was viewed as a form of seduction (see Barlow 1985b; Barlow and Lipset 1997: 24),[25] travel itself remains a metaphor of male desire (see Chap. 5). In these courtship narratives, obviously trysts and trade goods are not the prizes of travel. Nevertheless, the employed, wandering hero is drawn out of the familiar, familial demands of village life. He traverses a heterogeneous environment in which value and time are measured in terms of an impersonal matrix. The hero endures the experience, and the challenges to his identity it entails, only to return home completely unchanged. Travel is depicted externally, objectively: the hero moves through modern space and time unmistakably. His emotions are strong and instantaneous.

Beldon saw Sarah and knew she might be available to him. The narratives are constructed in terms of foregrounds. Tabanus decided that having won a fistfight, he should go and propose marriage to a stranger. The meanings of events are definite. Elements in the stories are placed in vivid relation to one another. Conjunctions make for an uninterrupted flow of action leading to no epiphanies. Makus rode a bus to the mango girl. Travel is instrumental, not a moral education. Its outcome does not disentangle the marital bond from kinship and economy. It does not change the self. But just the opposite: actors marry and begin to take their place in the community, a transition they construe in unproblematic terms.

As a phase of life, Octavio Paz once observed that youth is a time of love (1993). Particularly for young PNG men, I would say, youth ought to be a time of agency and individualism. I have privileged their voices in this chapter because young men seem to seek encountering and engaging life outside the village, where norms of community appear to slack down, no longer to constrain the self, more so than women, children or the elderly in their society. They are compelled by the tantalizing allure of freedom urban modernity seems to offer. However, instead of independence and opportunity, not to mention, autobiographical narrative, contemporary PNG alienates male youth. In the era during which they live, education has disembedded ritual seclusion, because the state and Christianity have replaced the Male Cult. But neither education, nor the state, nor the missions typically lead them to permanent employment, that is, to membership in a modern life. More frequently, they lead them back to an arena in which they vie for status through devalued village relationships, rather than prestigious, modern ones. At the same time, the world is increasingly disembedded by commodities; it is a world of mobile phones, wristwatches and outboard motors. They find themselves in difficult economic and political circumstances in which they have few resources or control to use them. Not surprisingly, the reckoning of such young men with modernity leaves them preoccupied by athletic matches and small-stakes card games played amid the bittersweet odors of marijuana smoke (see Chap. 3).

However, when depicted in Murik courtship stories, the self does not appear lonely and formal, like in an Edward Hopper painting.[26] While employed in town, while traveling among strangers on buses, the self does indeed take on a more isolated and anonymous position that is separated from the other. But these moments are short-lived. Courtship returns narrators to gifts, reciprocities and reproduction, that is, to representations of collective moral agency. Alan MacFarlane (1986) rightly points out that the experience of "marrying for love" elevates the marital relationship above other relationships, such as those with children or a wider kin network. In so far as their voices reliably disclose their subjectivities, these young men did not "marry for love." They did not see either their motivations or the relationship of their marriages to kin in terms of the modern, romantic chronotope. The point of orientation among these young men is the Murik village; small, animist/Christian communities in which life is not in the least anonymous but is becoming increasingly commoditized and connected to mass media and mobile networks. In spite of the twentieth century, Murik masculinity remains imagined and conducted in, as well as through, an ethos in which the resemblance of self and other is taken for granted.

As a consequence, marriage remains an undaunting, unproblematic project, whose purpose is not to assert adherence to a modern lifestyle, an optative independence, or to compress the self into a microcosmic world with the other. No. The narrators come to marry in chronological time and move about abstract, postcolonial space, to be sure. However, their experiences in this Melanesian modernity seem to matter little and do not persuade their hearts. Jobs and travel seem to leave them untouched, as if nothing had happened to challenge or change the shape of their desires. Instead, if anything, the boundaries of their archaic identities as young men appear to become shored up in these stories, rather than given up.

More generally, what do these courtship stories, and their chronotopic uniformity, suggest about their dialogue with modernity in PNG? I think at least two things. One is that the self may respond compartmentally, rather than comprehensively. That is, a young man may report to work five days a week, listen to the radio, talk on mobile phones, go to market, ride the bus, attend church services, write and read correspondence, yet marry a stranger. The other point to which these stories attest is the more general proposition that how masculinity is configured may be a measure of the historical pressures to which it has been subjected. In other words, the male self may be configured in terms of diverse and discrepant values and voices. Instead of a hegemonic masculinity, Murik masculinity combines individualism and kinship, capitalist relations of production and gift exchange, Christianity and ancestor worship, Western education and the Male Cult and so forth. It is therefore not at all consistent or predictable. While young men exert moral agency by courting and marrying, the absence of direct expressions of desire in their stories is an important dimension of a characteristically Melanesian subject position in, and now a measure of their alienation from, the modernity with which they are in dialogue.

In the next chapter, I turn to ambivalences in this dialogue expressed in the context of marijuana trade and consumption. I shall argue that the drug elicits longstanding alienations of young men from Murik society but hints at the emergence of a new subject-centered voice as well.

NOTES

1. Moreover, "[t]he rise of romantic love more or less coincided with the emergence of the novel: the connection was one of a newly discovered narrative form" (Giddens: 1992: 40). This association led him to arrive at a startling conclusion: "romantic love [i]s essentially feminized love" (1992: 43; see also F. Cancian 1987). That is, beginning in the nineteenth century, as women became increasingly domestic, they became "specialists of the heart" (Giddens 1992: 44), who read and were influenced by romantic novels.
2. Thus Goode: "Love is a pattern found only in the US" (1959: 40).
3. "Love is a passion to the Melanesian as to the European and torments mind and body to a greater or lesser extent; it leads to many an impasse, scandal, or tragedy; more rarely, it illuminates life and makes the heart expand and overflow" (Malinowski 1929: 69). See also Ruth Landes on Ojibwa courtship (1937); see Berndt (1976) who affirms the paramount import of romantic love in northern Arnhem Land as having both religious significance in certain contexts and also secular meanings in others; see Harris (1995) on romantic love among the Mangaians; Plotnicov (1995) on romantic love among urban Nigerians; Bell (1995) on the presence of romantic love in precontact courtship among the Taita despite the claims of missionaries that Africans were incapable of feeling any emotion other than lust, thus promoting the view that love was caused by European influence.
4. In some instances, these emotions must be reconciled with the demands of collective obligation, as among the Kutali of Sri Lanka, for example, where love is a silent precondition for arranging a cross-cousin marriage (de Munck 1998). Among the Kalasha of the Hindukush, child betrothal coexists with the right of a woman to elope, which right Maggi has called "the prototypic act that defines Kalasha women's freedom" (2001: 168). Authority in both cultures is challenged to fit the needs of personal desire and attraction to those of kinship and alliance. Empirically, then, love among literate peoples cannot be opposed to love among preliterate

groups. Rather than only one exceptional construction of it, several different relations between romance and society seem to co-exist. The implication that there is a historical sequence of "progressively more loving society" (Gillis 1988: 89) is therefore unsustainable. If we dismiss geographic, historical and sociological dichotomies as false and Eurocentric, then perhaps new questions about romance ought to be raised.
5. More generally, Myers has argued that emotions are political (1979; 1986) and Abu-Lughod and Lutz (1990) have said that emotion-discourse establishes, asserts and contests power/status differences. Another use of romance has been discussed by Creighton in Japan (1991), where Valentine's Day was imported by a chocolate company executive in the late 1950s and became a unique opportunity for women to openly declare personal romantic attraction for men, which was viewed as Western, by gift-giving, dark chocolate in particular. Twenty years later, this imbalance was amended by the invention of a reciprocal holiday during which men give white chocolate to women.
6. Abu-Lughod (1990) reported how romantic discourse threatened male authority in an Egyptian Bedouin community, despite being inhibited by sentiments of shame and modesty as well as by arranged marriages. Nevertheless, love poetry (*ghinnawa*) is composed by both young men and women. "To love, or to express the sentiments of love, then, also signifies one's freedom" (Abu-Lughod 1990: 36). In the 1970s and 1980s, Bedouin men began to buy and sell land as individuals, either for agricultural purposes or for profit. Conflict over land ownership led them into greater relations with the state's legal system in search of land title. As a result, senior men got more power and wealth, leaving women more dependent and confined within domestic spaces. While all men had independent access to the market, women did not. Their power in society was further diminished. A generational conflict with elders was then asserted in their love poetry.

In rural Nepal, Ahearn (2001) has described a shift in marriage practices. Although romantic love is not new, it is becoming more common, a change that is reflected by an increase in elopements and a reduction in arranged or capture marriages. Ahearn sets this change in a context marked by monetization, democratization, a development discourse that has been emphasizing individualism and, as if to confirm Stone's, Giddens' and Goody's views, increased literacy, particularly among women. Amid a stress on personal agency over fate, to be modern is to choose a life-long partner in a companionate marriage. Modesty norms restricting young men and women from spending time alone together persist: a new form of courtship has resulted. Fatalism remains a strong conviction among elders. So youth assert freedom through love letters, which correspondences their parents bemoan.

7. Wardlow (1999) has described the two models of love practiced by both urbanized and rural Huli youth in the Highland fringe of Papua New Guinea. One is based in love magic cast by women upon men, a magic which is held to assault the latter's spiritual autonomy and agency. The other is based in a modern, independent kind of mutual attraction that reflects obedience to God and should result in companionate marriage. Both are promoted by women and reflect their increased agency in the contemporary period. But both create conflict and tension with prospective mates. Men reject the inhibitions required of Christianity and they experience the feeling of being "in love" as a frightening loss of autonomy "which suggests the possibility of spiritual assault" (Wardlow 1999: 7). Women too worry about the spiritual repercussions of using love magic, as a later cause of sickness. Couples later rededicate themselves to traditional menstrual taboos and Christian orthodoxy by way of fostering a companionate marriage.
8. See Clifford (1988), Hatfield (2002) and Ball and Harkness (2015) for other uses of the idea of chronotope.
9. In "Forms of Time and of the Chronotope in the Novel" (1981: 84-258), Bakhtin lays out an elaborate historical classification of chronotopes, for example, of the Ancient Greek romance, the chivalric romance in the Middle Ages, in Rabelais, and so on.
10. *Mimesis* was written while Auerbach was teaching in Istanbul, having fled there after being fired from his position in Romance Philology at the University of Marburg by the Nazis in 1935.
11. Now Auerbach (1957) contrasts Homeric narrative in *The Odyssey* with the narrative style of the Old Testament story of the sacrifice of Isaac. In the latter, only certain parts of the action are brought into relief, while others are left obscure, unexpressed and invisible. Divine forces, for example, influence the heroes. The narrative flow is subject to abrupt turns of events. Meaning is multiple and must be interpreted. People change in the course of narrative experience; and there is a preoccupation with what is morally problematic. Similarly, in the chronotope of romantic narrative, motivation arises from the unseen interior of the person, the heart. Boundaries between self and other become volatile. Narratives of romance become imbued with, or incarnated by, multilayered backgrounds, emotional complexity, only some of which is expressible, if imperfectly so. By contrast to the Homeric chronotope of the ancestors, events touch the hero and ecstatically transform him or her.
12. cf. Horkheimer and Adorno (1955). Their reading of Odysseus presented in *Dialectic of Enlightenment* is quite different; namely that he is "a prototype of the bourgeois individual…a figure of the protagonist compelled to wander" (1955: 43).

13. Marriages were also arranged with the goal of expanding lineage-based, ceremonial groups or intertribal trade networks.
14. Missionary views about the Taita were that the African was incapable of any emotion other than lust; this promoted Western racism and the view that romantic love were caused by European influence. But the Taita married for love before the arrival of the white man (Bell 1995). More specifically, a careful reading of Father Schmidt's Murik trilogy in *Anthropos* does not give the impression that he was that sort of racist missionary.
15. Residence was not rigidly specified, but could either go in patri- or matrilocal directions, depending on the relative resources of the kin groups. In other words, it too was a subject of negotiation. Upon moving in together, bride- and groomservices were expected, demanded and performed by both spouses. Taking a man's perspective, Somare writes: "We do not have big ceremonial exchanges of gifts. The husband's obligation toward his father-in-law really begins after the marriage. It is an obligation that lasts for the rest of his life. If the father-in-law says, 'Cut me a canoe,' the son-in-law has to go and carve a canoe" (Somare 1975: 45).
Affinal avoidances were established with senior kin of both spouses' extended families. A man was expected to abide by hierarchical respect relations with his wife's elder siblings of both sexes, her parents and their siblings. These affines immediately became *wandiik* to him, an avoidance and respect term that would be substituted for the personal names of the wife's senior kin. The same avoidance and respect relationships, terms and roles held for women vis à vis their husband's kin. A woman was, and continues to be, expected to remain on her knees in the presence of her husband's father. When the spouses of sons enter the houses of their father-in-law, they walked on their knees.
16. Thus Bataille: "I intend to speak of ...three types of eroticism in turn, to wit, physical, emotional and religious. My aim is to show that with all of them the concern is to substitute for the individual isolated discontinuity a feeling of profound continuity" (1962: 15).
17. My little sample certainly does not exhaust the polyphony of voices either in Murik or in PNG as a whole. Bateson (1936), Lipset and Stritecky (1994), and then Barlow and Lipset (1997), all argued that there are differences between male and female discourse in Sepik societies (Iatmul and Murik). Moreover, male-female differences in the expression of romance have been a subsidiary theme in the theoretical literature on the subject (see Cancian 1987; Goody 1998; Giddens 1992). There are also other male voices, more urbanized, more educated or more Christian, that might discuss courtship in more reflexive voices. Nevertheless, if the representations of desire and moral agency in these stories reflect courtship discourse, they do so, I think, for rural youth in general, rather than just on the Murik coast. Jenkins and

Alpers, for example, drew the following conclusion: "For most young people [in PNG] sexual encounters predate the emergence of deep feelings for one another. Romance, in the Western sense, does not figure prominently in the discourse of either male or female informants, but young women speak of longing for their boyfriends in terms similar to those found elsewhere. Young men, however, seem to have no vocabulary of love, no way to talk about their deeper feelings except in terms of sexual pleasure, that is, *kisim piling* (1996: 249). Thanks to Leslie Butt for pointing their work out to me.
18. The PNG Kina equaled about US$.45 at that time.
19. See the story of Murakau Wino's courtship of Minjamok above.
20. I am referring to rites of reversal that Gregory Bateson analyzed among Iatmul people of the middle Sepik River (1936; Silverman 2001; Lipset and Silverman 2005).
21. In Murik kin terminology, it is the case that a wife may be addressed as "mother" by her husband.
22. I found myself so surprised by events in his narrative that I could hardly refrain from pressing him rather baldly in order to ascertain how he viewed what had taken place as specifically as I could.
23. The interview went on as follows:

DL: Do the Boig have this custom? About marriage?
T: You are referring to payments?
DL: Yeah. What do they do?
T: I didn't pay for her.
DL: Ah.
T: Here, we usually exchange; you take my sister, I take your sister.
DL: Yeah.
DL: What did they say?
T: They said to never mind a payment.
DL: They said, 'forget it,' eh?
T: Yeah. They said, she could come live here and then we would go live there. OK. After we stayed up there, we would come back here. Go, come. If I did pay for her, I would pay using our [nautilus] seashells, we do not think that is too hard—
DL: They called for—
T: They wanted shells. They didn't talk about money—
DL: Just shells.
T: Shells. *Kev, kev.* They are in the lagoons and standup vertically like this.
DL: Yeah.
T: We have plenty in the lagoons.

24. In Murik culture, intertribal marriages may or may not assert personal choice over obligation, since lineage or village endogamy is neither required nor highly valued. Intertribal marriages are valued because of the reliable and generous, brideservice-based trading partnerships they instigate. In 2001, 17% of all marriages I counted in the village of Darapap were with non-Murik mates (n = 85), while 57% of all urban marriages involving Darapap villagers living in Wewak town were with non-Murik mates (n = 21).
25. Trading partners were symbolic women who had to be magically seduced to be generous. Foreign women were viewed as sexually aggressive or as willing to have their affections "stolen" by visiting Murik traders. Feathers, color-coded by geography and standing for specific overseas sexual affairs, were named for the donors' lovers as they were placed in the hair of young male initiates.
26. See, the ethos of isolation in Hopper's "The Intermission," "In a New York movie" or "Nighthawks" (Kranzfelder 1995). Thanks to Diana M. Dean for pointing these out to me.

CHAPTER 3

Marijuana, Youth and Society

Despite the alienation of their Homeric voices, young Murik men marry across the anonymity and abstractions of modern space and time in PNG. Meanwhile, modernity in PNG has impoverished Murik society. The Murik have come to see themselves as poor and to see the contemporary state of their economy as exacting and challenging (Allen et al. 2005). Why? Modernity has deprived the Murik of control over a crucial link in the means of production. Marx of course understood that such a loss comes at the cost of moral agency, a loss that is audible in marijuana discourse, which is the topic of this chapter.

Recall that for Marx, labor was a form of moral self-fashioning that became alienated in early capitalism when workers lost control of the means of production.[1] Now quite a little research has been done about the cultural consequences of state-based currency on Melanesian societies, research that suggests that the relationship of money, commodities, markets, formal labor and so forth to premodern, indigenous notions of the moral person is very complicated (Akin and Robbins 1999; McCormack and Barclay 2013). In the Murik Lakes, the modern economy has indeed given rise to alienation, that is to say, to a loss of moral agency. But capitalism's relationship to Murik labor, I should clarify, is not to the means of production per se. The Murik still harvest seafood from their lacustrine commons, the commons they still own and control, for its use value (Lipset 2014a). What they have lost is control over the exchange value of Murik fish.

Regionally, Murik men were once seen as prestigious, intertribal actors whose voyages were eagerly anticipated and generously received by their regional trading partners along the North Coast (see Chap. 5). And locally, the value of Murik seafood used to be prized by their inland trading partners, who offered sago flour and garden produce in return for it (see Chap. 2). Today, overseas trade has slowed down to a snail's pace, and sago flour, once imported through a combination of dyadic trade relations and barter, has largely been replaced by biweekly, monetized markets where the value of sago flour has come to exceed Murik fish (Fig. 3.1). In these outposts of modernity in PNG, in other words, the Murik have lost control of exchange rates. And like their seafood, they too have become devalued. From a perspective of economic development in modern PNG, the Murik have been reduced to little more than a land-poor, subsistence-based people. There is another, gendered implication of what has happened to the value of Murik fish. There is an occult meaning of their poverty. Men lack the magical agency (*timiit*) to bespell trading partners and make them generous and forthcoming with their foodstuffs (see Chap. 7).

Fig. 3.1 Rural fish and garden produce market. Photo: David Lipset (2001)

While modernity in PNG has subtracted value from the Murik economy, it has done little or nothing by way of inducting male youth into its labor force (see Chap. 2). Most, if not all, village-raised young men receive at least a minimal degree of Western education from which they come away with no shortage of goals in their sights. Most commonly, they want employment, more education, to travel, or at the very least, to own an outboard motor and a boat. A mobile phone goes without saying (see Chap. 4). But the means are lacking. One characteristic feature of modernity in PNG is that while the national economy may be booming, its prosperity is not widespread. It fails to produce jobs throughout the nation; and neither does the state provide youth with advanced, occupational training. Anomie, as Robert King Merton once redefined the term, is not just a state of normlessness as per Durkheim, it characterizes societies in which ambitions have no access to legitimate agency to fulfill them (1938, 1949, 1957a). The result is behavior in which means and ends are unclearly related, such as *raskolism* in PNG, which Merton would have classed as deviance, if not also as rebellion. Another result is what Merton called retreatism, retreatism that appears as a preoccupation in PNG with minor, nonutilitarian forms of play, such as penny-ante card games, athletics and substance abuse.

In this chapter, I will argue that the expression of masculine alienation from modernity in PNG in marijuana discourse differs from the alienation the young men spoke of in terms of a chronotope of Homeric courtship. Their voices were solely focused on constructing a relationship between self and other in a way that seemed to imply an indifference to the emotional pull in the chronotope of romance. In marijuana dialogue, their relationship to modernity appears as a combination of values in conflict. The drug is viewed as a kind of imported good that is both part, yet not part, of the Murik overseas trade network. It is viewed as a commodity; it has exchange value, being bought and sold. But rather than authorized by the state, its exchange value is illegitimate. At the same time, youth find its effects pleasurable. Athletes even value it as a performance enhancer (Jankowiak and Bradburd 1996). While youth voice approval, marijuana use is condemned by middle-aged and senior men as a cause of domestic abuse, as well as mistrust of the state (see Chap. 4).

As my concern in this chapter is with marijuana discourse, I mean to determine how the metaphors in terms of which this drug is understood by the different generations of men *are and are* not distinctively Murik, and how they answer the modernity that has brought marijuana to them.

I will begin by comparing marijuana talk with the cultural construction of tobacco, with reference to traffic and consumption, on the one hand, and then with reference to views about the decline of the legitimacy of both the postcolonial state and local-level morality, on the other.

TOBACCO, GOOD AND BAD

Elsewhere in the Sepik region, and of course elsewhere in PNG, tobacco is cultivated. Margaret Mead, for example, referred to large Mundugumor tobacco gardens maintained by women's labor (1963: 191, see also Riesenfeld 1947: 75–6). In keeping with their position in an intertidal environment and trade-based economy, the Murik import and purchase tobacco. Generally, they reckon its value in at least two ways: by origin and quality. Tobacco is said to come from multiple directions in regional space that they identify with named villages and hereditary trading partners (*asamot*) who are also referred to as "routes" (*yakabor*) to their communities.[2] In 1986, for example, I accompanied my adoptive elder brother, Murakau Wino, on a visit to his "trade-brother" living in Sub village on Muschu Island, about 50 miles west of the Murik Lakes.[3] As this was the era before mobile phones, we only discovered that his host happened to be away in Wewak town when we got there (see Chap. 4). But the man's daughter, who called Murakau "father," felt obligated to look after us. Murakau held Sub tobacco in very high regard and had brought three Murik baskets with him to exchange for it. In return, his "trade-daughter" presented him with three, thick bark covered, oval-shaped sheaths that contained a great many little bunches of dried leaves (this one-for-one exchange rate being regionally standard for Murik baskets and many goods, such as clay pots, wooden plates, buckets of *canarium* almonds and even pigs).

In addition, tobacco is also purchased at regional markets that regularly take place in and around the Murik Lakes or it may be obtained from hereditary trading partners, as I have just illustrated. However acquired, parcels of trade tobacco may be gifted to junior kin and presented as a ceremonial valuable (*mwaran*) during ritual events. They are also sold. There is an ongoing demand at the local level. When I returned in 2010, villagers were talking about a "tobacco crisis" going on at the time; smokers were desperate. Vendors were selling single leaves and cigarettes rolled in rectangular pieces of newspaper at village markets, or from their houses, and during card games and athletic events (Fig. 3.2). But the feeling was that there was little or no tobacco around the community.

Fig. 3.2 Cigarettes for sale in a jar alongside a card game. Photo: David Lipset (2014)

The general point I want to make is only that both overseas and local-level tobacco exchange and sales are not at all alienated. Both sales and exchange are a collectively organized, normative enterprise, an enterprise that is taken for granted, and invokes images of self and other constituted in terms of kinship, cultural geography and regional as well as ritual exchange, and increasingly, in terms of money.

As elsewhere in modern PNG (see Thomas 2006, see also Halvaksz and Lipset 2006), marijuana is called "drunken tobacco" in Tokpisin (*spak brus*) or just "the smoke" (*dispela simok*).[4] In the Murik vernacular, marijuana is also classed as a tobacco (*sakain*). It is alternatively called an intoxicating, or, literally, a "crazy tobacco" (*sakain baubau*), or, it is condemned as an "immoral" or, literally, a "bad tobacco" (*sakain mwaro*). It is also classified, along with all other purchasable tobacco products, as a "modern, or whiteman's, tobacco" (*yabar sakain*). By extension, it is therefore included in the larger class of things, occupations and ideologies that have long distinguished power inequities between Murik people and colonial modernity (see Preface and Chap. 6).

Marijuana is neither imported from hereditary trading partners, like trade tobacco (or sago flour and garden produce) nor is it purchased at regional markets. But it remains no less of an imported commodity than these other goods. The difference of course between it and them is that it is bought and sold illegitimately and in secret. Marijuana is thus a morally anomalous good. It is a tobacco that is not a tobacco. In the following sections of this chapter, I will examine this contradiction in traffic and consumption discourse. Doing so, I want to argue that it may be seen to stand for the estrangement of Murik youth from the two economies that comprise modernity in PNG.

Traffic

I will begin by reporting how three young men viewed marijuana traffic. One mentioned that it was imported into the community. Another criticized how it was smuggled into the village where, the third man allowed, it was not sold in the open. Raising the subject was, of course, a little touchy which may be evident in the following ethnography.

> During a discussion in the Male Cult House about marijuana as a performance enhancer in athletics, I asked how the drug usually reached the village. A youngish, middle-aged man called Harry was carving a hand drum at that moment. Without hesitation, in an offhand, matter-of-fact voice, he answered, "It is brought from the east, through Bogia, along the beach (Fig. 3.3). Here, it is sold for K1 per parcel, which adds up to good money very quickly."
>
> One week later, in the privacy of his house, I talked to Jakai Smith, a senior middle-aged man, about intravillage trafficking. After denying knowledge about the subject, because "what I can't see for myself, I can't know about for sure," he went on to affirm Harry's point, "that the marijuana comes [here] along the beach from Bogia, Madang and the Highlands (Fig. 3.3). But it is not just our youth who bring it into the village. There are many women who married husbands from far away places. These affines come here. We don't know what they bring with them. How many times have we said at [councilor's meetings] that these kinds of affines are no good!"
>
> In a separate interview conducted in the house where I was staying, I asked Tabanus, whom I have known basically since he was toddler, about marijuana in the village (see Chap. 2). The young man agreed about its point of origin and offered to show me, secretly and quietly, who was currently selling it. He also volunteered to bring me some to show me what it looked like. I declined, conceding that I knew only too well what it looked like.

MARIJUANA, YOUTH AND SOCIETY 63

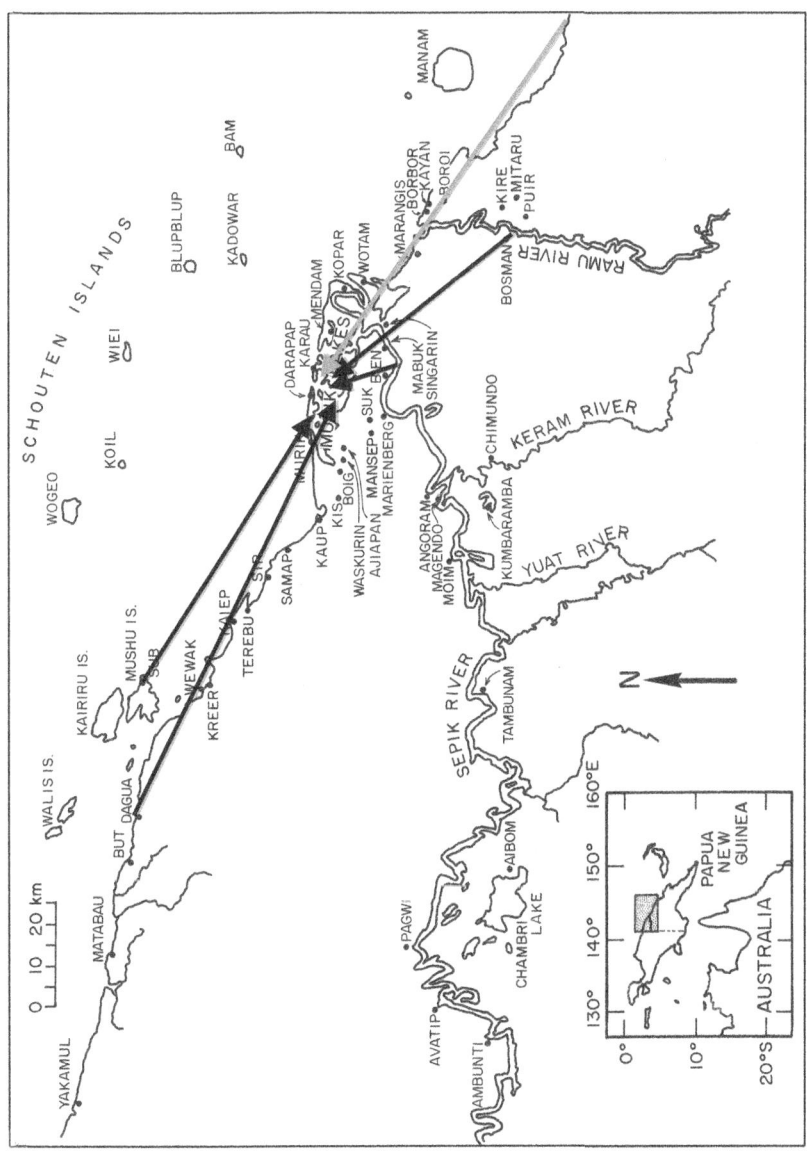

Fig. 3.3 Tobacco and marijuana flows to the Murik lakes, 2001

As I say, asking about the drug was a little dicey. The first informant, Harry, was willing to talk about marijuana traffic. Meanwhile, Jakai Smith, the second one, struck a culturally standard pose, momentarily declining to discuss the subject with me. His reticence, I got the sense, arose from its illegitimacy. Neither man volunteered to name which villagers might then be selling it, nor did I request to know. Tabanus, the last voice in this trio, possessed no such compunctions. In other words, attitudes about marijuana discourse are plural and delicate but seemed to divide along generational lines at the village level.

With respect to where the drug is imported from, all three men independently identified the same direction from which it entered the Murik Lakes. In this sense, they likened it, albeit implicitly, to an imported tobacco, which, as I say, is also spoken of in geographic terms. There are two other interesting details in their commentary: (1) that the drug is carried "along the beach," which is to imply, it is smuggled by couriers walking "by foot" rather than traveling by boat, and (2) that it comes "from the east" via urban centers, ultimately originating in the Highlands. The first point removed marijuana traffic from hereditary modes of transport and located it in the agency of individuals. The second one connected it to the nation and to the moral ambiguities of postcolonial modernity and state-guaranteed relationships, while removing it from the archaic world of "canoe-rollers" and the guarantees of hereditary trade partnerships (see Chap. 5). Marijuana was dissociated from collective forms of male agency, in other words. Thus, as both a commodity and a trade good, the meaning of the substance was double-voiced. Not only did it reflect an encounter between marketplace rationality and the peculiarities of the archaic Murik economy, but more generally it reflected the estrangement of young Murik men from modernity in PNG.

Marijuana parcels, as Harry and Tabanus went on to say, were sold in the villages. Harry specified a price: they were sold on a one-for-one basis, as a kind of incipient commoditized form that combined market exchange with archaic forms of balanced reciprocity, or barter. His casual tone, I think, suggested that he was implicitly including intravillage traffic as part of the micro-marketing of goods, like fish, cigarettes, betel nuts, baked goods and sago flour that goes on all the time. Although conducted in secret, my point is that marijuana sales were not entirely random or fully disaggregated from the informal economy in the villages. That is, it was part of the larger dialogue in which archaic and modern values were becoming morally conditional upon one another, composite and interrelated in a way that drew its norms from both while it did call the legitimacy of male youth into question, not for the first time, of course.

Two informants declined to name sellers. Harry also neglected to specify the genealogical category through which marijuana might be imported, however, as would be the case for tobacco. By contrast, Jakai Smith did accuse non-Murik husbands of village women. In doing so, we come upon another instance of how marijuana is seen as an immoral trade good. A long-standing and favored Murik tactic for instigating new trading partnerships is to claim brideservice obligations that tribally exogamous spouses are no less expected to fulfill than locally born ones (see Chap. 2). And one significant way they may do so is by arranging for the provision of trade goods from their villages of origin. But, of course, establishing trading partnerships through affinity is a legitimate rather than a bootleg mode of relationship. So yet another composite meaning of marijuana exchange has come to light. Although the "bad tobacco" is seen as a kind of modern commodity, this vision is not entirely full-fledged. Adhesions to archaic trade remain, although their moral value is reversed. Traffic discourse expresses the Janus-faced quality of Murik masculine alienation from modernity in PNG.

Consumption Discourse

Among the Gebusi, a formerly self-sufficient group of foragers and horticulturalists in the Western Province of PNG, tobacco smoking used to be a fundamental and essential symbol of "male social life" (Knauft 1987: 75). Except perhaps to differentiate children from adolescents and adults in Murik, smoking was and is not a privilege limited to a single social category either by generation or gender. It is enjoyed, as a cigarette wrapped in newspaper, or as a cigar or in a pipe, by all manner of men and women regardless of their status (Fig. 3.4). Earlier, I mentioned that trade tobacco is classed among the most morally significant goods in the culture; it is a ceremonial valuable (*mwaran*) that may be presented for the purposes of creating or renewing relationships in ritual settings. When a man returns to the hall of the Male Cult after a prolonged absence, he ought to offer a ritual gift (*kuup*) of tobacco and betel nuts to the assembly as a gesture of respect and sympathy for the interests of their collectivity which he has ignored while gone. As a token of reconciliation, a disputant, male or female, may also give tobacco to his or her rival, along with a meal. Tobacco leaves are used to decorate many types of ritual paraphernalia and

Fig. 3.4 Murik woman smoking a pipe. Photo: L.P. Ledoux (1936)

are distributed to guests as departure gifts (Fig. 3.5). Tobacco is part of the ordinary kit that adults carry in their baskets in public settings, such as mortuary vigils. It is consumed in public as a moral act that signals that one is participating in social life, rather than plotting against it.[5] Tobacco, in short, is construed as a "good thing" (*moran arito*).[6]

By contrast, attitudes about marijuana consumption elicited from young, middle-aged and senior generations of men cast the drug in morally contrary terms.

> About a conflict between a classificatory daughter and her husband in which marijuana intoxication was alleged to play a role, James Kaparo, a late, middle-aged, man, generalized that "many [rural] people try this stuff, but here in … [the village], the young men have adopted it as their own. They go to the beach, smoke it and play cards. If you see one of them alone, you can take for granted what he is doing. They come to ask us for money to buy food and they lie. They go spend it on marijuana. We tell them that it is no good. But they say that we are lying to them. They like it."
>
> I walked with Luke, my adoptive brother, to watch preparations for a grade-taking in the Gaingiin Society that was going on just near the beach (see Chap. 6). We encountered some young men in the overgrowth behind the beach who were making two masks. Nearby, a small-stakes game of cards was going on among some youth. Luke leaned over and, under his breath, quipped that he smelled marijuana. As for me, all I could detect was the fresh, ocean breeze.
>
> A bit later that day, Luke joined in a discussion of marijuana consumption among male youth that I started in the Male Cult House. He pointed out the exceptional case of "a senior man in [a neighboring village] who smokes it in a pipe … He likes it. He smokes it all the time."

Fig. 3.5 Tobacco leaves, newspaper and other foods hanging from a mortuary cape. Photo: David Lipset (2012)

Can I vouch for James Kaparo's claim about the unanimous approval of marijuana that he attributed to "male youth" in Darapap? Not exactly. But I can attest that male youth who smoke do not attend or belong to the Seventh Day Adventist (SDA) church. That they play cards and smoke indicates that they do not subscribe to SDA rules against doing so. How thoroughly the drug is associated with the young, and not with more senior generations of men, is highlighted by the exceptional case of the senior, marijuana smoking man Luke mentioned. Unlike tobacco, marijuana is thus a new category marker, albeit a minor one, that supplements a preexisting division in the community, that is, between male youth who are churchgoers and youth who aren't. While tobacco transaction and consumption is gender neutral and approved of, marijuana is associated with morally suspect, retreatist activities and illegitimate modes of disclosure. Smokers spend time alone and in secret, play cards and lie. They are often found in culturally liminal spaces, such as the beach or the coconut groves. What is more, notice that marijuana is said to disrupt normative reciprocities among kin and constitute mutual distrust and disrespect across generations of men, as opposed to tobacco, which is classed as a "good thing."

Lastly, I want to draw attention to the hedonistic motivation attributed to smoking marijuana: the pleasure of it. Now, I have not observed consumption practices, comportment, and so on. So, I cannot state, or cannot disentangle, what smokers may mean or what their senior interlocutors may be referring to when they claim that youth "like to smoke." But I can affirm, with some degree of certainty, that this declarative mode of subjective self-disclosure is extremely infrequent in Murik discourse. Mothers know the food preferences of husbands and children; it is true. "Komsing has never liked to eat sago pudding," a senior woman once remarked to me about her elder sister's son, who was by then well into his senior years. "He prefers sago pancakes." I suppose this muteness is consistent with the Homeric chronotope that I discussed in Chap. 2 or the stoicism attributed to Murik peoples' attitudes about environmental vulnerability that I will get to in Chap. 7. Only rarely does anyone ever hear anything said either about preferences for food, beverages, people or spaces. In the next two texts, a value of marijuana consumption as a performance enhancer—for example, as a source of agency—is broached and contested. These data will perhaps expand upon the general point that the young take pleasure from smoking the drug and like being under its influence.

> I stopped by the Male Cult House on a rainy afternoon. A few younger, middle-aged men were gathered there, among them a young man from the Markham Valley (Morobe Province), who had married a village woman. He had a soccer-coaching certificate, as do I, and we got to talking about training to coordinate runs by strikers in the attacking third. I then asked him how he had done with local youth at a recent tournament. Those "boys," he grumbled, "smoke too much marijuana before games and it blurs their vision, although they think it helps them play."
>
> In the midst of the interview I excerpted above, in which Jakai Smith assailed affinal traffickers, he also condemned the effects of drug use by citing an urban soccer team called "Murik United" that had to forfeit a match because the players were too high to play (see also Halvaksz 2006).

The attribution of agency to marijuana associates it with magic (*timiit*) which is also viewed as a morally ambiguous performance enhancer (see Chap. 7). For example, I attended a match between club teams from Vanuatu and Australia held in Port Moresby at the Pacific Club Championships in 2001. I observed that the Vanuatu players were not warming up, not getting touches on the ball, running or stretching their legs, unlike their rivals, the Wollongong Wolves from outside Sydney. My company, which included a retired captain of the PNG national team, advised me in knowing, but furtive, voices that the Vanuatu footballers had "warmed up another way." In other words, they went on to explain, the players had secretly anointed themselves with magic off of the pitch that ruled out their need for any further preparations. While there was little or no equivocation in their reading of the situation, or in their conviction in the efficacy of magical agency, marijuana discourse, by contrast, was nothing, if not thoroughly riddled with moral ambiguity. The emphatic condemnations of the drug's effects voiced by senior Murik men answered the positive views of the drug asserted by the young through their consumption discourse. Together, this dialogue about the values of marijuana both on hedonistic grounds and as a performance enhancer also gives voice to generational conflict in modern PNG. The alleged loss of moral agency of youth in the consumption discourse of middle-aged and senior men is also a reflection upon normative decline at the local level. That is to say, it portrays a vision of anomie.[7]

Pame, the last living member of the senior cohort of men that I first knew in the early 1980s, and Noah, one of his middle-aged sons, deplored marijuana consumption for causing an irreversible breakdown in lineage solidarity (cf. Smith 1994).

Noah: Now, we have changed. We used to send food to brothers and sisters. Now, there is no sense of family. Before, we respected lineage boundaries. Today, brothers marry sisters. The young men do not know how to carve. They know nothing about [Murik] culture. They … smoke at night and [then] beat their women. They smoke. We see them laugh about nothing, and then we know they have been smoking. The village has changed. It is a bush. Before you could go ask your brothers or your fathers, and they would help you without thought of getting anything back. Now, never. We have adopted the ways of foreigners. If your lineage can't help you, how can an individual make a business grow? [In] some [non-Murik] villages, [people] still help each other, the Maprik, the

> Yangoru, they still offer each other help. Also, our trading partners on the [offshore, Schouten] Islands cooperate together to go fishing. We have lost this custom of our ancestors.
> DL: What has overtaken the village?
> Pame: Marijuana has overtaken the village. Now we know nothing. The elders are dead. The women are ill. Now we don't have knowledge about the ancestor-spirits (*Kakar*). They are making women ill. When [young men] didn't have this marijuana, there were fewer fights with wives. Now that this marijuana has come here, they fight a lot with their wives.

While it attempts to affirm a ruptured view of moral time, except for the incorporation of marijuana into it, I must insist that there is little in these two men's views, or even its overall nostalgic tone, that is new. I mean to say that it does not constitute any kind of discursive discontinuity from older views of the state of Murik society.

Noah charged that the village had become normless beset by wife beating, defiance of incest taboos, a collapse of an ethos of reciprocity among kin and the loss of custom. Then he arrived at a curious conclusion about this bleak state of affairs: "We have adopted the ways of foreigners." Village morality, Noah seemed to be suggesting, had come to suffer from modern individualism. If not despair, at least there was a sense of dismay in his view of life along the Murik coast by contrast with the collectivist ethic and moral solidarity he thought abided elsewhere in the region. A breakdown, added his father, had also occurred in youths' understanding of the ancestor-spirits in the Male Cult, that is to say, of the taboos associated with their power such as the need to quarantine them from women. Lastly, the father chose to agree with his son about domestic violence: not only was it a problem but it was on the rise. How had all this come about? On account of marijuana consumption (cf. Bell 2006).

The alienation of senior Murik men from modernity, from individualism and from the preference of youth for marijuana, suggests the emergence of a moral divide between them, or at least the presumption of one. The objects of criticism, aimed at both moral decay at large and young men in particular, I want to argue, are generic rather than new: they predated the arrival of marijuana. In my view, such a discourse of rupture has been voiced by generation after generation of senior men throughout the colonial and the postcolonial eras, if not earlier. Now, marijuana is cited as a new corrosive influence on the community; it is a new symbol of moral disorder in contemporary modernity, to be sure, but one whose attributes are not at all new. Before, when the young were accused of defiance, genealogical ignorance and spousal abuse, before, when the solidarity of the lineage was depicted as unreliable, another external cause or combination of causes might have been cited (e.g., labor migration, education, alcohol, or missionization). Recall the unstable, short-lived quality of new marriages and associated blow-ups documented in Father Schmidt's diary entries from 1918 and 1919 that I cited in Chap. 2. Senior generations have long condemned "the nature" of Murik youth as jealous, petulant and ill-behaved, no less than they have disparaged the insolent character of Murik communities at large by contrast to their trading partners (see Lipset 1997: 217ff).

Their critique adopts the view that moral breakdown in society arises from both internal and external forces. Pame juxtaposed illnesses suffered by village women, which he attributed to ritual neglect of the Male Cult spirits, and the domestic violence he attributed to marijuana consumption. In the case of the former, the society is viewed as capable of reproducing moral order, and actors possess moral agency to do so. In the case of the latter, they do not. Now in part, this contrast is represented as a collapse of ultimate values: inattention to the Male Cult spirits, in the failure to fulfill norms of "conjugal morality" (Durkheim 1972: 173) and in the rise of individualism. Beset by broad-based value disorientation in modernity, marijuana consumption is a just proximate cause, a symptom of a larger estrangement.

Consumption Discourse in a Case of Domestic Violence

In 2001, the causal association of marijuana consumption to domestic violence had become a commonplace view, as well as a lived and experienced one. During fieldwork that year, a widow called Jamero looked after me, cooking for me, no less than she did for the rest of her family which included, among others, Nancy, one of her son's daughters, and Lauren, Nancy's husband, together with their three kids.[8] One morning, when I turned up (like a stray, hungry dog) for breakfast, Nancy had left home for Karau, a neighboring village, to stay with Joe Kabong, her classificatory father (FB, see Chap. 7).[9] Jamero and Jakai Smith, her neighbor and Nancy's mother's brother, explained why Nancy left.

Jamero (FM):	"Nancy (W) and Lauren (H) had a fight ... [yesterday] because Nancy wanted money to buy fish from her husband's family. She had also asked me for money, but I had just bought sago flour and had nothing left to give her. Lauren ridiculed Nancy."
Jakai Smith (MB):	"Nancy's husband insults her all the time. He swears at her. He isn't a good man at all. Nancy cried, took some of her things, and left for Karau."
Jamero:	"Now, I don't know what will happen. Will her husband go and get her, or will we just go on this way?"

Next day, however, Nancy returned, having been brought home by her "father" (FB). One week later, however, she had fled back to her "father" in the nearby village. Another one of Nancy's father's brothers told me that he was expecting her imminent return. Overhearing our conversation, Jamero volunteered that they had been fighting because Lauren was high. "He smoked and became very angry at Nancy." Nancy did come home that day, but a day or so afterwards, she was once again seeking refuge from her husband's abuse. This time, she went to stay with the family of a different "father" (FB). "Nancy came to me last night," he explained. "I hid her. It is an old story. Her husband smokes marijuana and thinks of her old boyfriends. The mind goes to the hand and the hand starts to bing, bom, bing! Good times [for her]? He doesn't beat her." After going back and forth several more times, Jamero, her grandmother (father's mother), allowed to me that Nancy had decided "to divorce him. She is tired of his anger, which is constant." A day or two later, when I reappeared at Jamero's house, again looking for breakfast, I found Nancy buying small parcels of sago flour at a little market that was being held in front of a nearby house.

In the course of the week or ten days that I was able to follow this case, the wife's kin blamed marijuana consumption for inducing jealous anger in the husband. They did not seem to view it as anything more than one of several motives of the conflict, however. Other causes they cited were the husband's contempt, his shameless character and finances. The drug provoked the husband's anger, in their view, because it disinhibited highly cathected memories about his wife's past lovers. Except for the addition of marijuana consumption, this latter view of spousal abuse, whose proximate cause is sexual jealousy, is nothing more than a conventional Murik explanation of conflict (see Chap. 4). In other words, the addition of marijuana to modern life had merely superimposed a modern idiom onto an archaic, or ongoing, struggle of male youth as they made their way into a post-initiation, post-cultic society (see Chap. 2).

Marijuana and the Postcolonial State

Inevitably, marijuana traffic and consumption discourse also featured in encounters with and attitudes about, the state, the preeminent institution in and of modernity. In the following two cases, the ineptitude of its legal system was impugned.

> James Kaparo recalled what happened when two young men, who were his trading partners, came to Darapap village seeking refuge in the aftermath of a murder that had taken place in Bin, a nearby village on the lower Sepik River. They had allegedly brought marijuana with them. Police came to the village in the course of their investigation and arrested Kaparo not for anything to do with the murder but for drug possession. At court, he denied having any knowledge about the drugs and was released.

By their inability to distinguish between traffickers and middle-aged bystanders, the informant implied police incompetence.

In a second instance, the police were accused of brutality, disrespect for custom, and lastly, of corruption.

> Jakai Smith connected an episode in which policemen came to the neighboring villages of Darapap and Karau at the behest of the Prime Minister, Sir Michael Somare, who had requested that they do something about the rampant drug use that he understood was going on there. The police beat up many young men, including Smith's own son. They dragged the youth off to jail in Angoram, the district seat. In the event, the police also desecrated the Male Cult House, for which Sir Michael eventually took responsibility. Adding that many policemen confiscate the drug, but then smoke or sell it themselves, Smith concluded, "We don't trust them."[10]

In this episode, the depiction of the state resembles young men. Police traffic in and consume marijuana just like youth. The state becomes an immoral and illegitimate equal, rather than a superior, neutral, third party. But, as I say, the state, in both its colonial and postcolonial forms, has been subject to criticism that reaches all the way back to the first decade of the twentieth century. In the past, the charge of police malfeasance, bias and favoritism of course did not include drug traffic allegations. This is a new, postcolonial expression of an old complaint (see Bell 2006). Alienation from the new modernity, in other words, is rooted in its colonial predecessor.

Conclusion: Marijuana, Modernity and Alienation

In the first phases of colonial rule, drug trade in the Pacific (and elsewhere in the world) was a deliberate tactic to make subordinate, indigenous peoples economically and psycho-physiologically dependent on traders, labor recruiters and the like. While American twist tobacco was used in colonial PNG (Hayes 2003: 59), alcohol was used nearly everywhere else in the world, except in Eurasia, where narcotics, like opium, were distributed.[11] Drugs continue to play a critical role in the expansion of the capitalist world economy (Mintz 1985, Wolf 1982, Lindstrom 1982).

Marijuana was not introduced to Murik youth by representatives of global capitalism however. It came to the Murik coast through national intermediaries rather than Western ones. This is not to say, of course, that global capitalism has anything less to do with the diffusion of this drug to this backwater of postcolonial modernity than it did with the introduction of alcohol anywhere else on this frontier. But it does suggest a more of egalitarian context of diffusion which perhaps has made the meaning of marijuana rather more dialogical than elsewhere.

Among the Murik, the likening of marijuana to a trade good, akin to tobacco, suggests that, although illegitimate, the drug is not distinguished either as a prestige symbol of modernity or as an extraordinary item of exchange, like an outboard motor (see Chap. 2). In the rapid spread of marijuana trafficking and consumption through postcolonial PNG, that is to say, I think that we may read a more subtle power relationship than that which informed relations between previous drug-bearing foreigners and their subjects (Halvaksz and Lipset 2006). Perhaps the cast of power relations between seller and buyer in postcolonial drug trafficking is more egalitarian than they were in colonial times when "natives" bought twist tobacco or beer. I do not really know what they were like. The data in this chapter do suggest, however, that they do not subordinate the buyer to the state, but rather reduce the state's perceived legitimacy, thus to make one more equal to the other. Another outcome would be similar to colonial manipulation of drugs: increased market integration, albeit illegitimately so.

As there was no psychogenic precursor of marijuana in either the precontact or the colonized culture in PNG, the hedonistic enjoyment by male youth of consumption is clearly new. Their view of it as a performance enhancer in athletics, by contrast, may be likened to persisting views of magical agency, although in a disenchanted form. Admittedly, these are only meager, superficial glimpses of the positive opinions that the young hold about the drug. What is unambiguous is that, however more elaborate their approval may be, youthful marijuana consumption seems almost unanimously rejected by age.

The anti-consumption rhetoric of middle-aged and senior Murik men does not suggest that the arrival of marijuana has produced a dramatic schism in their critique of modernity however. It rather suggests that marijuana has been assimilated into the preexisting genres of their distress, the decline of lineage solidarity, the insubordination of the young, sexual jealousy and domestic violence. Rather than novel, it is a contemporary successor to a host of past stressors that elders blamed for the moral condition of social life. In marijuana consumption, middle-aged and senior men perceive their uncertainties and mistrust, but they do so in terms of that which they have long feared. That is, they see their alienation from both the local community and the state at large. As such, they do not declare their allegiance to, but rather their ongoing ambivalences about, value transmission within the village and the legitimacy of the postcolonial state.

The contested value of marijuana, so I have argued, can only be understood in terms of generic cultural discourses into which the drug has been inserted (Mintz 1985: 6). But it would be wrong to suggest that understanding what marijuana means may be exhausted by such a static orientation. It would be wrong to suggest that marijuana, which is a new drug, can be fully comprehended from this self-enclosed point of view.

In particular, to the male youth who consume it, marijuana seems to offer a discursive shift in type and possibility, which is to say, it offers a shift to a new kind of voice. The idea of a commodity that yields personal pleasure and a secular form of agency offers a hint of an emerging modernist subject-centered voice, albeit an alienated one.

In the next chapter, the scene shall shift to Wewak town where mobile telephones started to become available in 2007. I will argue that uses of and attitudes about the new social media provide another context, along with courtship and marijuana, for dialogue in which Murik masculine alienation from modernity in PNG is audible.

Notes

1. The capitalist was alienated too, although in a way different from the laborer's. He was separated from his ability to experience himself. Producing nothing at all other than the capital he owned, he lost his quali-

ties and power as a human being and had to derive them from wealth. Marx imagined this pathology in an interior monologue.

What I am and can do is … not at all determined by my individuality … As an individual I am lame, but money provides me with twenty-four legs. Therefore, I am not lame. I am a detestable, dishonorable, and stupid man, but money is honored and so also is its possessor. Money is the highest good, and so its possessor is good. Besides, money saves me the trouble of being dishonest; therefore I am presumed honest. I am stupid, but since money is the real mind of all things, how should its possessor be stupid. (Marx quoted in Bottomore 1963: 191, Marx's emphases)

2. There are many "routes." Tobacco is exported to the Murik Lakes from "routes" in every village along the North Coast, west of Wewak between the Beach Arapesh villages of But and others all the way to the Austronesian-speaking Yakamul people who live just west of Aitape town (Barlow et al. 1988). Tobacco is also grown and exported to Murik villages by trading partners living on the Lower Sepik and to the east toward Bogia as well as up the Ramu River.
3. This was part of the "Sepik Documentation Project," K. Barlow, J. Salau, L. Bolton and I conducted under the auspices of the Australian Museum (1986–1988, see Lipset 2016).
4. Young Murik men, so far as I know, did not smoke marijuana, until approximately the early 1990s. I am unaware how it first came into use in the villages. That is, I do not know under what circumstances it was initially introduced, e.g., who was involved, where it was purchased, how people reacted to smoking it for the first times and how they learned to enjoy it (Becker 1953; Hallstone 2002). But I think it is safe to assume that the incidence of drug traffic and consumption at the mouth of the Sepik River mirrors the pace of its spread and the scope of its use throughout rural PNG.
5. I can still hear in my mind's ear, although I cannot recall the specific times when I was exhorted, young and affecting a pipe, not to sit idly by, but to "Eat tobacco!" (*Sakain komunk!*) during a lull in some festivity or other I attended.
6. There is increasing awareness among both Seventh Day Adventists and nonchurch people in Darapap of the health hazards, not only of cigarette smoking itself but also of proximity to secondhand smoke.
7. Herein, fathers and sons prey upon one another, the person is subject to a nightmare of horrifying, albeit plausible, dangers and the state conducts itself like a gang of *raskols*. I collected apocryphal stories of stunted growth, of plummeting blood pressure, of death, all caused by excessive consumption. I was told about breakdowns of morality, big and small. Red-eyed users asking for water or food indiscriminately, from whomever was with

them rather than from appropriate categories of kin, and of a murder committed in another Murik village by perpetrators alleged to have been high on marijuana. "They smoked it and didn't care what they were doing and killed the man, decapitated him and cut off his hands and feet." There was also a strong current of corrupted patrifiliation running through this discourse. I heard a story about a father who introduced his own son to the drug and about another father who habitually purchased marijuana from his sons. In the former instance, the boy became addicted to the drug and eventually died from the effects of withdrawal. A middle-aged widower also told me about his estrangement from an adopted son, who was then about 25 years old or so.

8. There is no strict postmarital residence rule in Darapap.
9. The Murik practice Hawaiian kin terms in which F = FB.
10. Pamé put his misgivings about the police another way: "Many of the police deal [drugs]. They check cars and the drugs that they confiscate, they take ... for their own kin and tribesmen."
11. Jankowiak and Bradburd (1996) surveyed a sample of frontier situations (n = 84). They concluded that drugs constituted a "primary force" (1996: 719) in the expansion of colonial power. They also argued that a correlation exists between the level of local political complexity and the used rugs as "inducers." Band and tribal societies were more likely to enter into an exchange relationship of goods and services for drugs than were chiefly or state-based ones. That is to say, drugs were introduced to people whose labor or property, in the eyes of the colonial agents, were otherwise difficult to control.

CHAPTER 4

Mobile Telephony in a Peri-urban Setting

The concept of "technology leapfrogging" refers to how people in developing countries adopt advanced or state-of-the-art technologies and skip over using older technologies, like landlines. It is usually associated with progress, that is, with the promotion of modern rationality (Antonelli 1991; Fong 2009) rather than with the reproduction of local processes and meanings (Appadurai 1996) that might otherwise counter or "overtrump" reason (Habermas 1987: 310)—much less associated with alienation or anomie. Unlikely as it may seem, however, the Murik adoption of mobile phones in modern PNG resembles courtship and marijuana in the sense that mobile telephones are being used and understood by peri-urban Murik people for their own, culturally defined, purposes. However, like marijuana, their use also seems to encourage the individuation of the subject, as well as mistrust in and of modernity. In other words, the moral status of mobile phones is no less double-edged than what we saw in Homeric courtship narratives and marijuana dialogue. Phones lend agency to the voice, to be sure, but that voice is also estranged from modernity in PNG.

Mobile Telephones in Modern PNG

Access to mobile phones began to take place in 2007 when the sector was liberalized and the Irish company Digicel entered the market (Stanley 2008). Consumer uptake was rapid and mobile networks expanded in the

Fig. 4.1 Street scene in Wewak. Photo: David Lipset (2012)

subsequent five years to cover about 75% of the country (Bruett and Firpo 2009). Phones are sold by street vendors, in trade stores and in company stores (Fig. 4.1). They vary in price of course and today the first generations of handsets are being replaced by "smart" technology that allows internet access. People do not subscribe to monthly or longer-term contracts but buy phone cards, phone cards that are no less available on the street and in stores, and enable users to download credit units to their phones.

Thus far, the few studies that have been done on mobile telephones in PNG suggest that the information channel they open up is an equivocal one, mostly beneficial for a variety of social and other purposes, such as healthcare (Yamo 2013) and banking (see Suwamaru 2014: 81), but as I say it has also been alienating.[1] One can see the latter in Telban and Vavrova's study of a relatively isolated, rural Sepik village, for example, where the mere possibility of a mobile phone network provided a strong motivation for people to try to register their land so the Digicel company might erect a tower on their particular property rather than somebody else's. At the same time, the prospect also gave rise to suspicions that white people had stolen the new technology from local ghosts. It also aroused hopes that deceased children might give their parents secret phone numbers they could then call to ask their ghosts to deposit money in bank accounts (Telban and Vavrova 2014: 234–5). Nancy Sullivan's surveys (2010, 2011) elicited similar attitudes. On the positive side, mobile phones were seen to facilitate communication that made people feel safer (see also Watson 2010, 2012, 2013). On the negative side, informants complained that the money spent on them was wasted (Watson 2011) and blamed them for enabling anonymous prank calls and harassment of women. Barbara Andersen's (2013) study of unmarried, nursing students living independently in an urban, Highlands setting shed light on an interesting twist of the moral panic ordinarily associated with new social media (Standage 1998). Young women she knew cultivated "phone friendships." That is, they accepted calls from anonymous men to whom they then made or received subsequent calls, in part by virtue of phone credit gifts received from these men. Such is the double-edged nature of alienation and agency in modernity in PNG that men target women by phone but isolation, indifference and anonymity apparently are a worse fate than harassment. Rather than simply hang up, the young women, notably communicating as individuals, use phones to domesticate their vulnerable, anxiety-riddled position among male strangers. Andersen put it well: the "phone friends" phenomenon is "a uniquely Papua New Guinean response to the communicative possibilities of the mobile phone" (Andersen 2013: 319; see also Lindstrom 2011).[2] I would put it a little differently: mobile phone friends are characteristic of the alienation of men and women in modern PNG.

Alienation in a Peri-urban Modernity

I discussed some of the main aspects of the peri-urban life among the Murik in Wewak town in the Introduction. Here, I would only reiterate that trust in these settings, the fundamental problem arising from the moral indeterminacy and freedom of the modern subject (Giddens 1990; Seligman 1997), remains largely (but of course not entirely) centered on *place*: it emanates from the Murik Lakes, the ancestors and the seashore communities that descend from them. The abiding value of the archaic implies several things.

One is that kinship, and the expectation that goods and ritual services be reciprocally exchanged within households, between lineages, with affines and trading partners, goes on informing relations among peri-urban Murik. Co-residential and dispersed kin ought to share food and provide each other material support—daily hospitality, transportation, help with the fulfillment of ritual obligations, and so on. Relationships constituted by marriage go on being restrained by customary avoidances of various kinds, not to mention brideservice obligations. And gift exchange with overseas trading partners, although its pace has decreased in modernity (see Chap. 3), still goes on in town and now incorporates money in addition to customary Murik goods, such as baskets, seafood as well as the occasional piece of folk theater (Mead 1935; Lipset 1985 and see Chap. 5).

A second implication of the ongoing significance of Murik values in town is a tendency to see not only urban life but modern life more generally, in Murik terms (see Chap. 6). According to this view, conflict is inevitably caused by sexual jealousy among the young or by substitute objects of desire among the aged. According to this view, intragenerational violence, motivated by infidelity, is part and parcel of growing up. But this view also finds humor in the reasons of the heart, and the impossibility of the id to prevent itself from risking everything for a moment of illicit pleasure (Lipset 2004a).

A third consequence of the persistence of the archaic in urban life is that, other than the prestige and power attributed to possessing its wealth and power, many people see little in modernity that is either credible or moral. In good van Gennepian fashion (1912), they view civil society as made up of "canoes" of kin who are threatened by the other—by strangers, pickpockets, drunken youth and carbon cowboys, whose unpredictable actions make public spaces risky.

Murik men (and women) travel to town for many reasons. But, as I say, they do not become modern by doing so. Their view of urban life is decidedly bittersweet, and this ambivalence informs their attitudes about and uses of mobile phones. The sentiments they express clearly arise from the collision of Murik values with the material appeal and the untrustworthy quality of life in modern PNG. They do not fit together. They rather combine in a dialogue whose meanings are not reducible to one voice or attitude.

Remind Him of the Almonds!

Very rarely do peri-urban Murik people refer to their mobile phones in their vernacular as the "white man's line" (*yabar makom*). Most call them *mobail*, the Tokpisin homonym. If the new technology has not achieved vernacular integration, it has nevertheless achieved a pervasive presence in daily life. For example, one senior man offered an intriguing comment about the proliferation of phones. "Here," he observed, "little children, old people, everybody has mobile phones. Only women in labor don't have them." The point of his hyperbole, if indeed it was hyperbole, is a little arcane. He seemed to be suggesting that nothing less than a condition that was as physically overwhelming, secluded and mystically polluting (to both women and men), as childbirth, would stop a person from using a phone. And, by implication therefore, he was indicating how very little, if anything, might come between an urban man and his phone, particularly in these post-initiation days.

The new medium has met with widespread approval. To cite another example, I watched a young man call his mother in Finchhafen, a town some 360 miles down the coast to the east of Wewak (cf. Uy-Tioco 2007). "Phones are good," remarked a middle-aged father, endorsing the sight. "Parents buy them for their children," a grandfather told me, "and buy credit units for them too. They are not too expensive." I once sat with a few men, when one of them, fingering his phone, noticed that he had missed a call from a village kinsman. Worrying aloud that some misfortune had befallen the caller, he instantly rang back to discover that the kinsman wanted nothing more than to ask for three prepaid units. He stood up immediately and quit our little gathering to go buy him a Flexcard. All of which is to say that Murik people, of both genders and all generations, have wholeheartedly adopted mobile phones and have put them to use on behalf of the kinship based networks they hold dear.

Calls are made to "micro-coordinate" comings and goings in daily life in town as well as with dispersed kin living elsewhere in the country (Ling and Yttri 2002: 139; Ling and Haddon 2003). In other words, they enable collective agency. Adults use phones, so one senior man told me, to "call kin at trade-stores to tell them to buy things or to check where someone is." I also saw a Murik man receive a call from the national capital, at the other end of the country from Wewak: a younger brother had rung to beg him to send betel nuts as soon as possible. A grandfather called his granddaughter to ask whether her little son was at home, and if so, he wanted to send him to buy some pastries from a street vendor because he was too tired to do it himself. A schoolteacher told me that he used his phone to call coworkers and people in the Seventh Day Adventist choir he sings in to plan activities, the timing of meetings and such. "I [also] ring my wife to ask her to come get our daughter so I can work a little more and record grades. Or I call her to arrange to meet me in town so we can go shopping together, which she likes to do." That is, phones diminish anomie: they provide kin with means to accomplish legitimate ends. They are functional tools that make daily life a little easier to micro-coordinate in space and time. They are a pragmatic mode of communicative action, in Habermas' terms, that promote normative life. In this view, they promote mutual comprehensibility of and conviction in collective values rather than strategic manipulation or control (1979). Of course, these are not necessarily culture-neutral, or modern, claims to rightness. But they do suggest that in this case, modern technology has reduced alienation from modernity in PNG.

Albeit in smaller numbers, Murik still voyage from village to town to access services and market. Men and women also move around the region to visit hereditary trading partners and kin. Mobile phones obviously extend their capacity for micro-coordination in space. On the one hand, they offer security. With the possibility of mobile phone use on the open seas, the signal being known to reach a certain spot along the coast and to be stronger than on land, it has become possible to call kin for help, if beached *en route* to town, having run out of gas, or having suffered a mechanical breakdown of some kind. "In the past, we would have had to sleep in the boat," a senior man recalled, touting this advantage of mobile telephones. On the other, I observed calls being made to regional trading partners. One man told me that he was intending to call a trading partner who had offered to help him pay for mortuary obligations he was trying to fulfill, in the aftermath of the death of his adult daughter. I saw a man call a brother who was visiting an offshore trading partner. He wanted to remind the trading partner that he owed him a bucket of *canarium* almonds to square a debt for a Murik basket he had previously given. Tell him, the man told his brother who was on the phone, "to [t]hink about [those] almonds for me."

Thus far, I have been illustrating how much mobile phones are seen to and do contribute to the solidarity and moral agency of men, women and children in peri-urban, Murik society, by increasing understanding and consensus, a form of rational action, as culturally defined. That is, I have more or less followed the kind of neo-functionalist framework that dominates the literature on the relationship of this new social medium to preexisting social values known as the domestication hypothesis (Silverstone and Haddon 1998; Woolgar 2005). But of course, there are other uses and consequences of mobile phones in modern PNG that create or exacerbate distance, tensions and frustrations between persons in society. Mobile phones, in other words, serve immoral purposes that also disrupt, violate, defy and betray society. Contra modernity, moreover, the new technology enables callers to communicate across expanded space and time, which has allowed them to expand archaic relationships, parochial values and local-level processes.

MOBILE PHONES AND MASCULINE ALIENATION

Let me offer an instance of what I mean. I had just arrived in Wewak town in 2011 and two senior men were helping me organize supplies and transport for some village-based fieldwork. They were classificatory brothers through their late fathers, who themselves had been rival siblings. Jakai Smith, a semiliterate villager, was temporarily living in town at the time (see Chap. 3). He owned one of the fiberglass boats and a 30-hp outboard motor in which I was hoping to make the 40 mile trip down the coast to the Murik coast. Jacob Sandar was an educated peri-urbanite who had not spent much of his childhood in the village. At one point as a young man, he had worked for Air Niugini, the national airline, and had been based in Melbourne Australia. Now in semi-retirement, he busied himself by using his literacy, numeracy and self-taught legal knowledge to help kin and friends deal with modernity in PNG in the form of its various bureaucracies in town and across the country. Although he kept close tabs on village life and politics, he had little or no sympathy for what he viewed as its dim-witted ways. He returned there as infrequently as possible, and then only for the briefest of visits.

In the yard of a kinsman's house, I was sitting and planning my departure with Jacob Sandar when Jakai Smith walked up, sat down on an old tire under the shade of a Starfruit tree and withdrew into a sulk (Fig. 4.2). Upset upon seeing Sandar, Jakai told me later, he had not wanted to speak. Eventually, as we went on discussing what all needed to be done to get ready for my trip, when Jakai did talk about using his boat, Sandar repeatedly interrupted him with characteristic impatience and rapid-fire speech. In exasperation, Jakai abruptly stood up and went back across town to Kreer Camp, where he and his family were staying with one of his "sons" (FBS).

Fig. 4.2 Jakai Smith (*left*) and Jacob Sandar. Photo: David Lipset (2012)

That afternoon, Sandar used his mobile phone to ring his younger sister Maggie, who lived there. He asked to speak with Jakai. Watching and listening intently to their ensuing conversation, I overheard Jakai repeatedly asking in a loud, clearly audible voice, "Who is calling? Who are you? Speak louder! I can't hear you! What do you want?" Jacob Sandar yelled out his name again and again but to no avail. Soon enough, Jakai apparently had handed the phone back to Maggie. "Jakai doesn't know how to speak on a mobile," Sandar explained to her in frustration. "Ask him what he wants to do about sending petrol to the village."

Somewhat later, Sandar told me that it wasn't only Jakai who couldn't manage the new technology but more generally, he derided "people like Jakai don't know how to speak on a mobile [phone because] … they aren't speaking face-to-face, so they can't understand speech on mobile phones. They are backward." Knowing the two men rather well, I took his contempt with a grain of salt. Subsequently, Jakai allowed to me that he had indeed known to whom he had been speaking on the phone but in his annoyance had not wanted to talk to him.

In this episode, the mobile phone served as a medium of communication in the ongoing rivalry between the two men while it also became a trope in their rancor—at least from Sandar's end. While provinciality and lack of sophistication have been in use to taunt and slight others long before the advent of a state, the mobile phone has refreshed the dig with a contemporary inflection. Feigned ignorance in general, which takes the form of deliberate misrecognition in this instance, I should not fail to add, is a commonplace tactic in customary Murik impression management and is even immortalized in one of the central Murik myths, "The Two Brothers," which is a tale about two sibling *yabar*-spirits who introduce many important forms of magical agency to society (see Chap. 7). The story is significant in this context because it depicts how deliberate misrecognition may be deployed to conceal anger not only in face-to-face encounters but today in mobile phone communication. In brief, the relevant scene goes as follows:

> After having had sexual intercourse with his elder brother's wife, the younger brother ancestor-spirit encounters his cuckolded elder brother upon the latter's return from a trading expedition to the islands. Knowing full well of the dalliance, the elder brother did not want to let his younger brother see his rage, or tip him off that he wanted to take revenge through a plan that he had yet to set in motion. Instead, the elder brother declined to recognize his sibling. 'Who are you?' he asked him, when they met.

In the myth, "elder brother" deliberately fails to recognize "younger brother." He knows him, of course. They are siblings, after all. Moreover, they are not merely mortals, but superior ancestor-spirits endowed with omniscience.

My point is that Jakai seems to have reenacted the tactic of the "elder brother" perfectly. He deliberately fails to recognize Sandar. Why? Not to further understanding but to veil resentment. Sandar, meanwhile, interpreted his misrecognition literally and turned it into a symptom of his rival's lack of modern sophistication. Not only was mobile telephone use detrimental to moral action, but mobile telephone skills had become a status marker, or, more specifically, an idiom of status derision, in relations between the two men.

What conclusions might be drawn from this incident? Initially, I suggested that mobile phones facilitate the micro-coordination of daily life among kin. Or, to put it in terms of the larger question, while mobile phones endow users the capacity to extend their voices through space, this greater agency does not necessarily open them up to more cosmopolitan, universal values that lie outside the archaic, the familiar and habitual. In this little incident, two men put a conventional, Murik mode of communication to use in the service not of rational understanding but of local-level conflict. And, by doing so, much like Murik courtship discussed in Chap. 2, they showed themselves hardly in the sway of modernity in PNG.

I want to refine Ling and Yttri's notion of micro-coordination (2002) in two ways. First, I want to suggest that micro-coordination the new communications technology enables may be seen to take place along two axes. In one, mobiles phones are used for purposes which are alienated and immoral while in the other, they make calls for moral and unalienated intentions. Secondly, in postcolonial contexts such as PNG, calls may be differentiated according to whether they are made for archaic and modern values and purposes. Obviously, when kin, as well as non-kin, use phones to meet or organize the provision of goods and services for each other, they are engaging in an unalienated, albeit archaic, form of micro-coordination. But the preceding episode illustrates that mobile phones may also be used to make trouble (see also MacDonald and Kirami 2015). Indeed, peri-urban Murik men and women complain rather bitterly that mobile phones assist what might be called the immoral micro-coordination of everyday life that amounts to an expression of alienation from modernity in PNG.

Like marijuana, the latter kinds of calls give rise to disaffection from and mistrust of contemporary society. The new technology has made it, and the state in particular, more illegitimate in their eyes, more violent and prone to racketeering (see Chap. 3). A senior man contrasted colonial with contemporary order in these very terms. "Under Australian rule," he told me, "there were strong laws. We were not allowed to drink. Now, we use mobile phones in the wrong way, to stage holdups and murders … Many men have been killed because of mobiles." Not only did he associate the new technology with the decline of institutional order, but the more general implication seems to be that modernity in PNG suffers from indiscipline, as if mobile telephony was, like marijuana, a symptom of a collective inebriation.

Two related lines of criticism also resonate with the alienation expressed in marijuana discourse: (1) mobile phones are put to use by a corrupt, criminal state and (2) they serve the delinquent purposes of youth. A senior man contended to me that "[g]overnment ministers employ youth gangs to stage bank robberies. They organize their crimes on their phones." Indeed, a young man snatched a bag off my shoulder in 2012 while I was walking down a relatively deserted street on a late Saturday afternoon, after businesses had closed down for the weekend. Next day, a few sympathetic youth approached me to ask for money to buy credit units so as to micro-coordinate their search for the thief. Mobile phone communication was necessary, they claimed, because they needed to match the linked network that supported the thief's fugitive movements. The collapse of state-based authority and failure of national character, with particular indictment of youth, criminals and politicians, are blamed on the new technology. These allegations, however, and the alienation they express, are not new. The breakdown of moral order in modern PNG, together with colonial nostalgia, has been a commonplace narrative ever since independence from Australia in 1975.

Another immoral kind of micro-coordination that goes hand in hand with marijuana discourse rebukes mobile phones for facilitating scandal (see Hijazi-Omarai and Ribak 2008). Talking about the difference between arranging and keeping extra-marital affairs secret in rural as opposed to urban settings, two men made the following contrast. "Before, [village] men and women used third-parties to carry messages to arrange to meet [a lover] (see Chap. 2) … Now, old men, married men, young men, students are all spoiled. They all have access. They commit adultery by mobile." If, as I suggested above, mobile telephones seem to enhance the moral agency of kin, immoral forms of micro-coordination would seem to be made on behalf of rendezvous in an ego-centered network created on behalf of ego-centered agency. The latter does not evoke Castells' network society in a synchronized and integrated information age that cheerfully supplants face-to-face community (1996). Nor does it quite recall mobile phone use in Jamaica, where "the most common form of … networking … revolves around the potential of sexual liaisons" (Horst and Miller 2006: 93), Jamaican calls not being viewed as adulterous but rather as an expedient way to maintain a moral network. In this narrative of modern PNG, mobile phones are seen as an alienating technology: they are criticized for expediting infidelity.

Speaking in a somewhat worried voice, a senior man charged the breakup of "many marriages … [to mobile phones]. Husbands check their wives phone numbers, become enraged and kill them." Of course, the actual relationship between mobile phone use and domestic abuse cannot be read off this general claim. But the view of the new technology as a metaphor for infidelity supports the side of my argument that, like marijuana, they are at least viewed to alienate rather than integrate the self from moral norms and institutions. A pair of men, sitting in the yard outside their house, reported having observed "a couple walk by arguing because of a mobile ... Yesterday, a provincial administrator ran by here, chased by his wife." Village life is no less rent by rendezvous than town. Domestic violence, motivated by sexual jealousy, is viewed as intrinsic to both venues (see Chap. 2). The suggestion seems to be that "recent call lists" make affairs a bit more legible and vulnerable than they are in off-the-grid, rural settings.

If infidelity is said to be made both simpler to arrange but also harder to deny because of mobile phone use, I also heard this view broadened to denounce urban youth more generally. According to this charge, desire is separated from conjugal duty, as it is in Murik joking relations (Lipset 2004a). As such, the moral condition of modernity is said to suffer for the selfsame reasons that both beset and also entertain archaic Murik communities. In both, age is virtuous, while youth is criticized as libidinous (see Lemish and Cohen 2005: 194). "Adults," said a senior man, "use mobile phones ... to check where someone is ... Youth have a 'different kind of work' with their phones." Or, as another informant, fetishizing phones in an appealing way, put it:

> Youth have problems because of mobiles. Young women ... get pregnant easily and quickly because of mobiles. They go the hospital to give birth and are asked who is the father? They call the name of a grandfather, not the father (see Kraemer 2015: 190).

Borrowing terms from Ling and Yttri (2002), I distinguished immoral and alienated micro-coordination of everyday life from moral uses of and attitudes about mobile phones. The new technology may thus be seen to enable normative voices while it simultaneously facilitates alienated or irrational voices. Ling and Yttri also discriminate another kind of micro-coordination that they associate with mobile phone use. Rather than practical, they observe that mobile phones are also used for expressive purposes they call "hyper-coordination" (2002: 147). Such calls voice emotional self-report. Ling and Yttri link this personal, and of course, by its nature, very local, sort of communication with domestic relations, particularly between parents and teens, as well as within adolescent cohorts. Thus, Norwegian youth gossip, flirt and chat idly on their mobile phones. In addition to whatever the content of their calls may be about, that is to say, they express and define subject-positions in relationships.[3]

I have shown that in PNG, mobile telephones are associated with the micro-coordination of illegitimate desire. At the same time, I have also suggested that specifically for the Murik, this sort of charge has a cultural reference to how joking partners conventionally taunt each other for separating desire from conjugal duty. Not unexpectedly, I heard a mother's brother ridicule an unemployed sister's son (his hereditary joking partner) for talking "on the phone all the time. If a woman rings, he runs off. Upon return, I ask him, "Who called? Was it a man or a woman?" What work does he have to do? Sex, sex, that's all! Hey! Hey!"

In the village, joking partners often assimilate modern institutions in their discourse. I once saw them gleefully improvise a mock "trial," complete with judge and formal discourse during which one of their number was "indicted" for infidelity with his "wife's mother" (Lipset 2004a). And in Chap. 3, I showed that senior Murik men viewed marijuana as a stressor in marital relations. Now, I find this same impulse and irreverent attitude in the context of mobile phones. In town, the new communications technology has also entered into their comedy. Another mode of hyper-coordination, and another double-voiced mode of alienation, is revealed: mobile phones lend a new trope to their humor about Murik masculinity

"What's Up?": Mobile Phones and the Modern Subject

I have been arguing that mobile phones provoke equivocal attitudes about modernity, but I must point out that they also seem to be encouraging a new kind of voice. This takes the form of a (Tokpisin) greeting that requests self-disclosure, as in "what's up" (*watsap*)? Or, "are you ok" (*yu stap gut*)? Of course, these salutations are put to use by persons who for the most part still take it for granted that they are part of, rather than separate from, a kin group, just as they continue to view agency as not being power solely exerted by and under the control of the autonomous, individuated self. So how they answer and report on their state of being, in other words, will report upon the solidarity of collective relationships, social duties or responsibilities, rather than mere emotion. Nevertheless, the use of this greeting on dyadic mobile telephones does seem to be opening up a mode of modern reflexivity in which the person is called upon to try and sustain a "continuously revised, biographical narrative" (Giddens 1991: 5).

For instance, I was walking with Jacob Sandar (see the conflict with Smith Jakai, above) along a road in town, when he received a call from an affine, a kinsman of his wife. The caller explained that he was in the hospital where he was about to have surgery. Sandar thanked him politely for updating him and promised to call back after five (at off-peak rates).

Sandar then received a second call. This was from a daughter living in a small town about 90 miles west of Wewak. She had access to the network, she said, and just wanted to check and see whether her father was "OK." Or, to cite one more example of an attitude rather than a case: I was talking to a middle-aged school teacher who was visiting his parents in a Murik village where there was no signal reception. He praised the liberation from spatial constraints that mobile communication allowed. In town, he said,

> they do not know how we are doing and we don't know how they are doing. If mobile service were to come [to the village], we would be able to know … In my thinking, what is good is that I can ask my *"what's up"* and the question can go to whomever I want. And their *"what's up"* may come to me.

One might liken forms of address such as these to the "link-up call" that Horst and Miller nominated as the most characteristic call poor Jamaicans make to each other (2006: 89f), but for a crucial difference. The "link-up call," consisting of little other than a brief greeting, is meant to stay in touch, thus to maintain a relationship, but it was in use long before the arrival of the Digicel Company in the Caribbean. In PNG, by contrast, this kind of salutation departs from archaic modes of talk.

Neither rural Murik men nor their urban counterparts express subjective states outside of formal collective contexts, like mourning or public oratory. I made this very point about courtship in Chap. 2 and again about marijuana in the last chapter. Face-to-face encounters, whether on village footpaths or city streets, do not prompt people to ask each other, "Are you OK?" or "How are you?" The conventional greeting is rather, "Where are you going?" or, a person might answer where they have come from or where they are headed as if the question had been asked. Pinpointing the discursive change that seems to be going on here is a little tricky. Mobile phone technology, perhaps in conjunction with other modern ideologies and goods, such as healthcare and marijuana, seems to be shifting the reference of relationships from place—in which the relationship of self to other is externalized in visible and palpable movements (see Chap. 2) to the person—in which self and other are interiorized, intimate and reflexively evaluated.[4] If the new technology is eliciting a modern voice, or at least a hint of modernist self-narrative, I might as well go on to ask how person relate to mobile phones as possessions, that is, as purchased goods (Macpherson 1962).

Mobile phones are prestigious commodities, of course, and high-end smartphones are valued as luxury goods. During my 2010 field season, a young man who had assisted me asked me to bring him a pair of football boots upon my return the following year. The following year, I failed to purchase the boots. "Never mind them," he replied to my apology. "Buy me a phone." The phone, clearly, was an equivalent, if not a superior, substitute.

Both in town and the villages, in addition to their communicative value, phones are endlessly fiddled with and studied, signal or no, particularly by the young, who also listen to the radio on them, make use of their flashlights and cameras, and of course, send and receive texts on them. Due to fears of theft, when not in use, phones are hidden in pockets and string bags hung around the neck or shoulders; quite a bit less often, one sees them attached to lanyards around the neck, or hand carried. They are highly valued. The quality of comparative brands is debated. In 2014, I saw how much the multi-functionality of a new smartphone was admired by its owner and her kin, especially for affording internet access, Facebook in particular. Yet never have I heard people complain about feeling incomplete or lost without their phone, as North American youth are reported to do (Luhrmann 2010). That is to say, while its uses are appreciated, peri-urban Murik did not fetishize mobile phones as extensions of the self (Fig. 4.3).

Fig. 4.3 Two sisters with mobile phones. Photo: David Lipset (2014)

For example, a senior couple told me that their classificatory son, a bus driver, had his phone stolen. Momentarily forgetting that he had put it down next to his seat, they said, when he brought the bus to a halt, it was promptly swept up by an exiting passenger who apparently saw an opportunity and took advantage of it. The bus driver, upon seeing it had disappeared, got angry but eventually blamed himself for carelessness, and drove on stoically. His kin, accustomed as they were to being picked up to do errands during or after the workday, now griped that they couldn't get hold of him.

Of interest was that they did not care to speculate that his forgetfulness was caused by sorcery. This might easily have happened with another object, like a netbag or, since a sorcery attack on mental attention is an otherwise commonplace explanation for unexpected lapses of focus. My point is that the mobile phone does not seem to be incorporated as an extension of Man (McLuhan 1964). Nor is it, for that matter, ornamentally valued. People do not use their phones as fashion statements. Rather, they are primarily understood as modern tools that extend moral or immoral agency. Note that, in a similar vein, I have never heard anybody complain about inappropriate uses of mobile phone in "public" space, in stores, on the street, or in a bus.[5] That is to say, the private boundaries of the self's space are not seen as vulnerable to or violated by mobile phone use in such places because identity is defined less by subject-centered persons in individuated bodies than by a network of relationships that are not relevant to, much less threatened by, the proximity of an anonymous caller talking on his or her mobile phone in "public." If anything, talk by the other arouses curiosity.

Conclusion: Mobile Telephones as Modernity in PNG

In this chapter, I have begun to show how mobile telephones are understood and used in the peri-urban Murik diaspora in Wewak town. Compressing space and time as they do, mobile phones have been viewed to afford kin a greater ability to fulfill and claim moral obligations to help each other. They have also been shown to play a role in their conflict and to lend a new trope to hereditary joking relations. At the same time, mobile phones are also faulted for risks they are deemed to be creating in the postcolonial ethos, in particular by facilitating infidelity among youth, by giving rise to domestic violence and for expediting lawlessness and antisocial behavior.

While they seem to be abetting a modernist form of self-narrative, that of dyadic self-disclosure, they also seem to be bringing modern anonymity a bit closer, in the form of the so-called *gaspaia* prank calls and "phone friendships" that others have reported (Jorgensen n.d., Andersen 2013). Clearly, for all their morally ambivalent consequences upon society, both perceived and in practice, it seems that one of their broadest results must express the particular relationship of Papua New Guineans, or at least of Murik men, to the kind of modernity they are inhabiting but also creating. The very first attribute of this modernity is that their appetite for mobile phone communication appears nothing short of insatiable.

There have been a few political demonstrations in PNG, but nothing akin to "smart mobs" trying to overthrow a government (Rheingold 2002; cf. Logan 2012). In the diffused, extremely provincialized political context of this modernity in PNG, perpetual connectivity rather encourages local-level communication (Campbell and Park 2008),[6] rather than cosmopolitanization or context-neutral values. The pragmatics and value of mobile telephony are thus not reducible either to its value as a commodity, to "the spirit" of its materiality (Katz and Aakhus 2002) or to any single value, for that matter. The value of mobile phones is not just rational or irrational. As a medium of communication for Murik voices, that value must be understood in archaic, as well as in modernist, terms (McGuigan 2005: 46). That is to say, it would seem that mobile telephony permits kin and non-kin to maintain contact for ongoing reasons *of their own* as well as to express their equivocal alienation from the modernity which would otherwise encompass them.

If modernity compresses space and time and thereby increases the significance of the subject-centered, rather than the place-centered, self in society, then mobile phones and mobile phone communication, being commodities, might also be expected to inform, reshape or impact the voice (see also Foster 2005). How has mobile telephony extended the reach of exchange value, thus to quantify communication in relationships? Not really very much so far. A commodified concept of value has not redefined the subject in culture in PNG to any wholesale way. Instead, my view is that archaic forms and practices apprehend the commodity no less than *vice versa*. Have relationships, for example, become measured in any way or fashion? Are they being calculated as having a monetary value equal to the cost of making a call? While one hears the phrase, "I don't have credits," (Tokpisin, *nogat unit*) with ever increasing frequency in town, I have never heard anyone complain that making a call was either too expensive, or a waste of money. Relationships, I would argue, and credit units, are not seen as commensurate forms of value. The mobile age is no metamorphosis in this corner of the Global South, although, as I say, together with other dimensions of modernity, it is provoking long-standing communication patterns to begin to change in small, but significant, ways.

What do mobile phones convey about modernity in PNG?[7] They clearly demonstrate the presence of one of its key elements, namely, what Simmel called the process of "distancing" or separation (1950: 476), which in this case refers to two things: the detachment of time and space from face-to-face relationships and the deterritorialization of global capital. But this kind of distance causes trouble for modernity in PNG: the new communications technology enhances moral agency over time and space but that agency simultaneously creates alienation. In PNG, alienation may be read in the appropriation of mobile phones for the micro-coordination of everyday life, informed as everyday life is by collective values—the "localizing process" that willy-nilly creates distance from modernity (see also Appadurai 1996: 17). It may also be read in a way the Murik criticize the appropriation of mobile telephones by youth, criminals and politicians. By analogy to marijuana, they suspect that their interests are jeopardized, put at risk, plain and simple, by unruly and dangerous constituencies that not only inhabit their modernity but define their very estrangement from its postcolonial irrationality. And lastly, by contrast to alienation, there is the widespread use of mobiles phones. Domestic voices answer one another on handsets nearly without regard for age, gender and class differences.

The voices enabled by the new technology, the technology which has saturated the communications landscape of modernity in PNG, might be likened to Bakhtin's egalitarian sense of the voice in medieval carnival. In the latter, moral boundaries between performers and audience, as well as between "the people" and sovereign institutions, were seen to be reduced and at least momentarily replaced by an inclusive ethos of collective satire, comedy, saturnalia and so forth (Bakhtin 1984b). Now it is true that mobile telephone use crisscrosses all social categories in modern PNG, not necessarily to enable people just to mock and challenge the authority of their betters, like a weapon of the weak (Scott 1985), but to micro-manage daily life for a variety of their own purposes, moral and/or immoral. If so, this chapter seems to support the conclusion that the relationship of mobile phones to modernity in PNG contributes to an ambivalent kind of dialogue. Rather than a temporary release from or reversal of modern inequalities, by freeing the voice from the constraints of face-to-face time and space, the new communication technology recapitulates both the good and the bad in modern PNG. It enables moral voices, of both men and women (see Kraemer 2015), while it simultaneously enables antagonism, suspicion and mistrust in their archaic relationships as well as for the nation-state at large.

* * *

More broadly, the three ethnographic chapters in Part I of this book have argued that Homeric courtship narratives, marijuana discourse and mobile telephones may be seen to express dimensions of the alienation of Murik men in their dialogue with modernity in PNG. I have suggested that this alienation is double-edged. On one hand, estranged from romantic love, young men engage in furtive, unlawful exchange and are criticized by elders who extend their criticism to the nation-state. But, on the other, they engage in moral action. Men marry. Men use mobile phones to talk to wives, kin and trading partners in pursuit of collective goals. And not least, a modern, subject-centered voice has begun to emerge.

Now in Part II, I adopt another view of modernity. I want to take exception to the widely held assumption that modernity squeezed moral life out of the archaic. Instead of seeing one as the damaged, but autonomous and sovereign, counterpart of the other, for example, as Marx did in his view of the proletariat in nineteenth-century industrial capitalism, as Weber did in his lament that modernity was nothing but a Faustian bargain, or as Mauss did in his view of exchange, I want to develop a view that *both* Murik and modern society give rise to alienation, to a dual alienation that I want to see in combination, or in what I call dialogue. To elaborate this argument, the three ethnographic chapters in Part II draw theoretical traction from Jacques Lacan's view that the signification of moral order is informed by a hidden, prediscursive core which is irretrievably lost yet meaningful.

Notes

1. See also Singh and Nadarajah (2011) on the use of mobile phones for monetary transactions; Logan (2012) on the impacts of mobile phones on PNG politics; Temple (2009) on the impacts of texting on language, and Yamo (2013) on mobile phones and health care delivery in the Western Highlands Province, and Suwamaru 2014.
2. Sullivan (2010) reported the apparently widespread phenomenon of what is termed *gaspaia* calls in Tokpisin. These are random, anonymous, prank calls by young men in the hope of just getting to hear a woman's voice on the line.

3. Their analysis of these kinds of calls recalls Bateson's concept of meta-message (1973).
4. Wellman has argued that in the West mobile phone use is dispersing connectivity away from the household and the group. "The person has become the portal" (2001: 238).
5. Chelsea Wentworth (personal communication) told me that she observed people answer phone calls during outdoor church services in urban Vanuatu, although they do make an effort to do so quietly. Dan Jorgensen also reported (personal communication) that one informant said that people who receive calls or text during church services in the Telefomin area "get shame."
6. *Apparatgeist*, or the spirit of the machine, is a notion developed to explain consistencies in social change that come out of the adoption and use of mobile phones and other personal communication technologies. According to Katz and Aakhus (2002), human beings share a universal orientation toward communication, which manifests in how we think about and use mobile phones. The symbolic nature of mobile phones is one of the most prominent areas of social change to which apparatgeist draws attention. What lies at the core of their framework is the increasingly personal nature of communication technology they term "perpetual contact". Similarly, Oldyzko's (2000) historical review of mediated communication reveals a traditional preference for interpersonal contact as opposed to person–machine or broadcast forms of communication.
7. A qualification: other communities in PNG, elites or young women, or more rural villagers, for example, may find other kinds of agency in their phones and subject them to different kinds of moral evaluation. Instead of a single picture, that is to say, my claim in this chapter must be restricted to what peri-urban Murik men are doing with the new communications technology. They expose one kind of voice, at one point in time, although I suspect their kind of particularistic agency, together with the emerging reflexive voice, alongside their alienation has a broad diffusion not only in the country but in the global South as well.

PART II

In the Time and Space of the Other

This is our starting point: through his relationship to the signifier, the subject is deprived of something of himself, of his very life, which has assumed the value of that which binds him to the signifier. The phallus is our term for the signifier of his alienation in signification (Lacan 1977b: 28).

CHAPTER 5

Folk Theater and the Signifier

In the late nineteenth century, with the intrusion of the first of several colonial states, Sepik/North Coast cultures became more regionally integrated than perhaps they already were in the late precontact era. There were no norms of the sort Malinowski found in the Massim in which shell valuables were exchanged in intertribal circuits of delayed reciprocity (1922; Leach and Leach 1983). But it was organized. Regional trade included goods, both material and symbolic, established exchange rates and hereditary partnerships who shared ways to set up meeting times and expectations for hospitality (Lipset 1985; Barlow 1985b; Tiesler 1969/70: 70). In the 1930s, Murik men were the leading impresarios of the most valued of all regional goods in the Sepik/Northcoast region. They specialized in the trade of folk theater, or what Margaret Mead called "dance-complexes," to local-level leaders (1963: 8). Perhaps surprisingly, perhaps not, one of the important male voices in the 1990s and the new millennium expressed itself in terms of this very practice—that of theatrical representation and performance. Following the argument I developed in Part 1 of the book, the ethnographic project in this chapter will analyze the meanings of *Woyon's Mother*, a new piece of folk theater that was not merely an extension of Murik men's renown à la Nancy Munn's argument about "the fame" that accrued to Gawa Islanders by virtue of their participation in regional trade (1986), but rather expressed their alienation from modernity in PNG. However, here and in the next two chapters, I want to elaborate upon this point by using Lacanian psychoanalysis to argue that the new show also expressed men's alienation from archaic Murik culture and society.

Before getting on to the ethnography of the new show and developing my notion of the dual alienation in men's dialogue in the course of analyzing it, I must provide some background. First, I will introduce the new show, which was in my view a kind of Murik Pygmalion. Second, I return to the Lacanian framework and its concept of signification. And third, I shall illustrate that framework with reference to Ovid's Pygmalion and the archaic agency of the steersman on Murik outrigger canoes.

A Murik Pygmalion

I first saw this Murik Pygmalion right after it had been created in 1993. As so much of my research in the Murik Lakes has involved the Male Cult, each time I return, I pay respects to it by not entering its hall until I sponsor the appropriate ritual feast for my joking partners in it, my adoptive sisters' sons (see Lipset 2004a).[1] Once the food and other gifts are consumed and distributed to women waiting in their houses, I am then called upon to stand and greet the assembly of men, explain my current research agenda and begin to take stock of the community since my last visit.[2] In this instance, after the food was eaten and plates were cleared away and returned to their owners, I could hardly fail to notice the rather garishly decorated mask that stood surmounted on a pole in the middle of the large hall (see Fig. 5.1). Asking about it, I was told that the mask was called *Woyon's Mother*, and that it was the eponymous centerpiece of a brand new show. Two of my sister's sons instantly vowed to perform something from it in honor of my departure a month or so later. No less eagerly did other men report that performances were pending in several villages in the region. Sitting amid the excluded presence of women and beneath the shadow of this new maternal spectacle, I could not help but ask how "she" had burst upon the scene.

I was told to wait. Peter Kaango, brother-in-law of Yanda, the man nominated as the show's "author," had to tell the story. In mourning, Yanda was confining himself to his house. As a personality, in any case, Yanda was known as a shy, reticent man who was "not given to saying much." Although the author was alive and named, a characteristically Murik notion of the voice restricted narrative rights to the story. It could not be recounted by just any proxy voice. The substitute narrator had to be legitimate, and in this instance his legitimacy was claimed in terms of an affinal relationship to the author.

Fig. 5.1 Yanda, "the author" of *Woyon's Mother*, sitting with the mask and headdresses of his show. Photo: David Lipset (2001)

Modern creativity is sometimes viewed as an unalienated expression of freedom; the individual artist controls the means of production. His or her agency is autonomous. It is located in a bounded self that may defy authority and convention. That is, it is either seen to arise from voluntary intention, or else it may be said to come from "inspiration," a nonspecific source, but one that is no less located somewhere in the self (Cohen 2007). Either way, modern creativity bestows various kinds of property rights in the individual artist. By contrast, the agency associated with the creation of Murik folk theater is dispersed in kinship networks and exchange practices of various sorts. The repertoire is extensive. Some shows were imported from regional trading partners prior to first contact. However, most were imported at one point or another during subsequent periods of colonial rule in the twentieth century in plantations, mines or mission stations, where men from multiple tribal backgrounds were thrown together while doing contract labor.[3] A few pieces originated in the Murik Lakes. But they too emerged from exchange relationships—with ancestors.

Woyon's Mother, the new Murik show that is the focus of the present chapter, was not understood as the creative outcome of individually based agency. Rather, its authorship, meaning and performance were understood to have arisen from an exchange between human and ancestral voices, an instance of dialogue with archaic Murik culture. A kind of Murik version of the Pygmalion story, the new show brought a beautiful woman to life, a woman who answered the desire of which "her author" was deprived. "She" acknowledged her author's Janus-faced emasculation not only in modernity in PNG, but I will go on to argue that the new show was an expression of men's emasculation in Murik culture as well. In other words, as a revival of the signifying virility of their Male Cult, *Woyon's Mother* gave voice to men's dual alienation. To make this argument, I must first return to Lacan's view of signification.

THE LACANIAN SIGNIFIER

As the epigraph to this section suggests, Lacanian psychoanalysis centers the subject in semiotics—in relationships of the signifier to the signified—rather than in the Oedipal injunctions Freud favored. In addition, the epigraph also suggests that regardless of capitalist penetration, regardless of history, regardless of cultural difference, the position of the subject-in-culture involves a prediscursive absence, or void, the signifier of which Lacan calls "the phallus." Several points must be made clear about the signifier for which Lacanian psychoanalysis is well known. First of all, despite its masculine register, it does not stand for itself in any simple kind of way. It is, yet it is not, an anatomical organ. For Lacan, the phallus is an enigmatic signifier that does not define reality/discourse in and of itself, like capital, God or the state. It is a trope that stands for its dependency on the "desire of the other, not so much because the other holds the key to the object desired, ... [but] because the first object of desire is to be recognized by the other" (Lacan 1977b: 58). Rather than autonomous, the phallus remains part of a lost relationship. In a key step in his argument, Lacan imagines this relationship in conditional terms, but also in terms of a phallic mother: "If the desire of the mother *is* the phallus, [then] the child wishes to be the phallus in order to satisfy that desire" (Lacan 1977b: 289). But such a wish cannot be fulfilled.

A taboo is imposed, but not by the father himself. The taboo is more abstract according to Lacan. It involves a semiotic substitution. The "name of the father" (1977b: 67) takes the place of the desire of the child to be loved by the mother. This patriarchal substitution both is and opens up the world of language, law and normative action, the world of culture or the world Lacan calls "the Symbolic." The *name of the father*, that is to say, is a linguistic, discursive and metaphorical intervention by means of which a symbolic "cut" is made and the "phallus" is left symbolically "castrated" (Lacan 1977b: 289). Signification now starts to become possible, signification in which the phallus may misrecognize itself, and be misrecognized, as a powerful and self-sufficient male subject rather than one tied to an absent apron. The Lacanian psychologist, Dany Nobus, succinctly summed up this illusion: the "function of the phallus is to pass for the signifier of the desire of the other" (1999: 113).

While the English translation of the Lacanian term for the lost desire of the other is "lack," it seems, at least to me, that this lack has to do with a social and moral emptiness, or a loneliness that consists in a loss of love and a sense, not of being suspended in a web of significance of the subject's own creation, à la Weber (1958a) and Geertz (1973), but of being caught up, like Hamlet, in the time and space of the other (Lacan 1977a). However, this "otherwise" metaphysic is creative and embraces fictions of indestructibility and unity, not to mention, moral order, rather than just despair and existential immobility (de Certeau 1983). Although stuck in a state of irretrievable, yet ambivalent, dispossession from the desire of an other, the phallus abides. Its modality is one of incongruity, rupture and tragedy—as well as integration, agency and direction. "The ... signifier," as Žižek put this peculiar quality, "is ... an index of its own impossibility. In its very positivity it is the signifier of 'castration'—that is, of its own lack ... In the phallus, loss as such attains a positive existence" (1989: 157).

Pygmalion's Statue, the Murik Steersman and the Lacanian Signifier

Ovid's Pygmalion presented a famous case in point of the Lacanian contradiction. In his version of the story, which had earlier references to a Phoenician monarch, his hero is a lonely, Cypriot sculptor. In a relevant passage that is set in a city in turmoil, Pygmalion comes upon the first prostitutes in ancient Greek society, women called the Propoetides, who had rejected Venus as their goddess and lost the power to blush.

> When Pygmalion saw these women, living such wicked lives, he was revolted by the many faults which nature has implanted in the female sex, and long lived a bachelor existence, without any wife to share his home. But meanwhile, with marvelous artistry, he skillfully carved a snowy ivory statue. He made it lovelier than any woman born, and fell in love with his own creation. The statue had all the appearance of a real girl, so that it seemed to be alive, to want to move, did not modesty forbid. So cleverly did his art conceal its art. Pygmalion gazed in wonder, and in his heart there rose a passionate love for this image of a human form, issuing from the semblance of a woman (Ovid 1955: 231).

From a Lacanian perspective, Pygmalion's revulsion is not motivated by feminine "wickedness." Instead, it is a denial of his dependency on the desire of women who do not desire him. Pygmalion is subjected to the signifier of their errant desire. He is suspended in a time and space of the other. What does he do? He fashions a life-size statue of a woman out of a slab of white ivory. Such is the very impossibility of the Lacanian phallus. The statue, inanimate and lacking desire, is an object that can desire him like no other, and vice versa, he desires it more than "any woman born." Subsequently taking pity on such exemplary pathos, the goddess of love, Venus, intervenes—as the statue's mother—to bring Galatea, the statue, to life. But Galatea is more than a trope of Pygmalion's symbolic castration. That is to say, the desire incarnated in his art was created by and created, a burning, yet unattainable, fantasy that can never restore the phallus, even though Ovid esteems Pygmalion's skill, the skill that made Galatea "lovelier than any woman born" (1955: 243). Lovelier, that is to say, than woman born of a real woman. Pygmalion's art, his signifier, created a substitute for the lost object, a real woman, only to recreate the loss of "her" desire and his symbolic castration.

What insight does a Lacanian view of Pygmalion offer our understanding of the alienation of Murik masculinity in the new piece of folk theater, *Woyon's Mother*? As it is a visual and performative answer in their dialogue, before answering this question, I want to briefly reflect on another Lacanian concept of the subject, the moment he called the "mirror stage" (1977b).

At the moment a mother holds her infant up to a mirror for the first time, Lacan suggests, the child glimpses his whole body and gets a false impression of coordination and autonomy, a *gestalt* in which he delights *as if* the image he sees were someone else. Once again, Lacan locates the subject not in the self but in recognition, or in this case, misrecognition by the other. The mirror offers an enthralling but false image that positions subjectivity in an irresolvable gap between appearances of unity and mastery, and experiences of a lack of control. The "gestalt ... statue" in the mirror masks infantile incapacity and dependency (Lacan 1977b: 5). Subsequent images of wholeness, permanence and autonomy sustain this illusion. I am not evoking the old evolutionary saw: Murik men are no more babies than any of the rest of us. My conceit is rather that the Lacanian mirror-stage is a useful view of a devastating, but thematic, dimension of their subjective and political predicament in Murik culture and modernity in PNG.

The imagery of the self in a modern mirror, as employee, Christian and consumer, constitutes a new jeopardy, a new illusion of order set atop the old one. The new *gestalt* does not cut men off from an archaic, precolonial immortality. It deprives men of a Symbolic in which they were castrated, yet privileged, and then ushers them into a new Symbolic in which they would be privileged as citizens in their own nation-state, their modernity. In both Symbolics, the masculine subject suffers a rude awakening. It is confronted by an inescapable question, which is, who does the other desire, if not me?

For Lacan, the intervention of *the name of the father* and the notion of the mirror-stage are replayed over and again in the Symbolic, so personal and historical loss become epiphenomenal to a built-in defect. This is the crucial difference between Lacan's concept of Symbolic and my view of Murik masculinity in modern PNG: while the Lacanian subject is ahistorical, the predicament of men in modern PNG is precisely the result of their position in Murik culture combined with colonial and global processes. So today, men respond to two lacks. One is archaic and consists of the absent desire of the Murik other. The second is from a modernity whose gaze and desire are also fixed elsewhere. Still, as Lacan would anticipate, Murik masculinity may not be reduced to alienation and loss, either personal or institutional. Its voices and attitudes must not be understood as a single-toned tragedy.

Like Pygmalion's statue-woman, masculine creativity arises from lack, or perceived lack, of its constitutive object, the desire of women. But unlike the melancholic Pygmalion, Murik men are chronically incensed, but also chronically wounded, by an expectation that women desire other men, rather than themselves. They are quick-tempered, prone to domestic violence and to magically augment their attractiveness and virility. In this jealous register, the phallus—in both individual and collective forms—immerses "himself" in the work of creating substitutions for the desire "he" lacks, however empty these signifiers turn out to be. And while doing so, in order to concentrate, they quarantine themselves from the immoral and impure desires of women. They reenact symbolic castration, the castration by which they became men.

A telling example I have written about before concerns premodern overseas trade, when Murik outrigger canoes were still powered by the wind blowing into their sails, rather than outboard motors. Should the wife of the steersman cuckold him while he was at sea, the prow of the outrigger canoe was understood to mimic the rhythm of her body during intercourse and bob up and down in the water (see Chap. 7). If the crew quickly replaced the man before his wife finished having intercourse, they could save the canoe. Upon returning home, the original steersman would disembark and, without bothering to investigate, beat his wife, certain of her adultery, certain that she had desired a rival. Preventing "the castration" of his phallus/canoe was understood (in part) to depend on her staying "quietly" at home during the voyage. Or, as Marilyn Strathern once put it: "the image of the active agent at the creative or created, center of relations is missing" in Melanesian manhood (1988: 269). In Lacanian terms, Murik voyagers as much as acknowledged the vulnerability of the phallus to the desire of the other in their view of the steersman's agency on the high seas.

Ostensibly "unmanned" by the wantonness of sentient women, Pygmalion created a "pure" woman. Prestate Murik men likewise desired "to cure" the emptiness of the phallus by substituting, or insisting upon, a "pure," or chaste, woman to make them men. But of course in contemporary PNG a second lack has come into play. Pygmalion's creativity, impugned by agents of modernity as "Satanic," "backward" or a "waste of time," is neither resolved nor effaced. Instead, the signifier that was dependent on feminine desire has now became dependent on modern, global desire and men find themselves tangled up in a dialogue contesting both. I would say this: like Pygmalion, the new piece of Murik folk theater answered masculine alienation by creating a fictional woman. But instead of answering one archaic lack, "she" simultaneously answered modernity, a contemporary lack.

The Murik Phallus, A Brief History

In Chap. 2, I argued that in the broader context of a declining Male Cult, courtship had taken on increased significance for the gender identity or maturation of young Murik men, although its mode of agency, which I called a Homeric chronotope, alienated them from modernity in PNG. Now Male Cults were certainly being "dismembered" in the name of law, the father or the son all over the nation, and not just at the mouth of the Sepik (Tuzin 1997; Robbins 2004). But I want to emphasize that these institutions were not being "severed" from an archaic symbiosis in which they were objects of desire in any simple way. Rather, cultic signifiers of masculine agency, sacred flute-spirits and the like, were being "cut off" from Symbolics in which they already lacked the other, in which they were already alienated. And now, they were being ushered into a second Symbolic where they were desired even less. For Lacan, the relationship of the signifier to itself was always a bit unclear. In prestate Murik, however, the link between the two, although occult, was indisputable. Initiation into the cultic phallus—an enchanted domain of warrior ancestor-spirits called Kakar—required an astonishing penetration. In the dead of night, the initiates' wives entered the cult *sanctum* through a small service door, in desire of their husbands' initiators (Lipset 1997: 187f). Their motive was understood in several ways. A senior woman to whom I once spoke about the practice shrugged her shoulders and dismissed it as nothing more than "our way." But I think that the presence of Murik women inside the Male Cult House can be put a little more specifically. In a cultural sense, the sexual intercourse they offered the men was a form of reciprocity, an erotic counter gift for the work of initiating their husbands that they had once performed. The wives "gave" their husbands' partners the same sexual service that the partners' wives had given their initiators when the latter men were admitted into the cult. In a psychoanalytic sense, the women recreated a tale of Oedipal exile into the Lacanian symbolic, the cost of which was nothing less than that "pound of flesh which is mortgaged in … relationship to the signifier" (Lacan 1977b: 28).

The women personified Arake, the mother of the warrior ancestor-spirits, the Kakar. The men who received the pleasure of her desire, took it from "her" sons, who suffered, or were meant to suffer, their jealous rage with Homeric stoicism (see Chap. 2). Perhaps, they were mollified by the prospect of getting "her desire" back in the form of the cultic signifier, the individually named, wooden spear-spirits, and then literally, at some time in the future, when a new cohort of young men sought initiation into the cult and had to send their wives to have sex with them. The symbolic castration to which the husbands submitted did and did not go unheeded. They received status, power and prestige in the Symbolic, and they received the *name of the father* in the form of their specific ceremonial Kakar spear-spirit. However the "cost" of the process wounded them, they were to that selfsame extent bound to the signifier.

In the course of the twentieth century, however, the Kakar ancestor-spirits, and the military-political autonomy and sexual exchanges for which they stood, withered in power and value. Condemned by missionary Christianity (as fornication), ritual intercourse had all but ended by the 1970s. Today, the Male Cult no longer goes to war. Today, instead of giving wives' sexual services, men pay money in exchange for Cultic initiation (see Chap. 6). In modernity, moreover, they have also abandoned the Cult's great "floating signifier," the outrigger canoe, whose overabundant meaning expressed—for men, if not for women—the great symbolic power of their signifier (Barlow and Lipset 1997). The little fiberglass boats that replaced the outriggers Murik Male Cults used to launch as if they were initiating young warriors (thus involving ceremonial exchange of sexual intercourse by the wives of the latter men) require nothing of the sort when first brought home from town. These boats (and outboard motors) are understood as little other than commodities, remittances of kin, gifts from politicians, or as part of development projects sponsored by the National Fisheries Authority. They are a disenchanted, instrumental form of mechanical transportation.

Illusions in a Lacanian Mirror

As I suggested in Chaps. 3 and 4, Murik men tend to see themselves as alienated men who are impoverished by, as well as disconnected and estranged from, modernity in PNG. Whatever resources their intertidal environment and small-scale fishery may fail to provide, like other Sepik peoples, they have a lot of models of objects in their minds or actually stored in dwellings and cult houses. All of it, what we in the West would call intellectual property (Malinowski 1922: 185–6), are associated with use rights and privileges that are limited by norms and magical sanctions, rather than by copyright law (Harrison 1992; Coombe 1998).

In 1993, the reason that I was in the Male Cult House in the Murik village of Darapap and first saw one of the masks in *Woyon's Mother* was because the Fowler Museum (at UCLA) had sent me there to canvass local opinion about the prospect of installing an exhibit of Murik art, some of which remained subject to the aforementioned property rights. I went from village to village and broached the Museum's intention in each Male Cult House where the men answered more or less in unison: should we want to do a show, I ought to be initiated. They were making two points. First, they did not object to the project but rather wanted to facilitate it. Second, they imagined the agency necessary to install a museum exhibit in terms of the magic (*timiit*) elders teach initiates to arouse women's desire, make them invincible in battle and, among other things, empower the stage management of shows. In return for their magical support, I would host a lavish feast.

Basically, the significance of their view of the museum installation for this chapter is this: the men were applying a model of property rights drawn from the intertribal trade of shows to it. According to this model, the exchange of folk theater is an act of lineage reproduction and Male Cult initiation. On the one hand, in return for a big prestation, the recipient of a show is adopted into the donor's lineage, more or less at equal rank to him or her, and may thus go ahead and trade the show at his own discretion. On the other, from the viewpoint of the Male Cult, the recipient is endowed with its signifier. He may be given an ornamental loincloth (see Fig. 5.2) as well as training in the occult mode of preserving masculine potency from the impurities of feminine sexuality.

But, I want to say that these shows resemble Lacanian mirrors. That is, they are reflexive, libidinal images of the self as other that dramatize illusions of aesthetic coherence, such as orderly exchange and cosmological reenactments of how they came to be, or at least of episodes from it. In the event that the show was imported, it is sung in the original vernacular that may not be fully, or even partially, understood by either donors or recipients. A show's primary, performative meaning is as a visual object of desire. Although not all shows feature fantastic, masked effigies (*murup*; Tokpisin: *tumbuan*), all have libidinal associations, particularly for men. In many, serenaded by a small chorus of senior men, a troupe of young

Fig. 5.2 A senior man at his retirement, decorated in the insignia of his lineage and the Male Cult. Note the snake's head motif on the apron of his loincloth. Photo: Helen Dennett (1984)

men and women perform the particular choreography of the show. Each of them has been bespelled to enhance the power of their dancing and their bodies have been rubbed with red ochre and profusely decorated in shell and teeth ornaments, to arouse the gaze of opposite-sex spectators. This is the illusion of lineage reproduction, beauty and agency that appears in the mirror. Not only coherence, but a petition for the lost desire of the other.

Many expressive genres flourish in Murik culture, besides folk theatricals. One of them called "Mangrove Songs" (*Woyon kor*) consists of sorrowful laments whose lyrics are said to be made up by men (and women) as they paddle alone in their canoes in the privacy of the lakes' expanse (see Harrison 1986). These songs, a genre of maudlin autobiography, are exclusively composed in the Murik vernacular and are sung in a single melody. They commemorate how the self became separated, whether from kin or lover, although often from the latter. In Lacanian terms, that is to say, rather than an appeal for, they are commemoration of, lost desire.[4] Sentiments like these, of human authorship, and being entirely made up of local reference and language, used to disqualify *Woyon* songs as "merely," or, no more than, a form of domestic expression that was "just" performed at home, and never exported to regional trading partners or disclosed to modernity in PNG. What is more, while folk theater is corporate property of individual lineages, *Woyon* songs, *qua* melody, are considered to be the common property of everyone living in the five Murik villages. Individual composers are acknowledged during informal, late-night gatherings of small cohorts of age-mates, or as part of end-of-mourning celebrations, when kin gather in same-sex groups in the men's (and women's) Cult Houses and remain in each others' company, eating and singing together until dawn. In such contexts, a Woyon song might be started by its author, or his or her sibling, whose voice is then joined by the company, although some songs become so popular that they enter the general repertoire.

As this musical genre is performed in a collectively owned melody, it is notable that the Murik devalued *Woyon* songs. They did not convey essential information. They were not a means of ancestral power. They were not, like Aboriginal songs, "the authoritative guide to social relationships and to relationships with the land" (Wild 1987: 106). They were not a link to a great past, mythic or historical. They were not even a necessary part of ceremonial performances. Nor were they said to be part of an emerging Murik ethnicity in the new nation. They were just seen as an informal kind of folk music. If the theatricals were regionally desired, *Woyon* songs were merely subject to local desire, that is, until the early 1990s, when Yanda, the shy, grieving artist, "created" nothing less than a beautiful image of their "mother."

Who was the author of *Woyon's Mother*?

In 1993, as I sat with Yanda's brother-in-law, Peter Kaango, I recalled knowing this proxy narrator some ten years earlier. He was then an active deacon in the Seventh Day Adventist (SDA) mission in the Murik village of Darapap who observed the church's rules banning participation in the Male Cult, folk theater or any form of dancing. Although SDA theology condemned such activities as Satanic, I never got a sense that Kaango himself did so. Still, I worried that his Christianity might distort his retelling of his brother-in-law's story although I got no sense that it actually did so (any more than the story may have been distorted in its original recital). True enough, he would not perform in the show. But there was no tone of condescension or reproach in his rendering of his affine's story. On the contrary, he told it matter-of-factly, in the mix of *Tokpisin* and the Murik vernacular that senior people tend to speak with me. To orient the reader, let me summarize the main points of "his" narrative.

> Yanda first saw ancestor-spirits dancing and singing Woyon songs in a dream. In the center of their performance, two spirit-women danced with his recently deceased grandson. Next morning, Yanda got up and started to carve masks of these two ancestors and teach the songs and the new choreography to the Male Cult.

Like Ovid's Pygmalion, Yanda's story accounts for "the artist's creation" of a woman. But unlike Pygmalion, the story locates Yanda's creativity, not in the sentient artist, but in a presentation from "the ancestors." Moreover, the artist does not exactly seem to have been motivated by symbolic castration, that is, by the loss of the desire of a maternal other, but from the loss of a different kind of attachment, the premature death of a child. I shall argue that this latter difference is more apparent than real however. The more significant difference between the two stories arises from the contemporary and archaic forms of alienation, to which Yanda's new show responded. I will now develop this argument in a close reading of his brother-in-law's narrative.

> Many people tried to invent a dance step to *Woyon*, but all they could do was sing the … songs with a hand drum. Darapap [villagers] went to Manam [Island] and tried to do it. But it did not look good.

I do not know who first tried to create a show around Woyon songs. But clearly, the critical attention being paid to the project dismissed initial attempts for failing to meet standards: "It did not look good." It was not yet seen as desirable, that is to say, to the other. Yanda set sights on this empty mirror, a visual field, and political prize, not by admiring the unity of his own reflection, but by going to sleep.

> Yanda had a dream. One of his grandsons, a twelve-year-old, named Porer, had just died. Yanda was in mourning.

Now, the narrator positions his brother-in-law's authorship within a particular moral field. First, he associates the new show with the collective space, not of the living, but the dead, the Murik afterlife being encountered through dreams (*aga'orub*). Then, he points out that the dream took place in the aftermath of a premature death. In Murik terms, Yanda was living in close proximity to his grandson's spirit (*nabran*), was beset by death pollution (*mwak*) and was observing mourning taboos until he celebrated the Washing Feast (*Arabopera Gar*).

While the SDAs did not establish their mission until the early 1950s, as I mentioned in Chap. 2, the Catholic Church started serving Murik communities during the first years of the twentieth century. Even so, as late as the 1990s, the Murik still viewed dreams as part of a loosely integrated, ancestor-based cosmology in which the relationship of culture heroes and the spirits of the recently dead to everyday, human society (*noramot*) remained little differentiated. In daily life, one's spirit was still visible as a reflection in water and as one's shadow. Ethnographically, nothing is particularly unusual about these sorts of emanations either by night or by day (Frazer 2009). However, there is one aspect of overlap between ordinary experience and cosmology that is culturally distinctive so far as I know.

Recall that in the Introduction, I labeled Murik a "canoe people" for their fascination with canoes, not just as vehicles of transportation but as metaphors for social identity that they deploy in modernity (see also Lipset 2014b). For the Murik, the body is a canoe (*gai'iin*). And vice versa, they see canoes as bodies. Human spirits travel through daily life in multiple canoe-bodies, physical, material and cosmological. By day, a person's spirit may move about in his or her physical canoe-body and as "passengers" in wooden dugouts or other boats. By night, human spirits are thought to "disembark" from their physical canoe-bodies when they fall asleep or lose consciousness and then move about in their dreams where they readily encounter recently dead kin or other spirits. The dead more or less relate to each other and to the living the same way the living do, except perhaps for a few differences. For one, spirits are known to travel through the waking world and the afterlife in more kinds of "canoe-bodies"—human, aquatic and zoomorphic—than do the living. As a result of this greater mobility, their knowledge of social life is likely to be more far-reaching than that of the living. A third difference is that, unlike men, the libidos of the dead are inexhaustible. Or, perhaps one might say that the spirits encountered in dreams are seen as rather less alienated from the signifier, or less suspended in the time and space of the other, than living, married men (see Chap. 7). If so, it is not surprising that dream-reports are sometimes attributed a special kind of legitimacy. The dead offer tutelary portents as well as omens and oracular knowledge about the sick and the dying in dreams. Moreover, as in Yanda's case, dreams may even become a source of creativity. The meaning of dreams, in other words, is saturated with a desire for the desire of the other, and an elaborate code of symbolic equivalences, which may also be seen as motivated by this selfsame longing, is used to interpret them.

Although psychological anthropologists (Stephen 1979; Tedlock 1991; Lohmann 2003), as well as of course many other rather more well-known social theorists, have sought to interpret what dreams mean, I think that one dimension of their meaning has been given less attention—which is the paradoxical point about their legitimacy as a source and form of power/knowledge. Dreams may fulfill desire otherwise frustrated in waking life, but in so doing they may also be said to be expressions of agency outside of the boundaries of the sovereign discipline of the state (Foucault 1977). That is, in a space where the reach of the law gives way to subjectivity, there we find revelations of more detailed—or, again, less symbolically castrated—desire for desire. Perhaps the degree to which fulfillment of desire for desire becomes possible is not only a measure of its impossibility under the sun but also a measure of the broader context of political authority that would inhibit it. I will return to this point below. For the moment, I want to expand on the ambivalent representation of desire in Murik dreams and mourning.

In Murik dreams, desire is sometimes depicted as fulfilled, as a loss overcome. For example, a spell I once learned enables one's spirit to dream-travel to visit kin living at a distance and (secretly) check up on their well-being. For the most part, however, human spirits are said to dream-travel to the afterlife, where the deceased go on living. Here, they become contaminated with mystical "dirt" (*mwak*) associated with contacting the dead. A daily bath in the sea is therefore not just part of a regimen of physical hygiene, it cleanses the canoe-body of the impurities by which its spirit has been profaned during the night. Like a dream, mourning is also understood as a polluted state of embodiment.

Death opens up a disturbance in the symbolic order that exposes the emptiness of the signifier.[5] Rules rush in to distract collective attention from it. To wit: the mourning taboos Yanda and other close kin of his grandson observed reduced and inhibited them socially and jurally. They did not wear new clothes. They stopped doing their hair. Men did not shave (note Yanda's beard and hat in Fig. 5.1). Women covered their heads with towels or bandanas when outside the house. They could not engage in ceremonial exchange involving the lineage. That is, they submit to a term under the signifier. They inhabit a time and space during which they are deprived, and deprive themselves, of the desire of the other. Why? In defense against death, perhaps the ultimate signifier of the loss of the desire of the other. Not to observe the mourning taboos would arouse suspicion of having had something to do with causing the death and would thus provoke sorcery vengeance. By withdrawing from society, they also hide away from the desire of the dead to lure the living to join their company in the afterlife, killing them as they do.

Yanda and kin were lingering about their houses. They would quit this liminal state during the Washing Rite which culminates at dawn when mourners squeeze inside a cone-shaped, faceless effigy made of coniferous branches, run across the beach, cast off the effigy and take a plunge in the sea (see Fig. 5.3). Ritual and daily life momentarily coincide: the

Fig. 5.3 At a Washing Feast, mourners squeeze inside a spirit effigy as they cleanse themselves of death pollution. Photo: David Lipset (1981)

end of mourning is an awakening from a dream (and vice versa). Both end at dawn with immersion in seawater, an act of ablution. Mourners are then plied with food and drink, given gifts of new clothes and a haircut (Leach 1958). In Lacanian terms, they return from the time and space of the other in mourning to the time and space of the other in everyday life. They move from alienation to alienation.

Drawing upon the work of van Gennep (1960) and Max Gluckman (1955), Victor Turner used to make a related point. During interludes defined by what he called "structural liminality," people are permitted to act in ways that do not conform with norms and expectations associated with ordinary moral status (such as during Mardi Gras in New Orleans or Carnival in Rio). For him, such times and spaces free up the moral imagination to be socialized and prepared for new, future relationships or to be creative and playful (Turner 1974; see also Lavie et al. 1993). Mourning in Murik certainly prompts celebrations that combine both, like the Washing Rite. Related sentiments of loss and longing are also understood to motivate the self to seek solitude on the lakes, there to compose Woyon songs. But Turner's sociological argument ignores the dangers, or alienation, involved in liminality: the risk that violence of one sort or another may break out. In the Murik ethnotheory, persons inevitably end up in states of mourning due to the loss of the desire of the other and the intense sexual jealousies that such a loss provokes (see also Chap. 4). Never, or very rarely, is illness, misfortune in love or premature death deemed accidental, "organic" or otherwise unrelated to the loss of the desire of the other; the loss of the other's desire is always understood as mystical retaliation for infidelity, that is, it is the triangulated retribution by a jealous rival (see Chap. 2). The victim may be the consort himself, or, more likely, one of his kin. An untimely death, such as the death of Porer, Yanda's grandson, must therefore have resulted from vengeance by sorcery attack. When the desire of the other is lured away, conflict results. In Woyon lyrics, however, rancor is repressed, or sublimated, in favor of an elegiac tone of longing and loneliness. By contrast, in grief, it is transformed into fears of and persecutory dangers from ghosts and sorcerers that threaten the moral boundaries of society (Lipset 2016).

Initial performances of Yanda's new show evidently were well received. His brother-in-law, however, did *not* exactly attribute its authorship to him. *Woyon's Mother* did not result from his autonomous, individual creativity. He copied what he saw in a dreamscape to which he traveled while asleep. Let me now return to Kaango's narrative of what Yanda apparently saw there.

[Yanda] ... saw some trees ... [to which some] spirits ... travelled as fish, others came as birds, others ... as butterflies. The fish went ashore, ... left their canoes and joined the show ... as ... ancestor-spirit men. [They] dressed up [in secret] on top of a *talis* tree[6] and when they were ready, they came down from the tree with two masked ancestor-spirit women, one with a [figure of a] butterfly on top of her head and the other with a [figure of a] fish on top of her head.

If the alienation of the living and the dead are just distinguishable by degree rather than in kind, perhaps it should not be surprising that the setting of, and the agency represented in, Yanda's dream are decidedly ordinary—in Murik terms, at least. Travel occurs. An arrival scene takes place. Yanda's vantage point, whether arriving with, or simply watching the approach of, the spirits, is left ambiguous. In any case, trees on the shoreline are visible to him. Perhaps the space is not Murik territory, *talis* trees being relatively uncommon on the Murik coast. Moreover, senior people, such as Yanda and Kaango, do not view Murik society as having originated in the Sepik estuary. Rather, they see their relationship to space, which is, in their case, a relationship to the Murik Lakes, as the result of ethnohistorical events rather than mythology. They view themselves as strangers, that is, as descendants of immigrants and refugees who made their ways there in precolonial times from different parts of the Lower Sepik/North Coast region. The dead, being a bit less alienated, return "home" in the afterlife. They are expected to go to live with their lineage ancestor-spirits who continue to reside in the spirit-communities (*pot kaban*) from which they migrated to the Murik Lakes. One therefore encounters them in nondomestic spaces outside the estuary of the Sepik. The immigrant topography of the afterlife entails a few more taken-for-granted ways in which the dead are thought to mimic the alienation of the living men.

No less than the human persons, the ancestor-spirits rely on "canoes." Some travelled "as fish, others ... as birds, others ... as butterflies. The fish went ashore and left their canoes."[7] In other words, they disembarked from zoomorphic embodiments and reentered humanoid ones. Upon doing so, they proceeded to engage in ordinary stagecraft. They climbed up a *talis* tree so as to hide within its thick foliage. Their reasons for wanting privacy are entirely about desire for desire. They do not want to be seen by the audience prior to their entrance. They do not want to diminish the magnificence of their entry and they also want to safeguard the secrecy of spells they cast that ensure the success of the show. Needless to say, their concerns for concealment and dramatization also relate to the alienation of the signifier. The spectacle, no less than the magic, are expressly meant to attract audiences, but particularly the gaze and desire of young women.

Their performance featured the spirit of Yanda's grandson standing in between two groups, each of which was associated either with the "fish" or the "butterfly" ancestor-spirits.

> Two spirit-women ... danced in the middle of the show. The dancers put the deceased grandson in ... [between the] the two spirit-women ... Two groups danced, one on one side, the other ... on the other side of the grandson (Tokpisin: *tumbwan*). They sang [the Woyon songs] and ... then returned to the water. They approached the water and then all the dancers went inside the two spirit-women. The woman with the fish on top of her head received all the fish spirits inside her. The woman with the butterfly on top of her head received all the spirit-dancers who were butterflies. The two ancestor-spirits went down into the water [together] with all the dancers. The dancers went into water inside of these two effigies, like an effigy during the Washing Feast. (see Fig. 5.3)

Elements in this image, the two dancing masks, the two groups and the manner of their exit, were informed by sociological anxieties with which Yanda had gone to bed. Let me explain. Sir Michael Somare once recalled the first time he was taken to the Male Cult House as a child in his autobiography (1975). "During the height of the festivities, ... masks were dancing, [and] my father picked me up and placed me between the [masks] ... The masks lifted me up and, between them, carried me over to my Uncle" (1975: 2). According to Somare, his delivery by the masks signaled his official adoption by his father's brother. My point here is that the death of his grandson seemed to provoke a culturally normative apprehension in Yanda: who would adopt the boy's spirit, one of Yanda's lineages, or one of his mother's?

The spirits ended their performance and reentered the water. Here, the brother-in-law narrator implicitly likened their stage exit to the moment when mourners squeeze inside an effigy as they perform ritual ablutions that bring this liminal period to a close (Fig. 5.3). There are other culturally self-evident associations to their departure: the Male Cult, as well as several other shows, are divided into paired groups. In other words, Yanda dreamed solutions to his waking concerns in terms of prestate ritual processes, sociology and institutions. The masks and choreography drew from men's alienation from the Murik archaic. Subsequent analysis of lyrics and performances not only support this conclusion but, like marijuana, also illustrate how the new show became another context for Murik men's alienation from modernity in PNG.

As I say, alienation is a contradictory state of estrangement and capacity. Thus it is that at the end of the narrative, it is clear that the dream left Yanda feeling no uncertainty or compunctions about what to do.

> Yanda got up in the morning and set to work making the headdresses of the two ancestor-spiritesses. And then he began to carve the mask with breasts that we use for the *Woyon's Mother* figure today.

This is obviously a decisive moment, but observe that although authorship remains carefully attributed, it is nevertheless left entailed rather than specified. Yanda did not imagine the images from scratch. Rather, he "got up in the morning" and essentially copied them from what he had seen in his dream. His authorship, in this sense, was a shamanic act of mediumship between himself and his ancestors. As such, the new show was lineage rather than individual property (see Fig. 5.1).

Despite being no more than a broker for his ancestor-spirits, or in Murik terms, their "canoe," Yanda is also said, quite explicitly, to have begun work on *three* figures, although only two appear in his brother-in-law's dream narrative. That is, the sculptural authorship of the third figure—the mask of *Woyon's Mother* herself—was perhaps a bit more located in him. Apparently combining the two images in the third headdress, "he began to carve the mask with breasts." Yanda's individual agency, in other words, was restricted or confined to this latter act of craft.

If "the mask with breasts" was an act of independent creation, I must add a word about its relationship to the Murik work of mourning, which, in my interpretation, mobilized and shaped its maternal imagery. Mourning in Murik is a response to a loss, not only of a specific loved one, but I would argue that it simultaneously entails a broader sentiment of loss of the bearer of care and love that the specific deceased signifies (cf. Klein and Riviere 1953). According to this logic of deprivation and exclusion, death arouses and denies an ideal of archaic desire, that is, it reconstitutes the empty signifier. On the one side is the figure of a doting mother, the figure of desire, nurture and caretaking, a young, full-breasted beauty (Lipset 1997). On the other is the dependent, vulnerable incapacity of infancy, her little object of desire, or, as Lacan would say, her phallus. While the mother's desire is intensely focused on her baby, the father is yet absent, having been exiled into postpartum obscurity. Rather than dismembered, the little phallus remains attached to his or her maternal presence. Every death therefore invokes the loss of her desire. In this sense, death rehearses the injunction of *the name of the father* that severs the child from the desire of his mother. What ensues? Impure and unkempt, mourners take refuge in the house, whose spirit is said to be maternal. Mourning regresses the self to a dilapidated state, not just in appearance, but also by enfeebling it (cf. Gell 1998). This is not the intervention that expels the self into language and the moral order of the Symbolic; it rather expels the self from the Symbolic into a liminal status offstage. In mourning, perhaps Yanda's creativity may have been a bid to repair the grieving self by reintegrating it with the desire of the lost other (see Klein 1929; Kligerman 1980).[8] As a steadfast, maternal image, *Woyon's Mother* was not in the least independent of archaic Murik culture. If anything, it confirmed a longing to restore, or incorporate, the good mother—or rather, her desire. Although in differing forms, both Yanda and Pygmalion were motivated by loss of the desire of the other.

This interpretation raises a related question: does the water from which the spirits emerge to perform and to which they return after the show ends have any significance in the context of mourning? Elsewhere, I argued that immersion in seawater is a metonym of the birthing process (Lipset 1997: 167f). In Yanda's dream, the ancestor-spirits travel through water, go ashore, turn into men, dress up, dance and go back into the water, to return to their zoomorphic forms, butterflies and fish. That is, the ancestor-spirits who were reborn as men, are reborn as ancestor-spirits. They are subject to multiple births, and thus bathe repeatedly in the desire of the mother, which might account for the inexhaustible quality of their libidos as well as lending support to my contention that the ancestral world of dreams is a time and space in which the other is at least somewhat less dissociated from the desire of the other and therefore less alienated.

We can now see how *Woyon's Mother* expressed loss. In the community, the show signified that the deceased grandchild remained accounted for, not only among the ancestors but among the living. However, by turning this musical genre into folk theater, Yanda was simultaneously recuperating the Male Cult's ability to be desired in terms of the archaic, prestate cosmology. Partly for this reason, I suggest, *Woyon's Mother* was judged beautiful. I say "partly" because the new show also answered desires that were "cut off" by men's ongoing struggle in modernity in PNG (Eng and Kazanjian 2003). The songs that serenade *Woyon's Mother*, as well as its performance contexts, make it plain that the show answered these larger losses, as well as local ones.

A Theater of Alienation

While the lyrics seem to refer to the immediate circumstances in which Yanda created *Woyon's Mother*, they do not narrate a linear plot that begins and ends. Nevertheless, I was given to understand that the following three songs are each named and sung in order during performances before giving way to anything else in the vast *Woyon* repertoire. The first one is entitled *Gamairo*, Gamairo being the name of the hamlet in the Murik village of Wokomot where Yanda's son-in-law, the father of Porer, his deceased grandson, was born.[9] Here, a voice, likely that of *Woyon's Mother* herself, possibly addresses the deceased grandson. By doing so, "she" is honoring the boy's father.

Ai, ai Gamairo	Ai, ai Gamairo
O'o a o abai awaro	O'o a o from there your father comes
Ai yo oi	Ai yo oi
Ai, abai awaro awaro	Ai, from there your father comes, from there

Why must the child's spirit know to trace his paternal lineage back to this locale? Because death, as I suggested above, is riven by custody disputes, or to put it in Lacanian terms, by the desire of the other. Among the living, divorce, adoption and ceremonial exchange all give rise to competing claims to rights in children. No less death. Although the lyrics of Gamairo appear to privilege an agnatic relationship, I must emphasize that they do so as a petition, and a desire, in the context of an actor-centered, cognatic social structure, rather than a patrilineal one (Lipset and Stritecky 1994). The voice confides to the grandson's spirit: Gamairo is the *name of the father*, or at least, the name of his hamlet of birth. "When you go there, that is, when you go to this spirit-community," the singer seems to be saying, "you will be recognized and accepted by the ancestors of your father's kin who will make a place for you." Death creates a time and space of the other: the ancestors contest the new ghost. The lyrics of Gamairo connote the emptiness of the signifier: They express a lack that arises from, and gives rise to, a rivalry, that is not fixed by one, unilineal concept of descent.

The second song, called "Silau!," or "Sail-ho!" in English, does not seem to bear any explicit narrative connection to the first. It does not develop the theme of identity politics after death, but rather calls attention to prestate conventions of overseas trade, thus perhaps to evoke the arrival scene in Yanda's dream. In the lyrics, a young man's voice calls out to the community. Having been the first to spot the approach of a boatload of trading partners, his message consists of nothing more than one word, but that word, needless to say, is the voice of the Lacanian phallus expressing a desire to be desired by an unobtainable object. The lyrics do not identify the guests. They may be the ancestors in Yanda's dream traveling as birds, butterflies and fish. They seem to be generic men and women. Perhaps they are the former having turned into the latter. They are said, in either case, to be nearing the shores of a village, the prospect of which arouses both desire and the expectation of loss.

Silau-o! Silau-o!	Sail-ho! Sail-ho!
Samanga numbunge'te'ara	They see us as they arrive
A ai Silau-o!	A ai Sail-ho!
Silau-o! Silau-o! Silau-o! Silau!	Sail-ho! Sail-ho! Sail-ho! Sail-ho!
Ipuro ipuro ipuro!	Fuck, Fuck, Fuck!
Nononga nimbwenge twara e'ai-i-pro	They will think of us as they depart for home

Like the first song, "Silau" opens by evoking an archaic ethos—now of visiting trade. "*They* see us," sing the hosts, acknowledging the gaze of their guests, "as *they* arrive." The guests disembark and anticipate the bounty that they hope their visit will yield. They go to their hosts, call out names of ancestors and present them big baskets of garden produce, as well as other gifts in which they specialize (e.g., clay pots, wooden dishes, tobacco). In turn, Murik hosts become obliged to fulfill their desire for desire: they must guarantee their safety, feed them bounteously and keep them entertained until everything they have come for has been assembled—in other words, the bags they have brought have been refilled with seafood to which they may add imported Lower Sepik sago flour and Murik baskets. A few days, or a week or two, may pass, like an extended holiday for the guests. The night before leave-taking, this lavish hospitality should climax in a departure feast.

Their gaze and gifts create work for hosts and kin, which basically radiates out to enlist the whole community. For male youth, however, the meaning of their gaze differs. For male youth, the undertone of this Maussian ethos is not a mystical threat but their desire for the desire of the other. Visiting trade they imagine as an opportunity for love, or at least a fling. Thus the excited call "*Silau-o, silau-o!*" may as well be understood as a call to the phallus, a call to the signifier. From their viewpoint, the lyric might be translated to mean, "They [young women] see us [male youth] as they arrive," which interpretation is confirmed by the subsequent line. Visiting trade is here imagined to give rise not just to the exchange of goods but to intimacy (see Balme 2007). If so, the hosts' expectations that the guests "will think of us" when they leave for home have a double meaning, or as Bakhtin would say, it is "double-voiced." It refers to the shame the visitors are meant to feel upon departure because of the extraordinary hospitality to which their hosts have treated them, a sentiment that is meant to loom over them and motivate them to reciprocate in kind later on. But the line is bittersweet too. The transience of visiting trade becomes tinged with the impossibility of desire. This latter tone is drawn out more personally in "You Depart," the last song of the trilogy.

Mwasiro ira'o	You leave your house
Ma pi'li ganu nemar'e	I get ready and then I go to the lakes
Ngonga ur i nganga'me	You will meet me
Eh gawen'ira poro	I go to your mother's house
Ma baron'a ngasema ain'a.	"I have come at your daughter's request"
Ma mogevbo nononga nemana tonagana	At the dock, I think about the woman as she leaves

Now, a young man imagines or recalls his rendezvous with a girl in the trading party. The space of desire is left unmarked. Where did they arrange to meet? In some secluded spot on the beach? Or, did the young man just venture over to the house where the girl was boarding, having returned from fishing on her behalf? In either case, he speaks to a woman whom he refers to as her "mother" and explains he is calling at her daughter's request, which is to say, for honorable reasons, perhaps to bid her farewell. The rueful tone of the whole Woyon genre is now given voice here. The song ends in a dejected feeling of abandonment. What begins in excited desire ends in a horizon of departure, a signifier of lack.

However ineffectively, another voice has implicitly imposed itself on this emptiness. In the second two songs, desire is given local inflection. Yet the era when hosts were obliged to ensure their guests' security has now become a duty that is shared with the state (see Chap. 4). Murik men persist as regional exporters of premodern valuables—woven baskets, shell ornaments, carvings and folk theater—in the context of visiting trade (Lipset 2016). For many, its reciprocities have become a nuisance and a symptom of the degree of their failure to turn their small-scale fishery into a sustainable business. In reference to this wider context, the elegiac image of a lover's departure is not only an image of desire fulfilled, but now lost. Her departure has also become a comment on the wane of the era in which Murik men once possessed magical agency and resources that made them renowned objects of regional desire. In this sense, the departing woman stands for men's economic weakness amid a composite modernity, made up of gifts and commodities, wherein they find themselves suspended in a time and space of both the archaic and the modern other. This dual alienation is *not* voiced in the lyrics. But it becomes quite audible in some of the contexts in which *Woyon's Mother* was subsequently performed.

Let me go back to the original scene of my return to the Male Cult House for a moment. Why was the mask of *Woyon's Mother* on display at that time? Why was it not hanging along with props from other shows (see Fig. 5.7)? Why was it affixed to a pole in the middle of the Cult House decorated in full regalia? Because the show had just been staged to celebrate the release of three village men from prison, after murder charges against them had been dropped for lack of evidence. In this setting, that is to say, *Woyon's Mother* had been the Male Cult's expression of moral vindication against the postcolonial state. It also expressed another, related attitude about modernity.

Despite suspicions held in some quarters about the moral status of cultural anthropology in the Pacific (Trask 1991), it cannot persuasively be argued that in PNG this discipline has represented the state's sovereignty or interests, in any, but a superficial sense. There is, however, a way in which fieldworkers and anthropology have stood, and continue to stand, in the thinking of globally marginalized, but thoroughly engaged, rural communities for the equivocal charms of modernity (cf. Rodman 1991). All attempts to domesticate ourselves as equals to the contrary, field anthropologists remain privileged, if perhaps not exactly exotic. Although adopted as kin, given personal names and made the object of moral claims, for example, to requests for remittances small and large, we remain different, a difference that can rub some actors, rural men in particular, the wrong way, showing them up, entirely by example, as *kanaka*, or, now, as *grassroots*, that is, as underclass, inferior and backward (see Smith 2013).

The day before my leave-taking in 1993, a small, departure feast (*sassan*) was held for me in the Male Cult House. The meal was to feature a brief performance of *Woyon's Mother* that had been promised upon my arrival several weeks earlier. I was to be recognized, people insisted, not as a departing American, much less a departing anthropologist, but as a "son of the village" (*nemot goan*). Despite its inclusive and benevolent ethos, the celebration nonetheless had an instrumental edge. These kinds of gatherings, as I mentioned above, are part of a strategy of desire. The guest of honor is meant to be endowed with a memory that will motivate him "to worry" about those left behind, and generously honor the debt with which he is leaving. The departure feast was a claim on me, in other words, as someone with modern resources, that I "not forget" my hosts and be sure to repay them, at a later date. If one performance of the new show celebrated the Male Cult's triumph over the state, in this context, *Woyon's Mother* sought to obligate me as a signifier of the modernity to which I was then returning. That is, in addition to what it meant to its grieving "author," the new show spoke of the decline of Murik men in the contemporary regional and capitalist economy, as well as to the diminishing value of the Male Cult in modernity.

In the event, only a few plates of sago pudding and rice topped with smoked or sautéed fish were brought to the Male Cult House. I myself was honored with the exemplary figure of Murik hospitality, a huge, boiled sandcrab (*kajak titiken*) over a large dish of sago pudding. Men clustered about each plate and started to eat. Speeches followed crediting my adoptive status in particular families in the community. A young man then donned the *Woyon Mother's* costume. From the waist down, "she" was covered by thick, hot pink, raffia skirts. The wooden mask, with its brown torso and perky breasts were exposed without Christian shame. A headdress, decorated with feathers and the butterfly and the fish motifs, sat on top of the mask. "She" then danced, flanked by my matrilateral joking partners. The two young men were also decorated with teeth and shell ornaments, as well as *Woyon's Mother* headdresses, one with a butterfly and a bird image and the other with the figure of a butterfly and a fish. At first, senior men serenaded them inside the hall. Subsequently, the junior men took a turn and began to sing the *Woyon* songs. The show was then taken outside, so women, who kept their distance, could see it (see Figs. 5.4 and 5.5).

Fig. 5.4 *Woyon's Mother* being readied inside the Male Cult House, Darapap village. Photo: David Lipset (2001)

Once in public, the performance took a decidedly Lacanian turn. The dancers displayed a resplendent form of masculinity that bristled with desire for desire. When I asked the two dancers why they clenched nautilus shell mouthpieces between their teeth, one of them answered that it was a way not to smile. Translation: their enchanted glamour so charmed the female gaze that it was hard for them to maintain composure (cf. Mulvey 1975, see also Chap. 2). Being desired, they had entered a virile, single-sexed state of masculine embodiment. Of course, in another sense, the *double entendre* of a man disguised as *Woyon's Mother* with a phallus nonetheless hidden beneath her extravagant skirts, and her two

Fig. 5.5 *Woyon's Mother* performed in Darapap village. Photo: David Lipset (2001)

sons trailing behind her, could hardly fail to recall *nggariik*, the pantomime of birthing/coitus that middle-river Sepik men perform for their sisters' sons in honor of first accomplishments. Initially reported in the 1930s, their pantomime was then analyzed in terms of local processes and gender categories (Bateson 1936; cf. Silverman 2001; see also Lipset and Silverman 2005). Here, my point is that in the more than 80 years since this sort of ritual cross-dressing was initially reported, *Woyon's Mother* did not just express local desire and local constructions of masculinity, and local alienation, it was also an answer to modernity in PNG (cf. Foster 2002: 16–17).

In another performance of *Woyon's Mother* I saw in Wewak town in 2008, its reference to both the archaic phallus and modernity was quite explicit. The show was performed during the provincial celebration of the 40th anniversary of the entry into national politics of Sir Michael Somare, who was then in the midst of his third term as Prime Minister (2002–2011). Troupes from all over the Sepik performed for the whole

Fig. 5.6 *Woyon's Mother* performed in honor of Sir Michael Somare's 40 years of service to the nation. Photo: David Lipset (2008)

afternoon in a large dance ground near the middle of town. While the rest of the ethnic/tribal groups staged a single show, each of the five Murik villages performed a different show, among which were *Dragon, Sea Eagle, The Fog Men, Double War* and *Woyon's Mother*. For the latter, no mask danced. Instead, the show featured a different image of women as its centerpiece: the troupe itself, which danced in several rows, was entirely made up of about 35 women. Doused with red ochre, each woman wore shell anklets, armbands with aromatic basil and other leaves, necklaces and bandoliers as well as the butterfly/fish headdress (Fig. 5.6). As they danced, a small coterie of middle-aged and senior men, dressed casually in shorts, T-shirts or polos, played hand drums and serenaded them with Woyon songs. Immersed as it was in a great ripple of regional dance-troupes, not to mention dignitaries of the postcolonial state, exemplified by Sir Michael Somare, their native son, *Woyon's Mother* expressed a dual alienation. It expressed Pygmalion's desire to create the desire of the other as well as their contradictory, motley position in modernity in PNG.

Pygmalion's Desire in the Postcolonial Moment

In the archaic, pre-state economy, Murik men funded their ceremonial economy and status rivalries through overseas trade. They relied on the Male Cult to provide the magical agency for their purposes. Under the weight of modernity, the requisite taboos have been abandoned, and the most significant Cultic transaction, the provision of sexual intercourse to senior patrons by the wives of the junior ranks, had come to an end (see Chap. 6). Meanwhile, the decline of ceremonial exchange among regional trading partners reduced the value of Murik shell ornaments and folk theater. Then, the 1990s saw fiberglass boats replace outrigger canoes, the great, floating signifiers of the Male Cult.

Murik men more or less answered this masculine nightmare in two voices. On the one hand, they replied with a commitment to modern universalisms. Speaking *Tokpisin* (and English) in front of children instead of the Murik vernacular, they sent them to school in the hope they would find jobs. They worshipped in churches. They held an endless round of micro-markets within the villages. They even began to ignore norms of kinship-based reciprocity and sold each other fish in the late afternoons. Youth smoked (and sold) marijuana (see Chap. 3) and one also saw the young, the ones who haden't left for town, absorbed by penny ante card games. They fiddled with mobile phones that had no signal or wore unplugged earbuds ornamentally. They took pride in wristwatches, radios, solar panels and other signs of modernity that came their way (see Chap. 4). On the other hand, they also answered modernity in voices that would recuperate the cultic signifier. If I were to compile a list of the latter sort of ritual actions, objects and relationships that have been created in the past several decades, I would further subdivide it all into two kinds of voices. In the one, new instances of old types of masculine agency and expressive genres have been created, or recreated, such as the revival of customary modes of social control (Lipset 1997) and the invention of new folk theatricals. In the other, men incorporated modern, state-based values into locally constituted forms of cultural discourse (see Chaps. 3, 4 and 6; see also Lipset 2004a).

Now in addition to the point that these two kinds of masculine voices combine both to affirm and repudiate modernity in PNG, by distinguishing them, I want to stress that Yanda's new piece of folk theater was no anomaly. It did not answer a specific change that was taking place in the wider scene in the early 1990s. It was rather one kind of intermittent, but persistent, answer Murik men have been formulating since the early twentieth century. In a festive, rather than an incapacitated, doleful voice, they created new signifiers whose disposition toward modernity was not empty but rather contradictory.

To a certain extent, *Woyon's Mother*, sung in the vernacular, danced by men and women adorned in archaic valuables, resisted the authoritative, universalizing voices of modernity. What is more, the authorship of Yanda's show might be likened to a kind of weak legal pluralism (Griffiths 1986). His dream took place in unofficial space (see Lattas 1993). The territory, the dreamscape in which the spirits staged their show, was inside yet outside the state. His ancestor-spirits were not citizen-subjects of the Eurocentric modernity. They neither voted nor pay taxes. The state does not guarantee their equality or security. Yet the ancestors were creative, or as Appadurai once put it, they were "context-generative" (1995: 64). Their spectacular agency subverted one of the crucial projects of the state, which is to standardize the moral action of its citizenry and gain the consent of the governed. If the creativity of the ancestors and Yanda, their withdrawn representative, did not explicitly repudiate or at least impugn this project, it was surely athwart it in several ways, all of which congealed in a single image. The dream performance of the new show was not offered on a pay-per-view basis; it was a gift the ancestors made to Yanda, their kinsman.

As a theater of the ancestors' resiliency, or perhaps as a weapon of the weak (Scott 1985), *Woyon's Mother* portrayed the Murik Male Cult as an indestructible and entertaining signifier amid modernity in PNG. The new piece, as well as the rest of the folk theater genre, particularly when performed for and exported to intertribal trading partners, celebrated archaic languages and masculinity, as well as the icons of archaic desire, shell and teeth valuables. Its fantasy of a beautiful mother and her sons and daughters was thus, in formal terms, comedy. The heroine survives and escapes impossible obstacles without the slightest scratch, much less pain, to reintegrate society (Frye 1957). But *Woyon's Mother* must be simultaneously understood as tragedy, as theater in which the work of detachment is being done. Yanda's mourning framed it in the anxieties to which Murik people feel prone during this difficult transition when the spirit-other leaves living kin for the world of the ancestors.

When the show was performed in the village to celebrate the release of two wrongly jailed kinsmen, or on behalf of my departure, its representation of Pygmalion's desire still remained somewhat detached from and disdainful of modernity. In 2008, it was unapologetically performed in celebration of the nation-state. The shifting reference of the show to modernity went on alongside its offer of a gratifying image of beauty and coherence that both performers and audiences might still embrace however much it might also be dismissed as little more than an increasingly irrelevant form of archaic masculinity.

Disgusted at the shamelessness of women, Ovid has Pygmalion sculpt a beautiful woman, as if to allegorize (and satirize?) the very impossibility of male desire. Pygmalion substitutes his art for his loneliness by turning this lack into a figure whose presence fills his heart and gaze. Like Pygmalion, *Woyon's Mother* also said something about the impossibility of male desire. Both creations answer lack, although of different kinds. Like Pygmalion, Yanda and the Murik Male Cult created an illusory object of desire, feminine completeness and aesthetic continuity. Like Pygmalion, perhaps *Woyon's Mother* was a masculine *cri de coeur*, a somewhat woeful longing to be desired. Not a recuperation, of course, or even a deferral, but an expression of men's persistent yearning for the other. Indeed, as recently as 2014, I noted that two of "her" distinctive torso-masks were still hanging from the rafters in the Male Cult House in Darapap village, along with props from other shows (see Fig. 5.7). The allure of

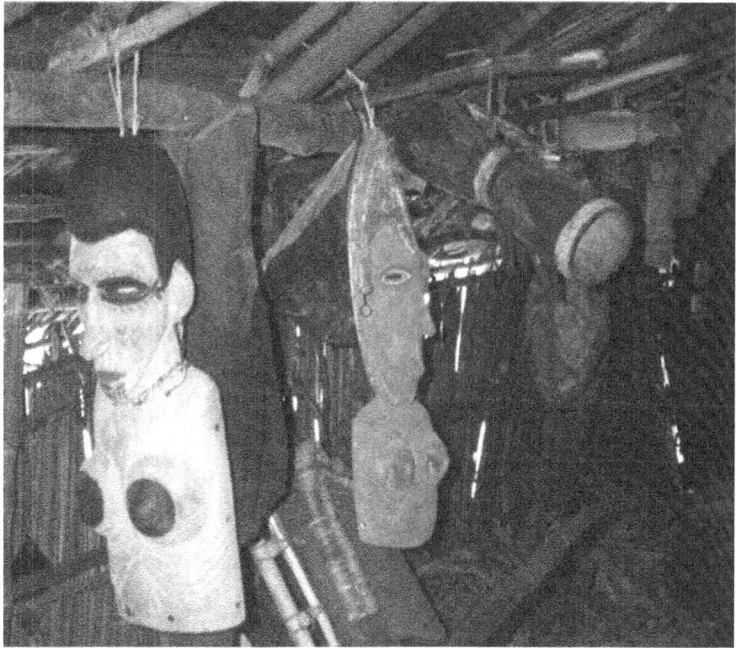

Fig. 5.7 *Woyon's Mother* masks hang in the Male Cult House in Darapap village along with props from other shows. Photo: David Lipset (2001)

Pygmalion's agency, for example, men's hopeless desire to create and encompass feminine desire, evidently continued to attract men amid the turbulent, troubled present.

The next chapter continues to focus on the dual alienation of the Murik signifier in modern PNG. It concerns a crucial moment in its dialogue that took place in 2001—when money was substituted as acceptable payment for grade-taking in the public masking society.

NOTES

1. They reciprocate in like manner (or, at least, are supposed to reciprocate in like manner) the day before I leave the village to start off for home.
2. This practice is part of conventional avoidance relations that are assumed by parties in conflict until they share a meal together and resolve their dispute. The meal was prepared by wives and daughters by whom I was adopted.
3. For example, "Aimaru," which is a widely traded show that features two fish set on poles, as well as masks of their parents, dancing through and about rows of festooned dancers, is said to have originated near Aitape, prior to World War I. The story of this show was recounted to me in 1982 by Marabo Game. "A Tumleo Islander had a dream. A kidnapped spirit, imprisoned in a cave, showed him the four effigies and taught him the music. Some years later [during the 1920s], the show reached the Murik Lakes as a gift from this man's sons to the children of their sister who had married a Murik man whom she had met while he was employed at the Catholic Mission in Tumleo. The couple later moved to live in the Murik Lakes. Aimaru was performed for the first time during the interwar period, after which the family traded it elsewhere [in] the Sepik region."
4. The songs inevitably tell of the landscape. By contrast to Biangai songs (see Halvaksz 2003), the landscape in Woyon songs are background to the elegiac recounting of specific incidents, and sentiments provoked by, the lost other.
5. Lacan called such disturbances "the real" (1993: 63f).
6. *Terminalia catappa*, a common tree in PNG, grows on foreshores and similar wetland environs and bears edible fruit.
7. Indeed, the fish, bird, and butterfly motifs that decorated the ancestor-spirit figures also appear throughout Murik art, most prominently as designs on canoe prows (Lipset 2005, 2014b).
8. See Rosaldo (1989), not for its contrary Ilongot construction of mourning, but as an example of the point that creativity may recuperate loss, in this case of the author's wife, Michelle.
9. Wokumot in turn is one of three communities which make up the village of "Big Murik."

CHAPTER 6

Money and Other Signifiers

Let me briefly restate what I find useful about Lacan's concept of "the signifier."[1] First of all, it is a symbol that does not stand for itself (cf. Wagner 1986) but rather refers to a prediscursive other that resists all "attempts at rational incorporation" (Habermas 1987: 102). In Lacan's view, the signifier, which is to say the phallus, does not define reality/discourse in and of itself, like Connell's notion of "hegemonic masculinity" is said to do. Instead, it has a structural defect, a defect that makes moral order possible but only in a way that misrecognizes itself, and is misrecognized, as powerful and self-sufficient. What is more, perhaps the most fundamental attribute of the signifier for understanding the dual alienation of Murik masculinity in modern PNG is that it positions the self in a time and space in which it neither belongs to nor controls the other.

However, as I argued, or rather began to argue, in the previous chapter, postcolonial settings like PNG require an alteration of the phallus. In modernities like these, everything—every illusory signifier of legitimacy and moral agency—is plural. Instead of a single Symbolic, multiple languages, names, cosmologies, laws, medical systems, currencies and so forth coexist, perhaps in competition with each other, as rival voices. So instead of one Symbolic into which the phallus is exiled, there are two Symbolics, both of which take their cut from the "very life" of the subject, thus to "bind him to the signifier." Two *names of the father*, that is to say, two discursive interventions, "symbolically castrate" the phallus, thus to bind the subject to plural sorts of alienation. Together, the two Symbolics, the one archaic and the other modern, give rise to unpredictable chains of meaning. The latter does not erase the former. Instead, they become superimposed upon one another in chains of signification which are both positive and productive as well as empty.

By way of taking this view of the dual alienation Murik masculinity a little further, I will proceed as follows. The first section of the chapter develops a couple of relevant dimensions of Murik personhood that need more ethnographic and theoretical attention. I will then turn to the public masquerade I call the "Gaingiin Society," in which rights to senior masks used to be exchanged in return for wives' sexual services. Next, I will analyze a moment in 1988 when money was substituted for sexual intercourse during a grade-taking rite. In conclusion, I argue that this substitution took place in the broader context of dialogue in which men's archaic signifier answered modernity with estrangement and desire.[2]

MOBILITY AND MORAL ORDER

I once saw a national election polling team at work in a Murik village in June 1982. They set up a folding table on a basketball court and opened a roll in which citizens' names were registered, the adult men and women of the community. People filed by the table, checked in, received a ballot and cast their vote, sheltered in the anonymity of nearby cardboard booths that had also been set up. This was one of the first national elections after Independence, and I recall that voting seemed to arouse villagers' anxiety. People stood around cheerlessly while waiting in line, and many of them scurried off to their bush toilets upon fulfilling this odd new duty. The very act of voting was in and of itself strange, despite the fact that it was now being managed by Papua New Guineans rather than Australians. However, I want to point out another disconnection or incongruity that made it an interesting double-voiced moment. Unlike the bureaucratic concept of state-based citizenship, status in Murik society is defined in terms that are resolutely parochial, but more importantly, they are resolutely human. This is not to say that personhood in Murik is more moral and authentic than postcolonial citizenship in PNG. It is rather to say that in PNG, the person is not simply a "citizen-isolate," as Ronald Berndt once put it (1962: 88). The person is rather a composite of archaic and modern values, idioms and practices that do not fit together (see Chap. 2). Voting exposed that dialogue and it gave rise to something akin to *angst*.

Instead of rights that stem from a universal constitution, or even from being a child of God, membership in Murik family groups and lineages is claimed in ways that appear to complement, challenge or at least answer nothing less than the essence of human particularism and interdependency, the birthing mother and her infant. Elsewhere, I argued that moral authority and status in archaic Murik society largely draw tactics and idioms from a kind of a "hidden dialogue" with a trope of maternal praxis (Lipset 1997). The Murik, that is to say, implicitly acknowledged that reproduction was a deeply heterosexual process. Therefore, men had to look elsewhere to forestall their dependency on the desire of the other. Among their interventions were the lineage insignia—an outfit of ornaments, most importantly a named basket (*sumon suun*) and/or a medallion of boars' tusks and bird of paradise plumage—which senior men, and senior women, brought out to display during rites of passage, particularly on behalf of the firstborn (Fig. 6.1). These insignia differentiated lineage membership, but significantly, they used to constitute incest taboos. That is, they were meant to limit desire. More broadly, the *sumon* ornaments signified moral order not only between lineages but within them. Senior men and women responsible for them were obliged to safeguard the solidarity of their group by keeping them out of harm's way, particularly should contested desire for the desire of the other break out when they were out on display during rites of passage.

The take-away point would be this: ritual elders are understood to serve as moral anchors of Murik communities. They fulfill ethical obligations incurred from the ritual "work" done on their behalf by a previous generation, by ritually indebting new generations and keeping the peace. Order is maintained within the lineage. It is reproduced not just by the other but by a ritual process of elimination. The child, whose loyalties are otherwise pushed and pulled by a welter of cognatic desires, is reduced to membership in one or two lineages, in which he or she becomes the "child" of its signifier (*sumon gwan/gnasen*) in addition to being a child of his or her mother. In Lacanian terms, these lineage signifiers, like the Symbolic more generally, are "cut off" from the desire of the other. They are alienated from her love and care and their morality is indelibly enchained to this prediscursive trauma.

In the previous chapter, I pointed out that the Murik person is understood as a spirit-passenger (*nabran*) travelling in a canoe-body (*gai'iin*). In daily life, when people (*nor*) paddle about the Murik Lakes in dugout canoes, they put this cosmological dimension of being into motion. At the

Fig. 6.1 Middle-class man decorated in lineage insignia for his initiation. Photo: David Lipset (2014).

same time as human spirits travel in dugouts, their ancestor-spirits do too. As we saw in Yanda's dream (see Chap. 5), they may make use of zoomorphic canoe-bodies in which they go meet up with the spirits of dead kin. Now I think that the concept of mobile spirits moving around in multiple canoe-bodies at night and by day does not just express or represent the Murik adaptation to their lacustrine environment: it also expresses their alienation from the desire of the other and a consequent desire to restore its unity.

There is an occult reference of the canoe-body that lends support to this interpretation. From a masculine viewpoint, if not necessarily a feminine one (see Barlow and Lipset 1997), the canoe-body is associated with the phallus. Carving requires chastity that mystically empowers the canoe-bodies of the carpenters to work effectively. Their chastity also safeguards the integrity of the wooden hull from sexual pollution by women. Canoe-prows are intricately adorned with phallus-like motifs (Fig. 6.2). Overseas voyages of outrigger canoes were protected from shipwreck by the chastity of the steersman's wife (see Chaps. 5 and 7). And, in the aftermath of a phase of male initiation, when a father learned that his son had stoically withstood the pain of learning how to expel the impure feminine blood from his penis, he might exclaim: "Oh! My canoe has come shore!" (Lipset 1997: 280).

The embodiment of the person in general, and the symbolic phallus in particular, is thus imbued with vehicular meaning, and *vice versa*, canoes have phallic attributes. These ideas coalesce into a single image. When a son is born, kin are said to observe with relief that "he will take his father's place" (*yan kaban osangait*). The idiom of "taking his place" acknowledges that youth may and should succeed age to occupy, or claim, the status,

Fig. 6.2 The Fog Man canoe prow. Photo: David Lipset (2001).

rights and obligations of the senior generation. But it also acknowledges that this succession is contingent upon Maussian reciprocity: it must be given, taken and returned to a future generation. However, this view of reproduction should not be mistaken for a concept of reincarnation. It surely involves generational succession among kin but one that is imagined as a process or sequence of status substitution that is oddly comparable to the transition of an officeholder in a bureaucracy (cf. Weiner 1980). These three images—the bestowal of lineage insignia, the canoe-body-phallus association and generational succession as X "taking the place of" Y—combine to envision a static, yet mobile, moral order in which passengers travel through the time and space of the other, a lacustrine/marine space, in the decorated canoe-bodies in which they temporarily have rights. In Murik terms, an heir is sometimes said to be her mother's or his father's "canoe." A son or daughter thus becomes a vehicle-metaphor in the social structure for the jural status of his or her same-sex parent. In this prestate concept of generation and person, the metaphor of reproduction is simultaneously the reproduction of a social metaphor: an heir should take over the helm of a canoe-body, the corporate lineage. Simultaneously, it is a cultural assertion that status substitution is not only possible but offers a kind of solace.

In the upside-down world of Lacanian signification, such an unequivocal view of reproduction is of course not the whole story. In addition to consolation, the appearance of an heir should also give rise to an expression of the *No!* by which the *name of the father* metaphorically expels the phallus into the Symbolic. For Lacan, the Symbolic is a form of dismemberment. It is a space of semiotic exile, or alienation, in which the phallus is cut off from the desire of the other in a way that motivates its commitment to language, convention and law, on the one hand, but also recreates this originary Oedipal intervention and the eternal gap between the pleasure of maternal desire and the impossibility of getting it back, on the other. We shall now see that the Murik do indeed value reproduction, which is to say, "replacement," both as comfort and as loss. To illustrate this view of the alienation in the two Symbolics in which Murik men find themselves estranged from both their own archaic as well as from modern PNG, I now turn to a discussion of their public masquerade.

The Postcolonial Gaingiin Society

The Gaingiin Society consists of ranked spirit-masks which afford men a measure of veiled agency in village space (Bernardi 1985). It is divided into seven age-grades, each of which is named for the particular spirit-masks it holds (Murik: murup, Tokpisin: tumbwan). Internally, grades are made up of one or several cohorts (*orub*) of men who are said to have been born around the same time. Adjacent grades are, or are said to be, related through matrilateral kin ties. Mothers' brothers have junior partners who are classificatory sisters' sons. However, they refer to themselves as "fathers" of the latter, whom they call "sons."

In precolonial times, when intertribal relations were potentially violent and self-governed, the Male Cult of each village was responsible for its defense. The Gaingiin Society then served the Male Cult. It trained youth in the skills and defensive postures appropriate to the ethos of *warre* when "every man is Enemy to every man" (Hobbes 1972: 223), prepared them for the rigors of Cultic initiation and instructed them in its organization. At the same time, its senior masks asserted authority in community spaces during certain circumstances in order to facilitate achieving specific ritual goals.

Over the past hundred years or so, the Gaingiin Society persisted, although Murik communities had long since ceded the right to defend their security to the state. In 1981–2015, the age-grades of the Gaingiin Society still asserted the right to make and don the spirit-masks that concealed their bearers' domestic identities, at least pseudoanonymously, in several villages.[3] As spirits, they remain mute and do not speak. As warriors, they still reserved rights to chase and attack anyone junior in grade to themselves. Until around 2010, when changing lake tides began to make footpaths, avenues and plazas rather too slippery to sprint around on, young men in the entry-level Gaingiin grade (see Fig. 6.3) regularly stalked, chased after and menaced uninitiated children by their appearance

Fig. 6.3 A newly initiated Gaingiin grade. Photo: David Lipset (2001).

and with throwing sticks. Gaingiin was a beloved, but earnest and scary, bogey from whom children would flee (in delight). He associated the public sphere, at least for young children, with the aforementioned Hobbesian posture, made into an intense game of chase. Once in a while, a young parent might even be seen handing a toddler over to the spirit-bogey, who would hold it up above its head, as the child screaming in terror, desperately struggled to be get back to its mother or father. When Gaingiin did return the toddler, he or she would cling to the parent for dear life. The public sphere was no bourgeois commons where order was guaranteed by a sovereign authority to promote commerce and communication (Habermas 1984). It was rather alive with frightening spirits whose *name* mothers and fathers would sometimes yell out in order to bring unruly children to heel.

Members of senior grades in the Gaingiin Society continue to impersonate the Dimbwan and Bananain spirits in several Murik villages (Figs. 6.4 and 6.5). Their unique privilege is to oversee a measure of *civitas* in them: they may install a community-wide taboo against the harvesting of coconuts. That is, the two spirit-masks may (temporarily) supersede the otherwise autonomous property rights held by lineages, which was, in pre-state terms, a nontrivial claim. During the run-up to major feasts, such as end-of-mourning festivals, ritual sponsors may oblige the Dimbwan and Bananain cohorts to fashion property markers (*jaba'iin*) out of the midribs of sago fronds (*saidug*). Grade members would beat them so that yellow streamers, three or more feet long, dangle down from the midrib shaft that is leftover. The two masks then erect the *jaba'iin* signs at the openings of channels and footpaths leading to coconut groves, which are then said to become "their property." Should coconuts be "stolen," the Dimbwan and Bananain maskers are not only entitled to chop down the entire grove where the theft took place but attack the whole village. In addition, the two mask-spirits may provide "security." In 1993, for example, I saw the Dimbwan mask "escort" a group of women through the coconut groves to a waterhole and then "bring" them back to the village. He did so, it was said, to make sure that no coconuts were stolen on the way. The two mask-spirits also reserve the right to suspend their taboo and temporarily allow the gathering of coconuts, should a contingency arise, such as a drought or a funeral. When the Dimbwan grade agree that sufficient coconuts have accumulated in "their groves" to supply the needs of a pending feast, they secretly go to a private spot in the bush where they decorate themselves with flowers before returning to the village to declare by their appearance that final preparations for the feast should get started.

MONEY AND OTHER SIGNIFIERS 143

Fig. 6.4   Bananain mask. Photo: David Lipset (1993).

The taboo the senior mask-spirits install exerts a supra-social, yet indirect, kind of authority over the whole community. The agency behind it is named, but masked and numinous rather than masculine and human. The question is: authority over what? Over property represented as *coconuts*. Coconuts are "property," to be sure, in Murik terms. However, they are also associated with the desire of the other. Specifically, coconuts evoke her unalienated desire before the intervention of *the name of the father*. This connection is visible (and audible) in the way Murik people drink its liquid (*dapag arum*). They literally suckle coconut milk from a small hole they open through the eye. It was made explicit in the effigy of an ancestor-spirit woman called Namiit, who appeared in a phase of Male Cult initiation, her breasts then being represented by coconut half shells attached to her torso. The association is given a grotesque inflection during a rite-of-reversal called

Fig. 6.5 Dimbwan mask. Photo: David Lipset (1993).

noganoga'sarii when women and men, armed with coconut half shells filled with a fetid concoction of animal feces mixed with mud, try and stuff this mixture into the mouths of affines (Lipset and Silverman 2005). More examples could be cited about the maternal symbolism of coconuts (Lipset 1997: 279). Suffice it to say that the taboo forbidding their harvest seems to evoke the intervention of *the name of the father*. The compensation that was given in return for promotion into the most senior grade confirms this interpretation in a Melanesian way, needless to say.

"The Snake Caught Me!"

Until the 1960s, grade-taking demanded a "total prestation" from the Bananain maskers in the classic Maussian sense in which a gift draws multiple values to it, thus to come to stand for society as a whole (Mauss 1967: 3).

As I explained above, the Gaingiin Society served as a kind of infrastructure for the Male Cult. The domain of the one was limited to within the community, while the other extended into the region. But both were identically organized. Men in the senior grades of each institution have a junior partner in the adjacent grade who is his classificatory sister's son, but who is ritually referred to as a "son." In both, the senior man will eventually yield his status and its associated rights to sacra to that "son." And in both, in order to compensate his ritual "father" for doing so, the "son" must permit his "mother," for example, his wife,[4] to "marry" his "father." This "marriage" which involved the provision of a wife's sexual services was called "sending his skirt" (*dago'timariin*) to his counterpart. That is, in the Gaingiin Society, a husband would make a request to his wife to have sexual intercourse with his senior masking partner.[5] In 1981, the late Murakau Wino outlined to me the sequence when the junior maskers succeeded the senior ones.

> Husbands and wives ... [belonging to] the Bananain grade paddle across the lakes to collect sago frond midribs. Upon returning to the village, they pile them up in an isolated spot in the coconut groves. That night, the leading member of the junior grade "sends his skirt" to his "father" [his classificatory mother's brother]. This [provision of sexual intercourse by the junior partner's "mother"] was meant 'to pick out the thorns of the sago fronds caught in his feet.' The woman would go to him carrying a sago frond over her shoulder. Placing the base of the frond on his shoulder, the husband's "father" acknowledged her [desire].
>
> The couple then went together to the pile of sago fronds that were to be used to make the [raffia for the] cloaks of the new Dimbwan masks. The couple had sex there. The woman returned to her husband [afterwards] and declared to him: 'The snake caught me!' (*Ma wakun tenangakum*). The leader of the junior grade—that is, the man who had just sent his wife—then gathered the rest of the couples in the [rising] cohort together to prepare a feast for the senior grade who then taught them how to assemble the Dimbwan costumes.

In this remarkable Lacanian reversal, rather than being cut off from the desire of a senior woman by *the name of the father*, thus to enter the Symbolic, at the behest of *the name of the son*, a junior woman offers her desire to a senior man in order to obligate him to retire from the Symbolic. Her desire, in good Melanesian fashion, is attributed a reciprocal value; for example, it is viewed as an act of compensation. Needless to say, my understanding is that her husband, the leader of the junior maskers, would not have agreed to or accepted this concession free and easily. Not at all. Alienated as he is in a time and space of the other, he would have done it jealously and anxiously, if not resentfully. However, once again, stoicism was called for. He must repress possessive sentiments of conjugal attachment (e.g., love). He must repress the pain of the symbolic castration, even though agreeing to send his wife/mother to his masking partner is a voluntary act and even if the return was winning the prestige of rank and authority in the Gaingiin Society. Notably, we shall also see that the subsequent grade-taking rite included birthing imagery of a kind, so in this sense the Murik formulation of desire as an act of reciprocal exchange that gave rise to status replacement was viewed in generative terms, that is, as a reproductive process.[6]

The senior man would *not* taboo his ritual "son" from his "mother's" desire permanently, but would rather *return* her to him. She goes back to her husband. Celebrating his partner's phallus and her successful seduction of it, she would announce (to him), "The snake caught me!" The dependency of the phallus upon the "desire of the other" could not have been stated any more plainly.

A Coconut Taboo

In the Gaingiin Society, "giving skirts" to compensate initiators ended for all intents and purposes in 1988 when a new gift—money—was substituted for sexual intercourse. In order to argue that money was superimposed on the archaic phallus in this context, and eventually that this substitution belongs to the larger alienation of the masculine signifier, I must return to that time when Kathleen Barlow, Lissant Bolton, John Salau and I had undertaken the "Sepik Documentation Project" on behalf of the Australian Museum in Sydney. We had set ourselves the task of studying Murik regional exchange, while purchasing artifacts and documenting existing Museum collections (Lipset 2016a). We called on selected villages along the North Coast and around the Lower Sepik River, conducted interviews about historical and contemporary exchange, elicited data about objects from photographs we brought along with us and bought a few things. In Murik village of Darapap, we purchased a Yangoron spirit-mask, Yangoron being the name of a family of spirit-masks held by a mid-level grade in the Gaingiin Society who appear in public from time to time dressed in coconut-bark capes and overalls made of the same fabric. "Father" and "son" masks are distinguished (from their "mother") by nothing less than a big, erect phallus that bounces up and down as they beg for food or dance for bemused audiences who may serenade them with song (see Fig. 6.6).

MONEY AND OTHER SIGNIFIERS 147

Fig. 6.6 Yangoron (right) begging for food. Photo: David Lipset (1988).

The agency of the Yangoron family in the community, that is to say, is transgressive and comic, rather than threatening or administrative.

In the course of negotiating to buy "the son," or rather his costume, from "his" grade, I went to a meeting in a Male Cult House in Darapap village. I found the Dimbwan grade there, having been tasked to install a coconut-harvesting taboo in the run-up to a Female Cult initiation rite (Barlow 1995). They had assigned the work to Bananain, the maskers in their adjacent, junior grade. As men waited for a feast that the rite's sponsors were preparing, heated charges of ritual negligence arose between the age-grades.

> Mikah Ker denounced the Dimbwan grade for failing to feed the Bananain maskers [of which he was a member]. He said that he did not want his [junior] grade to do the work of making and erecting the taboo markers (*jaba'iin*)—gathering stalks of sago palm and pounding fringe from them.
>
> Wapo, a senior Dimbwan masker, offered [to sponsor] a meal for the junior grade in the name of his cohort, so that the taboo could be properly mounted.

In general, this kind of exchange, in which work is done in return for food and support, is normative in Murik kinship. Houses are built this way. Canoe logs are cut this way. Children go buy fish and sago for their mothers this way. In other words: Mikah Ker was offended because his grade was hungry. So, given the state of their stomachs, why should they work? The tense meeting of the Gaingiin Society continued.

> Mikah Ker stood and demanded to be initiated into the Dimbwan grade. Too many junior men, he complained, had been promoted ahead of him. A firstborn son might replace his father in the senior man's grade, especially should his "wood have rotted." Sitting next to me, Joshua Sivik, who was a generation younger than Mikah Ker, whispered that he himself had taken his father's place in the Dimbwan grade this way. Sivik pointed to Kaibong, a man junior to Ker, who had been promoted ahead of his cohort after "giving" his wife to his mother's brother, and had taken the opportunity to pull several other junior men up with him, but not Ker.

Micah Ker's reproach, that he had been ritually ignored by the senior maskers, was based in an assumption that completely adheres to the norms of Murik kinship, an assumption which I need to make explicit. Not only are youth expected to be demanding; age fully acknowledges a desire to spoil them. But never vice versa. Age, once again, should be stoic and never ask anything directly of youth, apart perhaps of little, inconsequential errands. To do so would shame the self as "young." Cooperation from youth, in any case, should be gained on a voluntary basis, arising from an ongoing context of care and nurture. Micah Ker may have been protesting, in other words, but as he belonged to the junior grade, his grievance was not at all remarkable. Lacan associates language, discourse and moral order with the phallus that signifies the loss of the desire of the other. From his standpoint, the generous presence that youth demand evokes her loss. More generally, initiation into the senior grade of the Gaingiin Society signifies a lack, a lack that binds the subject to the phallus, as Lacan's epigraph to this Section of the book put it.

To wit: promotion in the Gaingiin Society is not fixed by chronological birth but is fungible. Why is grade-skipping warranted, and how is it compensated? It is justified in terms of the phallus. The substitution of the firstborn son, or other youth, for an aging father was meant to safeguard the phallus, not as metaphor, but now as organ, as a literal recipient of the desire of a junior masker's wife. It was also justified by the ambition of a junior man who wanted to advance ahead of his cohort, which required sending his "mother" to have intercourse with his "father." Grade-skipping explicitly denoted the phallus. The subject would enter a new level of 'the Symbolic' not by having to give up being the object of the desire of the other to the *name of the father* but rather by trading upon that desire with "him."

Meanwhile back at the Male Cult House: the co-sponsors of the women's initiation rite, Kaibong and Tasi, his co-wife, were serving a meal to the senior maskers. The food was meant to obligate them to taboo harvesting coconuts. A large number of leaf-covered wooden and porcelain plates of rice or sago pudding garnished with fish were set out in the middle of the floor. Before eating, discussion began about "the price" of grade-taking. Money, men acknowledged, had now replaced "skirts" in various contexts of ceremonial exchange. It had already been used at the highest level of moiety exchange in the Male Cult. However, in the Gaingiin Society, its reciprocal prerogatives remained in play. Having previously "sent" his wife to have sex with his mother's brother, Kaibong still held rank and authority in the senior grade. In addition to honoring his cohort with the ceremonial porridge of coconut milk and dried coconut meats (*aragen*), Kaibong held the right to set the price for grade-taking—which he put at K200.[7] Standing up, with all the great many dishes laid out on the floor in front of him, Kaibong said that he and his wife were offering a

> "little food [to compensate the senior, Dimbwan grade] to set up the taboo markers in both Darapap and Karau [villages]."
>
> Mathew Tamoane stood (as a junior, Bananain masker): "Our initiation [into the Dimbwan masks] should [take place] right away! It will take a bit of time to collect money from the grade-members. We must take [the] Dimbwan [grade] now and pay later!"
>
> Kaibong (in anger): "You [junior, Bananain masks] must pay us first!"
> Murakau (as a senior member of Dimbwan): "Right!"
> Mikah Ker (as grade leader of the junior, Bananain masks): "Food is easy. We can give you food now. But money is a little harder. Can you give us a

little time for it? The feast will be staged soon. If we want to get the money together, there will not be enough time to gather a lot of dry coconuts for the [ceremonial porridge]."

Wapo (an elder in the senior, Dimbwan grade): "We won't allow debt. We want the food and the money at once. Otherwise, we will just put the Dimbwan [costumes] together and wear them ourselves!"

Mikah Ker: "I will go to [town] and come back and get the [sago fronds for the coconut taboo and the costumes] and beat them with my grade."

The senior, Dimbwan grade distributed the plates and began to eat, acknowledging their obligation to set the taboo by doing so.

If their debate shows us anything, it is that the standing of the Gaingiin Society was relatively uncontested in 1988. Unlike the Revivalist Christians elsewhere in the Sepik region (Tuzin 1997; see also Robbins 2004), even Seventh Day Adventist (SDA) men in the village of Darapap were not out to disband it. The three men—Mikah Ker, Wapo and Mathew Tamoane—who advocated holding the grade-taking rite as early as possible, were all leading SDAs. Neither did anyone dismiss the Gaingiin Society as a waste of time that could be better spent on modern pursuits, like their fishery. Instead, men assumed that grade-taking in the Gaingiin Society ought to and would go on. Their issue was how to reproduce it within modernity. The problem was how to convert the value of the phallus, for example, "the desire of the other," into money? This was a nontrivial moment. The stakes in Murik men's dialogue with modernity were high: how many PNG kina was a "skirt" worth? Marking this equivalence, a characteristic problem of modernity immediately beset their debate: trust (Seligman 1997). Why? Because money is so contradictory. It allows for the "bracketing time-space by coupling instantaneity and deferral, presence and absence" (Giddens 1990: 25; see also Simmel 1978). In this particular situation, although the senior grade was not confident that they would get their money, they nevertheless agreed to let the junior grade owe it to them.

THE METAPHOR OF MONEY

Mistrust aside, the grade-taking took place a couple of days later. Unfortunately, I had gone back upriver to the Catholic Mission at Marienberg, to rejoin my Australian Museum colleagues based there. I did manage to collect an account of what happened when I subsequently spoke to Joshua Sivik, one of the retiring maskers, shortly thereafter.

We [the Dimbwan-mask grade] decided that K200 was too dear. We cut the price in half. They only paid us K30, and left the rest as debt. Enoch, Mikah Ker, and [another man] each paid K10 and became leaders of the grade. Kowre and Sauma [two senior maskers] accepted their money. The rest of us got nothing. Sauma gave his share of the money to Kiso, his wife, because she had [intercourse] with his mother's brother.

Joel Robbins and David Akin argued that "social reproduction is the heart of the matter where currencies are concerned" (1999: 17; see also Bloch and Parry 1989: 28). But although their point is well taken, it fails to emphasize the contested value of social reproduction which is to say, the contested value of reproducing collective identity through ritual action: throughout the history of colonial and postcolonial Melanesia, money and shells have been used for this purpose in different ways (Burridge 1969; Errington and Gewertz 1995: 49–76; Brison 1999). Cases have been reported in which efforts were made to "enclave" money (Appadurai 1986) from contexts of social reproduction in ceremonial and gift exchange so as to control its disruptive effects on social order (Akin 1999; Foster 1995). But other instances, like this one, have also been reported in which money replaced prestate valuables in order to protect the power of local-level leaders from the democratization of shells (Strathern 1979; Gewertz 1983).[8] Perhaps the question posed by the substitution of money for "skirts" in this context recalls Marx's concept of fetishism, or the extent to which money may be seen as "savage" or "bitter," or have the capacity "to talk" (Gregory 1997; Shipton 1989; see also Taussig 1980). That is, how is money understood to displace attributes ordinarily associated with people? How is money, more specifically, another signifier of the dual alienation of Murik men?

In my terms, if "skirts" were replaced by an asocial medium of exchange that was "cut off" from primordial relationships, times and spaces, to what extent did "money" still stand for the intervention of *the name of the father* and the loss of the desire of the other (Simmel 1978)? In its symbolic equivalence to the phallus, what, in this context at least, did money mean? Did it tip the arrival of the isolated, modern subject on the Murik coast? Did it erode social life, making it less moral and more abstract, as Mauss stressed (1967)? Did it make inner life more rationalized? Did it imply a Weberian shift from an otherworldly sexuality into a self-absorbed, erotic sensuality (1958c)? Suffice it to say, we have come upon an important event for my topic in this book.

What claim did this substitution make in the dialogue between Murik masculinity and modernity in PNG? The Male Cult House being what it is, needless to say, money was hardly being transacted for ritual privileges in the Gaingiin Society as between strangers in a marketplace. Mothers' brothers in the senior grade were not trying to maximize profit in return for the Dimbwan grade-taking. Indeed, they voluntarily reduced their "fee." What is more, the substitution of money reversed the vector of dismemberment. Instead of depriving the junior husband of the desire of his "mother," money deprived his senior partner of her desire, leaving him, and the rest of his grade, with little more than a few PNG kina, and an outstanding debt, to show for their largesse. Although tense, it was clearly no longer a moment made possible by the virtue of manly stoicism. But neither did it turn into an impersonal form of market exchange. That is to say, it did not immediately displace the desire of the other, its archaic predecessor. This is not saying enough however. Let me finish discussing my informant's narrative of the grade-taking and then try again.

As I stated, the senior maskers did give way to the junior, "children's grade" (*naje'orub*). In the event, the ritual work of installing the coconut taboo was combined with their initiation into the Bananain maskers. Joshua Sivik continued his account:

> The [junior grade] gathered sago palm fronds in a motor-canoe. Both husbands and wives of the senior grade then beat the fronds [for the cloaks of the costumes]. The men put together about twelve Dimbwan costumes inside the Male Cult Hall. Classificatory mothers' brothers made specific masks for their sisters' sons. I made the mask called Sabogandp for Andrew Komsing and made Dagodago for Luke Manambot. The Bananain grade gave a feast to [us] for this work. We, [the retiring] Dimbwan grade then beat them as they crawled through our legs (See Fig. 6.6).
>
> Mikah Ker paraded through the village as [the spirit-mask] Mware'nor; he wore the Mindamot lineage insignia (*sumon*) as a headdress. Coconuts were broken in his path [to honor the insignia]. The rest of the newly promoted Dimbwan masks followed him. Two masks [who were] their "mothers" trailed after the parade.
>
> The [senior, retiring] grade made ceremonial porridge for the new Dimbwan grade to oblige them to begin the coconut taboo. Eight coconuts were harvested to prepare the porridge. Next day, six Dimbwan masks went to Karau [village] to install a taboo on groves there. The grade was well fed there for their work.

The relations of production between the grades, that is to say, had assumed anything but a "fantastic form of a relation between things" (Marx 1990: 165). Rather than alienation, the prevailing ethos remained one of use-value, domestic relationships and personification of the spirits. The two grades were classed in patrifilial terms as "fathers" and "children." Married couples worked together as an age-grade to make the costumes. The Dimbwan masks were individually named, and one mask, called Mware'nor, was decorated like a firstborn child displaying lineage insignia on the occasion of his initiation (Lipset 1990). As I say, the junior grade's initiation by the senior maskers used to be contingent upon the oedipal intervention of the *name of the father* and the repression of the junior maskers. Today, as we have seen, "skirts" are no longer exchanged. But the rite still invoked a grotesque reenactment of birth; the "sons" succeeded the "fathers" by crawling through a gauntlet of their legs (see Fig. 6.7). All of which is to say this: the substitution of money, if seen as a state-based *name of the father*, "dismembered" the signifier for a second time. Heretofore, it had been deprived of the desire of the other. Now, money deprived it of that archaic deprivation. The dual lack of desire in which a new alienation was being superimposed upon an old one led to prestige and privileges in a Symbolic consisting of masks which may be seen as an alienated voice answering modernity.

The retiring senior grade fed and were fed by their successors, who then installed the coconut taboo in two villages. Despite the substitution

Fig. 6.7 A junior grade of maskers is beaten during their initiation rite. Photo: David Lipset (2001).

of money for "skirts," the relationship between people and masks seems to have remained relatively stable, in other words. The masks did not become governed by relations between people in a state of independence from each other. Nor had the subject suddenly become secularized. Outer life did not become disenchanted. Nor had inner life suddenly become spiritualized. The maskers of the Gaingiin Society had rather moved into a nether world, a neither/nor world in which men were doubly alienated, no longer quite Murik, but not quite modern.

How did their dual alienation fit the broader itinerary of the Murik signifier in modernity in PNG? Donald Tuzin, studying a rural Arapesh case, regarded a campaign mounted by Revivalist Christians against the Male Cult as a symbolic act of "murder" that "killed" ritual masculinity (1997). There were no metaphors, or chains of signification, by which he was able to conceive of the two institutions in mutual reference to each other. In that case, nostalgic and depressed post-cultic men were pitted against the Revivalists, who were desperately preparing for the Second Coming. In a time of millennial values, there was apparently little else than rifts and masculine anomie.

Toward the end of the last chapter, I distinguished two related kinds of answers to modernity in PNG from Murik men. In one, the cultic signifier is severed from the Murik Symbolic, by speaking in and for nothing other than modern values, for example, commodities and the market (see Lipset 2005). In the other, the cultic signifier articulates itself with modern ideas, objects and persons. The two may now be said to converge, I want to suggest, in a contradictory, double-voiced dialogue rather than the kind of monotoned tragedy Tuzin so eloquently lamented among traditional Arapesh men.

Yabar and Other Signifiers of Murik Modernity

Not unlike Sahlins' Hawaiians (1985), or innumerable other Pacific Islanders (Connolly and Anderson 1988, Schieffelin and Crittenden 1991), the Murik took to referring to whites as "children of ancestor-spirits" (*yabar goan*) at, or soon after, they began to have sustained contact with the West sometime during the nineteenth century. As I mentioned in the Preface, the *yabar* were a category of ancestor-spirits whose unsurpassed powers enabled them to change persons and the environment in ways that exceeded all other spirits and human beings. It was they who introduced outrigger canoe technology.

They could cause terminal illnesses. They caused big storms and earthquakes. In Durkheimian terms, the *yabar* ancestor-spirits were a representation of the autonomous mastery of society over its members (1995). In ethnohistorical terms, perhaps they represented Austronesian culture. In Lacanian terms, at any rate, they expressed the empty signifier and its residual desire for the desire of the lost other. Needless to say, the *yabar* ancestor-spirits have all but disappeared from Murik conviction, although the term *yabar goan* certainly remains in widespread use. Indeed, "white man" is its most commonplace meaning today, although the phrase is not afforded any presumptively racialized valence (Bashkow 2006). One hears it, for example, in reference to the Papua New Guinean middle class (see McGavin 2014). Moreover, as I pointed out in the Preface, *yabar* is also used as a noun to refer to the context of labor in the capitalist economy of the postcolonial state. In *yabar*, punctual subjects work for salaries, purchase goods and travel among strangers in modern "canoes," such as cars, buses, boats and airplanes (Lipset 2014b). In other words, now more or less emptied out of any allusion to the ancestors, the term *yabar* has come to stand for nothing less than a vernacular concept, not just of modernity but modern alienation (Umbach and Hüppauf 2005). Villagers and peri-urban Murik judge the space and inhabitants of *yabar* as morally challenging and difficult to deal with. Although they recognize and appreciate its vigor and wealth, they complain how uncomfortable, insecure and ignored it makes them feel (Martin 2013). The *yabar* ancestor-spirits may have become lost to Murik cosmology, but the superiority of the powers that were once attributed to them remains as a more or less disenchanted signifier of modernity in PNG. This semantic extension exemplifies a chain of substitution that does not just signify a rupture or a discontinuity but rather an extension or multiplication of Murik men's alienation. I shall add a few other instances of substitution in their material culture that further illustrate this kind of dual alienation of their masculinity.

Today, men prevail upon any makeshift kind of sealable container, for example, glass jars, little metal tins, even plastic bags, to hold the lime powder they add to a betel nut chew. In the past, the lime gourds engraved with geometrical designs, which only initiated men had the privilege to use, they named for the overseas lover who had given it to them (see Figs. 6.8 and 6.9). As signifiers of the lost desire of the other, the jars and tins no longer refer to "her" lack. Now, they refer to a second lack, one that figures men as poor and unsophisticated "grassroots" in the national slang (see Chap. 4).

Fig. 6.8 Man with lime gourd. Photo: David Lipset (1988).

In prestate society, rival moieties used to consecrate a new Male Cult House (*taab*) by competing to ignite fire by friction. Their rivalry was also part of an elaborate, archaic dialogue between male and female, in which the Male Cult asserted a claim on maternal nurture, the victorious side had the honor of relighting the hearth fires in the community, all of which had been extinguished prior to the event (a claim the Female Cult answered by attempting to shake down the new building by its pilings). The winning moiety also made a claim on light during the nighttime. In 2012, when Sir Michael Somare sponsored a consecration rite for the opening of a new Male Cult House for whose construction he had paid, some men complained that this particular piece of moiety competition was neglected. But, the Male Cult can no longer claim that women's cooking depends upon its internal rivalry. Today, while men and women go gathering firewood from the Murik Lakes, fire is started by disposable butane lighters and the night is illuminated by kerosene powered hurricane lamps, battery powered flashlights and lanterns, and lately by solar panels and solar powered lights. These commodities, I would propose, do not refer

Fig. 6.9 Man with glass jar, for lime powder. Photo: David Lipset (2001).

fire to the Male Cult and the rivalries in which "his" moieties once had occasion to "fight." Instead, they make daily life less dependent on "his" archaic signifier and more reliant on the time and space of a modern other.

The technology of sleep suggests a similar shift. Today, men and women sleep (alone or with children) inside mosquito nets bought in town and hung up in their houses. Until the mid-1950s, women and children slept in handwoven tube-like bags (*arug*), together with the skulls of their grandparents. In the morning, as they crawled out, they took the relics and "fed" them cigarettes and betel nuts. Men, for their part, used to sleep in *arug*-bags in their Male Cult Houses; now they sleep alone or with children in mosquito nets in their family houses. The nets are not completely disconnected from the lineage. Like Yanda, the "author" of *Woyon's Mother*, they still meet ancestors in dreams (see Chap. 5). But of course mosquito nets are disconnected from the hands of the Murik women who once wove them.

Today, moreover, most people sleep on foam pillows. Archaic pillows (*ara'moan*), were made of wood propped up by little bamboo legs. They were ornately engraved with imagery of ancestor-spirits and zoomorphic motifs, pigs in particular. Only initiated men (who had sent wives to their cultic partners) carved and had the right to use them, which is why they depicted the agency of the ancestors and male desire. Foam pillows do not signify their predecessors. Foam pillows are gender neutral. Needless to say, they are not cultic signifiers of lost desire. But they do signify the extent to which Murik material culture has become dependent on exchange value and consumer capitalism.

Taken together, glass jars of lime powder, foam pillows and mosquito nets, along with butane lighters and flashlights, are all links in a signifying chain of masculine alienation, or in Lacanian terms, of a modern symbolic castration that I want to argue has been superimposed upon the archaic one. In other words, Murik men now live in the time and space of the other—twice over. But, like the substitution of money for "skirts" in the Gaingiin Society, the alienation of the Murik signifier must be seen as contradictory. It must be seen as combining persistence with loss of agency. There is a Murik system of value called *mwaran* that includes several kinds of ceremonial goods, such as tobacco (see Chap. 3), betel nuts and pigs, as well as lineage ornaments and a great variety of ritual services, of which the most important used to be the provision of "skirts." Hereditary feasting partners who are expected to donate *mwaran* during rites of passage are said to be in the "valuables route." Today, *mwara*-kin place PNG bills and coins on the chests of corpses soon after death for the deceased to use *en route* to the afterlife. In the past, male *mwara*-kin used to give new loincloths—their apron panels decorated with snake motifs—to their partners when the latter ended their period of mourning seclusion (see Fig. 5.2). Today, they give them new (or used) shirts and shorts. Disenchanted exchange-value is certainly referenced by clothes, and use-value is no doubt being disembedded by the substitution of these goods. However, they are incorporated within, rather than displaced from, the Murik archaic and its reciprocities, thus to evoke, rather than erase, the empty signifier of the past amid the empty signifiers of the present (Gregory 1982, 1997).

Perhaps the most outstanding examples of men's duel alienation are the fiberglass boats which travel on the ocean along the coast from the lakes to the market town of Wewak and elsewhere. These relatively little 19–23 foot vessels replaced the 45–50 foot lineage outriggers during the 1990s. The prows of the latter vehicles were protected by male ancestor-spirits and their construction process and consecration rites convened a comprehensive ritual dialogue about nothing less than the relationship of the cultic phallus to the desire of the other (see Barlow and Lipset 1997). Today, very few traces of outrigger canoes remain on Murik shores. Wooden planks, perhaps evoking an outrigger platform, are laid down to cover the floors of the fiberglass boats, planks on which cargo is stored and people sit, loosely dividing themselves by gender as they used to do on outriggers where men sat near the prow and women sat aft. Outboard motors have long since replaced coconut-bark sails. And their steering arms have long since replaced the big wooden steering paddles helmsmen used to hold (see Figs. 6.10 and 6.11). Safe passage now depends on machinery, which of course, requires gasoline and clean sparkplugs, rather than conjugal fidelity, or tabooing the desire of the other. However, a bus named after a lineage-outrigger carried fare-paying passengers through the streets of the provincial capital for several years until it broke down in 2011 (see Figs. 6.12–6.13; see also Sharp 2016: 82). The outrigger name reemerged in 2014, perhaps not surprisingly, as the name of a money management company started by a young Murik man in the national capital. As a signifier of masculine alienation, the fiberglass boats, outboard motors, the bus and the firm all reference the archaic phallus for which they are substitutions. They add a new lack onto the old lack for which things like outrigger canoes, masks in the Gaingiin Society, headrests and lime gourds once stood. They shift the dependency of the signifier from the desire of the other and relocate that lack in modernity, where money now signifies both the old and the new lack. Today, the fiberglass boats ferry fewer and fewer passengers to market and stalls that used to be manned by Murik fishwives selling their wares have been taken by women selling fish from the Sepik River. The fare, tied to rising costs of gasoline, exceeds what most people can afford. Meanwhile, Highlands entrepreneurs pay young Murik men a flat rate to buy fuel and transport Sepik betel nuts from the provincial capital to a drop-off point about 100 miles down the coast to the east. From there, this cargo is trucked up to sell to strangers in Highlands towns the sailors have never visited. As these young men race up and down the coast at breakneck speeds, they enjoy the wind on their faces. But their alienation is not far to seek: they think bitterly about how little they are paid and worry about the wear and tear each voyage does

Fig. 6.10 Man steering an outboard in a fiberglass boat. Photo: David Lipset (2012).

to their outboard motors, wear and tear that their employers do not feel obligated to repair (Owen 2005, Sharp 2016).

The modern tokens of value that have entered Murik material culture and the semantic extensions of Murik meaning onto some of them have given voice to a fairly equivocal dialogue in which, I am arguing, men's

Fig. 6.11 Young man with steering paddle. Photo: Rene Gardi ©(F)Vb 12638; Museum der Kulturen Basel (1956).

alienation for all intents and purposes has doubled. In the next chapter, I turn to debate about the meaning of rising sea levels that began to erode the Murik coast during the wet season of 2007. Ensuing debate about their meaning exposed a new context of this dialogue in which men now found themselves in a time and space of a new other, that is coming to be known as the Anthropocene.

Fig. 6.12 The outrigger canoe, Diskum. Photo: David Lipset (1982).

Fig. 6.13 The bus, Diskum. Photo: David Lipset (2010).

NOTES

1. See, e.g., Mauss (1967), Derrida (1981), Foucault (1970), Baudrillard (1981).
2. It is commonplace to view postcolonial masculinity in Papua New Guinea (PNG) as an historical tragedy (Brison 1995; Zimmer-Tamakoshi 1997; Knauft 2002; Robbins 2004; Wardlow 2006).

3. However, the masks run barefoot through the tideflats and leave footprints that are said to be universally recognizable.
4. A wife may be addressed or referred to as "mother" in Murik kin terminology which is Hawaiian.
5. See Thurnwald (1916) and Fortune (1939) for two other accounts of the exchange of sexual intercourse in the context of warfare and Male Cult ritual in the Sepik region. And see also, Lipset (1997), for a discussion of wife-lending in the context the Murik Male Cult.
6. This view could not but recall the great Trobriand ethnography of Annette Weiner (1978, 1979, 1980). Weiner was concerned with how extending the temporal and material cycle of reciprocity might give rise to a new view of exchange, her central methodological point being to take local concepts into accounts of exchange. Like the Murik, the Trobriand Islanders view reproduction through the metaphor of "replacement," "replacement" being a gloss for the extensive transactions that result in sociological succession (Weiner 1980: 78f). My interest in prestate and modern signifiers of masculine alienation obviously differs from Weiner's focus on exchange theory.
7. 1988 PNG K1 = US$0.85.
8. On the reception of money in rural PNG societies, see Robbins and Akin (1999: 5–7; Salisbury 1962: 126–30; Gregory 1982; Healy 1985; LiPuma 1999).

CHAPTER 7

In the Anthropocene

Wet-season tides (November to May) began to extend to unusually high distances along the Murik coast in late 2007. Beaches were eroded. Knocked-down coconut palms littered them along with stands of skeletal, dead casuarina trees (Fig. 7.1). The tides have continued to run high since then, sometimes breaching the narrow seashore, opening up new channels into the lakes which then close up during the subsequent dry season when the tides recede and the width of the seashore expands. Meanwhile, the lake tides rose. In the 1980s, Murik villages typically dried out between diurnal tidal oscillations. Now they no longer do so. In Darapap, people were poling canoes from house to house when the lake tides reached high water or, as in Mendam village, they trudged matter-of-factly along slippery, slimy and mucky footpaths.

Ecological change, like the rising tides cutting the Murik coast, is widely seen as one of the defining features of the Anthropocene, the "human-dominated geologic epoch" in which centuries of damage blindly done by capitalism has disrupted biospheric cycles of the planet (Crutzen 2002: 23). The magnitude of the Anthropocene extends far beyond environmental damage and its principal drivers, however. The epoch has been seen as nothing less than the end of the nature/society (Cartesian) binary. It has also been seen as a measure of human injustice and as cause for a new history (Chakrabarty 2009). It has been seen as a motive for a new heroic kind of green activism. But although anthropologists have certainly started to study the experience of its consequences in various parts

Fig. 7.1 Stands of dead trees along the Murik coast. Photo: David Lipset (2014).

of the world,[1] an important dimension of the subject position entailed by the new era has not been appreciated, much less analyzed, either in anthropology or for that matter anywhere else in the social sciences. The Anthropocene may be the latest iteration of a long-standing critique of capitalist modernity for the alienation it produces in the people living in its space and time (cf. Moore 2014; Cunha 2015).

I want to develop this point a little. Marx's view of alienation in capitalist society and Lacan's notion of the empty signifier both presume the irretrievable loss of an archaic moral order, admittedly of very different sorts. In my view, the Anthropocene may also be a concept of alienation that likewise evokes an irretrievable loss of human agency in time and space. That is to say, not only does the Anthropocene proclaim itself as a new geologic epoch, it proclaims a new chronotope of man (see Chap. 2). In addition to environmental damage in a virtually millennial era, it condemns reason, particularly in its modern, rational forms (Weber 1978) as morally "other." Modern confidence is shaken, leaving behind a widespread suspicion that what has been taken for granted about man-in-nature was not only wrong but dangerous for the future of the planet. Moreover, as Andreas Malm and Alf Hornborg astutely pointed out, its cost, loss and hurt must be "differentiated … on all scales of human society" (2014: 67). In other words, the impacts of the Anthropocene must be seen to vary by degree. While the poor will go down with the *Titanic*, the rich, they predict, will inevitably have lifeboats, of one sort or another, to climb into. In my terms, the Anthropocene will create chronotopic inequities, which is to say, a range of alienation in time and space of the other.

In this final chapter, I shall ask how the Anthropocene is being experienced, understood and debated as a kind of moral dissonance among men in a segment of the class without lifeboats. Despite living on the far shores of global capitalism, the whole of Murik society now finds itself inhabiting a cutting edge of its risks and impacts. As I showed in my analyses of courtship, marijuana, mobile telephones, *Woyon's Mother* and grade-taking in the Gaingiin Society, the voices and gender identities of Murik men have been both estranged from yet engaged with modernity in PNG and Murik culture. Now, the rising tides have added a new field of alienation to their contrary subject positions in this equivocal dialogue. To develop this argument, I first elaborate a distinction between modern and Anthropocene-based chronotopes of human agency in time and space. Next, I introduce what I call the chronotopes of archaic Murik masculinity and alienation. I will then discuss how these four chronotopes shaped community-level dialogue about the meaning of rising sea levels. As a whole, I conclude that rising sea levels is a new context of the dual alienation of Murik men.

Chronotopes of Western Modernity and the Anthropocene

Particularly in the era of industrial capitalism, modernity was viewed to afford a heroic kind of freedom in, or unilateral power over, time and space. So much so that it presumed a "doctrine of human exceptionalism" in which human agency was superior *in kind* from that of all other species (Macnaghten and Urry 1998: 7). The Whig history of Western society, as a narrative of technological progress, confirmed this capacity to do so (Lash and Urry 1994). Reciprocally, the environment was reduced to an object-space "out there" where it was value-neutral, or asocial. Having no body, mind or purpose, it could be plundered without restraint (Bateson 1973).

If, as I proposed in Chap. 2, a chronotope is an image of man in time and space that organizes a narrative, then by contrast to the chronotope of Western modernity in which human agency is a "sovereign of nature" (Marx and Engels 2002), in the chronotope of the Anthropocene the relationship of man and nature becomes quite different. No longer *superior in kind* over nature, man in the chronotope of the Anthropocene appears at the temporal threshold of spatial destruction of an immense scale, a tragedy which he himself has created and whose consequences he will suffer. Where the pillars of modernity, the imperial state and universal clock time once superseded political and subjective boundaries (Landes 1983), now the prospect of global death reduces the authority of the state and the significance of private tragedy. That is, it reduces "human exceptionalism" in space and time. In the chronotope of the Anthropocene, space is fraught with global risks, or abstract-alien dangers. The risks that imperil society—to bodily health, security, prosperity and the environment—diminish human agency. On the one hand, they are unbounded. They are exceedingly complex in causation. They ignore temporality. They ignore territorial sovereignty. On the other hand—and this is the decisive point in the emergence of this chronotope—its risks are *anthropogenic*. They are the outcomes of human decisions, but *not*, like their capitalist predecessors, intentional consequences of them. In the chronotope of the Anthropocene, human agency in and over space and time is compromised, if not severely jeopardized.

Rather than unilateral agency over amoral space, what characterizes this chronotope is alienation. In the chronotope of the Anthropocene, man is vulnerable in a time and space of the (capitalist) other, the cause of which defies signification and narrativity. Nevertheless, even as global risks proliferate, the sociologist Ulrich Beck has predicted that this new chronotope may also offer a new kind of agency in time and space (2006a). That is, instead of being based in instrumental rationality, agency in the new chronotope shall concede the limits of rational knowledge. In the chronotope of the Anthropocene, agency in space will become interdependent and collaborative rather than autonomous. From a perspective of the global South, however, the two rival chronotopes, of modernity and the Anthropocene, appear decidedly Eurocentric. In PNG, as we shall see, they are questioned by chronotopes that reject both.

The Chronotope of Archaic Murik Masculinity

Although the integration of PNG in the global economy grew, even boomed, during the early twenty-first century, the postcolonial state remained an inconsistent and unpredictable institution at the rural level. The position of the Murik in the postcolony certainly illustrates this erratic relationship. Although the three-time Prime Minister, Sir Michael Somare, was a Murik native son, the impact of the state on the Murik coast has been small, by any measure. There were government schools in the villages. But there was no running water, no roads, no electricity. Health care was nonexistent. And there was no state-sponsored development (see Chap. 3). Once the tides began to swamp the villages of Big Murik, Darapap and Karau,[2] the prospect that their residents might become internally displaced climate refugees seemed imminent. With the future of these three communities in doubt, what services might the state now be able to provide?[3] An ambiguous promise of a level of government previously unseen either along the Murik Lakes, or really anywhere at all in PNG, had washed ashore with the tides. When the Somare government tabled its 2008 budget, funds were gazetted to purchase land on which to relocate these communities to higher ground just inland to the north of the lakes.[4] Needless to say, the prospect of resettlement was greeted with great interest by Murik stakeholders, among whom men still retained a privileged, if chastened, voice.

Recall for a moment my analysis of Yanda's dream and the creation of *Woyon's Mother* in the chapter before last. In the dream, persons, ancestor-spirits, fish and butterflies all travel through a landscape in which "no radical break [existed] between social and ecological relations" (Ingold 2000: 60). They move through local and regional space. But that space and time is not value-neutral. It is a space and time enshadowed by lost desire, the death of Yanda's grandson. In other words, the agency of the subject in space and time was represented as dependent on the signifier. Now, ever since Malinowski's day in the Trobriand Islands (1922), a question has been raised about how magic works, whether by means of the agency of ancestor-spirits, or by means of the power of words themselves, or a combination thereof (Mosko 2014). My point about magic differs: it has to do with its secrecy rather than with how its power works. My question is *why* is hereditary magic (*timiit*) secret knowledge?

It is hidden because both the ancestors and the living are made from the same cloth, the same lack. Both must be empowered to operate in a time and space in which desire is a kind of a "barred subject" that is acutely and inevitably vulnerable to the signifier of the other (Lacan 1977b: 14). So what agency, above all else, does magical *timiit* enable or augment? Both the story of Kumbun and Darua, as well as the courtship stories told by young men that I discussed in Chap. 2, showed that the ancestors and the living pursue the desire of the other in voices and practices that exclude the direct expression of love. Instead, desire is muted. At the same time, desire is the foremost field over which *timiit* spells, the most muted of all forms of masculine agency, is cast. Murik magic functions in secret because it expresses desire in a Homeric chronotope of time and space.

Timiit means "magic" in the Murik vernacular. The word is a noun form of the verb "to do or make" (*o'timiria*), so it also explicitly denotes agency, or power. *Timiit* magic is a form of knowledge/power that may be passed through any one of multiple (cognatic) relationships. As a mode of agency that is withheld from non-kin and may impact desire in space and time, it might be viewed as one of the foremost signifiers in the chronotope of archaic Murik masculinity. However, rather than a full-fledged, single-toned notion of masculine power, *timiit* magic was part of a larger ethos in which the signifier was imagined as vulnerable and alienated (see Chap. 5). Constructions of its empty agency in the material world to which I now turn make this ethos abundantly clear.

Warense's Revenge

Needless to say, the spatial and temporal context of this story is one of displacement. It is set during a time when Murik ancestor-spirits (*nagam*)[5] have only recently resettled along the lakes, having fled the middle Sepik River and after having repeatedly failed to reestablish themselves along the North Coast. Warense, the story's hero, founds a new village located nearby a non-Murik village called Gaut. Adhering to the expectations of pre-state *civitas* (and the archaic ethos of pre-state intertribal relations), Warense begins to build a new hall for the Male Cult. When time came to get ready to consecrate the new building, he leaves his wife Dom behind and sails off to visit offshore trading partners. In 1982, Mwandekama and Warense, the hero's namesake, recounted the shocking events that took place while he was away.

> [His wife] Dom went to the mangroves and fell asleep … The sun burned her skin red.
> Mistaking her for a sandcrab, the Gaut [men] killed Dom and cooked her. They divided the meat and ate her. One elderly woman, who had already lost her teeth, [was] only given one little leg. She could not eat it. So she threw it away.
> Warense returned from the islands and called for his wife for help, "Dom'o! You come and take everything from the canoe." The men [of Gaut shrugged and] … said they did not know what had happened to her. Some other women went to help Warense bring his goods to his house.

Setting aside the outrageous image of murder and cannibalism for a moment, implicit references are made in these two scenes to the Murk division of labor that deserve comment. First of all, Dom is associated with the mangrove to which Murik women still go to harvest shellfish. Sand crabs that they gather from the roots of mangroves at low tide will turn bright orange when boiled (again, by women). Is this perhaps why Dom, having been sunburned, could be mistaken for a cooked crab? Or, was this rather improbable association a caricature that called the morality of the indigenes, the people of Gaut, into question? What kind of people could mistake a sunburned woman for a boiled crab and then eat her? Only those of little or no virtue, "an other" living in the same space that the newly arrived Murik refugees wanted to claim for themselves. However territorially motivated, the point I want to stress is that the story affords both the nemesis and the hero ordinary, human, rather than extraordinary, qualities, and plausibly so. Although Warense is an ancestor-spirit, and not a mortal man, it depicts him and his wife, as well as the Gaut, in clearly human terms. The Gaut are more or less equal to the Murik. They harvest and cook shellfish from the lakes. They make an effort to distribute food among themselves. But perhaps they are depicted as moral inferiors.

In other words, realism is presumed in the story: Murik men are warriors, ritual leaders build Male Cult Houses, they make overseas trading expeditions to provision ritual feasting and expect that wives will meet their canoes upon their return (just as today, they do so upon their arrival from regional markets, or town) to offload cargo and haul it home. So, Dom's absence when Warense came back posed an obvious question: where was she?

> Warense searched for Dom in all the houses [although] he already knew what had happened to her because he was an ancestor-spirit. He asked the old woman. She explained how a crab had been eaten but the little leg [she had been given was] ... too hard [for her] to eat. She showed it to him and it was proof enough. Warense asked all the [Gaut] men. They admitted they had killed a crab. "That [crab]," Warense told them, "was my wife," and they were ashamed.

Murik ancestor-spirits are so thoroughly identified as living in the same world as human beings that the narrator feels he has to point out that the former are indeed superior, at least to the degree that their knowledge/power does exceed that of ordinary men. Despite being omniscient,

Warense is still depicted as like any skeptical man. He knows but, as in the instance of Jakai Smith, the mobile phone user in Chap. 4, he feigns ignorance, and goes to question the old lady. She shows him the crab leg as evidence of his wife's murder, evidence that he does not need to see, except that this is what men do. Warense then becomes enraged at the slaying of his wife. Although, again like a human man, he does not betray his agony, but instead sets a plan in motion to gain satisfaction.

> Warense decided to invite all the warrior ancestor-spirits (*brag*) to the feast for the consecration of his new Male Cult House. He … went to the Islands, to where the sun rises, and sent word to … the sea-spirits to come and flood the village … Then he went to find the bush-spirits where the sun sets and put out word to them. They too agreed. Then, he sent for the sun-spirits, to bring rain and wind. They too agreed. The people of Gaut did not know what he planned. The *brag* spirit-men waited until the day Warense … set … to arrive. All of them came. They ate. Clouds covered the sky. Rain, wind, high tides from the sea and the Sepik [River] rose up. Gaut went down. Sharks and crocodiles ate everyone. Some people tried to hide in trees. The village was destroyed; houses, coconuts, land. Everything went down.

No modern concept of causation, such as coincidence, or climatology, plays a role in the way the storm is portrayed. Rather than an amoral, non-human expanse outside the subject, the weather, the sea and its tidal events are a space and time of the other. Not that "the other" is very different. The motifs of commensality and assembly again tell us that the agency of "the other" is afforded a human form. The ancestor-spirits may impact the environment, the winds, the tides and so forth, but they are still cast as men. They must be solicited, like regional trading partners, to gather together at "the hour of the other" (Lacan 1977a: 18), for example, a time that Warense has set for them to wreck Gaut. Like a mother, he must feed them so as to obligate them to work for him and cast their weather and tidal spells over the space he wanted to destroy. And, of course, why do they convene in space and time? Not because of the death of the hero but because of the rage of a husband, because Warense has been caught in the time and space of the other. In the story, the storm has a moral epicenter rather than a meteorological one. Its culmination, an environmental tragedy of epic proportion, evokes the signifier. The storm is a man, a man who has been deprived of the desire of the other.

This intimate kind of loss preoccupies the subject in the chronotope of archaic masculinity. The center of the male subject as such, is an other, or more exactly, the center of the male subject is not the self but the signifier of lost desire.[6] The typification? Sexual exchanges in the Male Cult in return for authority over the military power of the Kakar, the ancestor-spirits whose signifiers were individually named ornamental spears, were "term[s] in a sexual configuration" (Lacan 1977b: 16). In Lacan's fantasy of dismemberment, the phallus is a symbol of contradiction, a figure both of agency and the absence of something or someone. Its meaning consists in the lack for which it stands, not just an emptiness, but a moral vacuum or loneliness in the center of the subject. If the phallus is a signifier of the lost desire of the other, it always conceals this absence by hiding behind imagery of purity, agency, indestructibility or dominance, for example, in signs of masculine presence. The Lacanian phallus thus appears as simultaneously obtainable yet unobtainable, or as unpossessable objects of desire. In the Murik case, it is dependent on women who must be given away in return for the authority of the Kakar spirits. Now in the chronotope of archaic masculinity, this Lacanian logic is not at all ambiguous. The agency of man in space and time is expressly vulnerable as if to nothing else.[7]

To conclude about Warense's vengeance: his wife Dom, the woman who otherwise desired him, and by her desire constituted him as a man, both conjugally and in the Male Cult, had herself become subordinate to the other, in this instance, to the non-Murik community of Gaut. In Lacanian terms, the storm expressed the lost other that of course could neither bring Dom back much less bring Warense satisfaction. The ancestor-spirits—identified with the sun, the sea and the wind—came and did his bidding. But Dom was still gone. If the storm was a manifestation of a time and space of the other, it went on signifying that kind of alienated space and time in the present. A few passersby may now and then notice and remark at the thick, verdant mangrove forest that has overgrown the former site of Gaut village, but it is just one among many places dispersed throughout the lakescape at which the lost desire of the other is inscribed (Lipset 2014a).

Puralima's Whirlpool

Let me cite another example of such an empty place (Weiner 1991): there is a small, eponymous inlet people call "Puralima" after an ancestress who is said to have drowned there. Marabo Game gave me a succinct account of the spirit-woman's demise in 1982.

One day, Puralima went out to dig for clams, decorated in her *sumon* ... [lineage ornaments]. Kakritena saw her. Pulling her leg, he tried to climb up into her canoe. The canoe sank. Puralima disappeared. Kakritena returned next day, but could not find her. One by one, Puralima's ornaments rose to the surface of the water.

In a terse cadence and stark imagery, the tale illustrates how an object of a man's desire may become lost in the very flutter of his jubilance. The image of Kakritena attempting to "climb up into her canoe" invokes the world of the salacious *double entendre* of Murik joking relations (see Chap. 4; Lipset 2004a). Puralima's "canoe" refers to both her vehicle and her body. The woman drowned because Kakritena, apparently overwhelmed by desire, pulls her overboard and capsizes "her canoe." The lady vanishes; all that remains of her identity and his desire is flotsam: ornamental signifiers of her corporate or jural identity. Paddling by the inlet today, adults look away and the young are reminded only to stroke on the side of their canoe opposite the inlet so as not to disturb the spirit of her grieving husband who continues to visit this space.

In the story, the lineage ornaments floating on the water appear in place of the desire of which Kakritena has been deprived. His phallus, lacking Puralima, still haunts the locale—now, in the present (see also Glass 1987). The moral hovering upon the water, that even in the absence of an other, the locus of masculine desire, the desire of the other, is unattainable, eluding a man's grasp precisely because he seeks her, would seem oblivious to the passage of time. Like Warense's revenge against the men of Gaut village, in other words, the story associated with the inlet suggests that men in the chronotope of their archaic masculinity are forever suspended in the shadow of an absent other.

The Steersman's Paddle in the Good Time

Time in the space of Puralima is static. Elsewhere in the chronotope of archaic masculinity it is conceived as cyclical, if no less reckoned in terms of the desire of the other (see Orlove 2003). The archaic year (*biriin*) is divided into two seasons (*akun*). When the monsoon winds blow from west to east (*buniim*), the tides are known to be high, the surf rough (December–May). Overseas travel is dangerous. This is the wet season called the "bad time" (*akun mwaro*). When the trade winds blew from east to west (*awar*), the tides recede, beaches expand, overseas travel is possible and erotic adventure is imagined (see Chap. 5; see also Barlow

1985b: 112). This is the dry season called the "good time" (*akun ariito*). Under moonlit nights during this latter time of the year, young people used to play guessing games about their gender. The community is full of desire and prospects for heroic signification (cf. Adam 1990: 120). Ceremonial exchange is provisioned through overseas trade (see the story of Warense's Revenge, above); men win rank and prestige, through the ritual deployment of their lineage ornaments. From the viewpoint of men competing in the ceremonial exchange, it is indeed the "good time." Really, from everyone's perspective, the dry season means good things to eat, places to go, and so forth. However, the word *akun* means "sun," not season or time, which are the modern glosses of the word. In the archaic era, that is to say, time was perceived in terms of local space, activities and relationships (Evans-Pritchard 1940: 104; Thompson 1967). The year was named after the Morning Star, days were "suns" and months were "moons." Setting the number of days until a future meeting with a trading partner was done by tying knots in a strip of dried grass equal to the number of suns that had to set before the event (see Lash and Urry 1994: 55). That is, as Giddens once put it, "time ... [was] connected through the situatedness of place" (1991: 16). Inevitably, Giddens missed understanding the logos (or perhaps, the phallo-logocentricity) of this concept of time. Murik time was embedded in the locality, to be sure. But, as in the destruction of Gaut, and now in the drowning of Puralima, the relationship of time to space invoked the signifying phallus, the iconic figure of which were the Kakar ancestor spear-spirits, but also the steersman piloting overseas voyages during the "good time" with his huge steering paddle (see Fig. 6.10). I discussed him briefly in Chaps. 5 and 6 but want to add a couple of more details about the relationship of his agency to the desire of the other here.

Sailing canoes, as I have said, were steered by big wooden paddles whose grip, shaft and blade might extend 12 or more feet in length (see Fig. 6.11). Holding the great paddle, the steersman's control was not exactly that of an automatic governor in a cybernetic apparatus (see Galison 1994). His direction of the vehicle was neither mechanical nor impersonal—to say the least. In archaic overseas trade, the safety of Murik outrigger canoes was understood to depend on the knowledge and skills of the steersman, to be sure, to evaluate the currents, the waves, the winds, and so on, but there was also a Lacanian sense in which the fate of the canoe was fundamentally understood to depend not on maritime knowledge but on his marriage—or, to put it bluntly, on the loss of the desire of his wife.

Preventing the "castration"/shipwreck of his phallus/canoe was therefore understood (at least in part) to depend on her staying "quietly" at home during the voyage where kin would attend her. She had to obey a great many taboos there, taboos that all added up to one and the same indictment of her: should anything unexpected, untoward or harmful take place during her husband's watch at sea, it did so because of her errant *desire*.

She shouldn't go and fetch water because the canoe would take in water and sink. She shouldn't chop firewood because the canoe would split open and sink. She shouldn't fall down because the canoe would mimic her and take on water, if sink. She shouldn't cut grass because the outrigger's lashings would break. She should not sit and dangle her legs off of her verandah so her skirts might blow in the breeze, which is a provocative pose for a woman to assume. If she did, "the canoe sails [would] ... blow like [her] ... skirt and the canoe will be swept away" (Barlow 1985b: 118). She should not, above all else, take a lover, lest the canoe imitate her hips while she had intercourse by pitching up and down, and then by sinking when she (and her lover) finished. On board, the sailors would promptly switch helmsmen in the event of any sudden change of course, or unanticipated winds, storms, or currents, covering him up for the rest of the voyage to "hide" him. Upon return, he would go directly to his wife and beat her, no questions asked. The weather and the seas, not to mention, the safety of the canoe, were understood with certainty and without mediation. The consequences of a wife's unfaithfulness did not require validation from expert opinion because loss of control of the canoe was assumed to be a metonym for the loss of her desire. In other words, the steersman's agency and the safety of the canoe were contingent upon her. The canoe was a signifying phallus that was dependent on her desire. Simbua, a senior man, with whom I spoke in 1981, could not have put it any more succinctly when, in the context of a discussion of archaic overseas trade, he recited the following adage to me:

> It is the woman who takes the canoe to the islands.
> It is the woman who brings it back.
> The canoe travels on the strength of women. (Barlow 1985b: 115)

As I reported in Chaps. 5 and 6, Murik men have stopped building and sailing outrigger canoes today and Murik women have basically stopped observing the canoe taboos they call "sitting quietly" (*asiiba o'sassa*). For the most part, masculine agency in overseas travel is now understood in climatological terms, technical knowledge and the monetary value of expenditures, in other words, through a chronotope of modernity. As a consequence, and here we have come to the main point of this chapter, and really, of the entire second section of the book, the agency of man in the chronotope of *timiit*, was alienated and is being alienated for a second time in and by modernity. The relationship of the signifier to time and space is becoming dependent upon the time and space of a second other. As male agency is becoming alienated from older vulnerabilities, it is *becoming* vulnerable to a new "other." This second alienation does not mean that the chronotope of *timiit* had been consigned to a past that has come to be viewed as if it were a foreign country (Hartley 1953; Lowenthal 1999) or that it may ever be.

In 1981–1982, I used to hear at least three Darapap men beat hand drums as part of a *timiit* spell to call their ancestor-spirits to stop rain. And then in 2011, I heard a young woman do the same thing. Voices speaking in the chronotope of *timiit* and the chronotope of modernity continue to question each other and went on doing so when the chronotope of the Anthropocene started to erode the Murik beaches. Dialogue ebbed and flowed with rising sea levels and now I shall turn to the different chronotopes that oriented understandings of the risk they posed.

The Tides Assessed

In February and September 2008, I returned to the Murik Lakes to assess the situation.[8] The beach was shocking. It had been cut down by about one-half to three-quarters of a mile, if not more (see Fig. 7.1). Severed trunks of coconut palms, some lying flaccidly on their sides, others, broken off just above their root systems, protruded out of the shallows and looked, for all the world, like a spectacle of dismemberment. In Murik villages, a perception was universally shared that something different was going on. "The tides are high!" (*Pwakan apo!*) was the refrain of the moment. Two widely held views of the risk they posed to space, time and the communities emerged as I talked with people (see Wildavsky and Dake 1990).

According to one perspective, time and space were uncertain. For example, in the village of Big Murik, where all the coconut palms were washed out, I spoke with a small group of men under the shade of a canoe-shed. A middle-aged man summed up this catastrophic sense of risk. "The sea is killing us … Now the distance between the sea and the lakes is very small … We don't know what will happen. We will drift," he worried, "like logs." Drifting logs, I hasten to add, are not only an image of alienation, that is, of displacement and lack of agency, but connote the phallus. Logs are associated to husbands without wives and to an initial phase in the process of canoe building when "female" logs had to be ritually transformed into "warriors" (Barlow and Lipset 1997: 10).

A second position was one of resignation. Regrettably, I elicited very few female voices. But I did visit Jamero at one point. Jamero, since deceased, was then a senior woman living in Darapap village. Sitting at home in the company of several kinswomen, she evaluated the situation in terms of one of the female roles in the division of labor. Like Dom and Puralima, Murik women harvest shellfish from the lakes. Jamero herself had retired from this not exactly exhausting, but still draining, kind of work, which involves standing neck-deep for extended periods of time in the lakes while inching about in a backward direction as feet feel for clams and clasp them one by one with toes, hands reach down to uplifted feet and put them into a shoulder bag. Jamero heard reports from younger women that while a clam called "*pwanjan*" had nearly disappeared, [another clam called] *mamab* remained plentiful." What she was saying was that something (presumably the salinity) in the lacustrine habitat was deteriorating, but not completely, and that life went on. One of Jamero's sons, Joe Kabong, a late middle-aged man who had retired to the village after a long career as a prison warder in various towns throughout PNG, seemed to share his mother's stalwart attitude. The Prime Minister, he acknowledged, was angry because villagers had rejected his resettlement plan. People were unwilling to move, he went on to say, because they were not disposed to "complain about the sea … [which] has always been a constant threat and battle." Indeed, the mood I detected was one of *angst* but not panic in the villages. For example, the ironic, lewd comedy from which so much of public and cultic interaction takes such egalitarian pleasure had by no means given way to dread (see Lipset 2004a). Were Murik joking relations now a discourse of denial of the chronotope of the Anthropocene, or had the latter not yet won the day? It was clear that most villagers were not living hounded and at bay. If a perception of risk had long been part of their intertidal, deltaic adaptation, then rising sea levels were not a crisis. They were rather more of the same.

The Chronotopes of Rising Sea Levels

Robert K. Merton once made a well-known distinction between leaders in mid-twentieth-century North America that may now seem a little quaint in light of the global economy that has developed since then

(1957b). Leaders, Merton argued, might be viewed as *local*, and inclined toward face-to-face relations with kin and community, or *cosmopolitan*, and inclined toward knowledge of and achievement in the outside world (see also Hannertz 1990). While middle-class elites in postcolonial PNG cannot be easily divided from rural villagers along this axis, Merton's distinction still offers a useful shorthand for making sociological distinctions both among the chronotopes of the tides that prevailed among them and where they overlapped (Martin 2013; Rudiak-Gold 2013; Rasmussen 2015). The three chronotopes might be summarized as follows:

1. One constituency of voices, made up of salaried, urban middle-class elites, as well as village cosmopolitans, spoke about the tides in a combination of modernist and Anthropocene-based chronotopes. For such people, the tides signified space defined by an abstract foreign, other, that is, by "nature" or "global warming," and time teetered on the brink of a disaster against which local forms of agency, masculine or otherwise, were fanciful at best.
2. Another position, held by villagers, was informed by a chronotope of archaic masculinity. Such people advocated magical explanations of, and proposed magical solutions for, the risks the tides posed. For them, rising sea levels resulted from vindictive, powerful men like Warense. They lived in a time and space of a local other.
3. A chronotope of alienation was also widespread among both middle-class elites and villagers: people expressed uncertainty about the causes of the tides and either wanted to ignore them or just did not know what the future might hold.

Taken together, dialogue about the tides might be viewed as made up of voices asserting contending concepts of agency in time and space, for example, contending chronotopes. I will now examine each one in detail as well as the disparate unity of the dialogue that they constituted.

The Chronotopes of Modernity
and the Anthropocene

If the dangers posed by the Anthropocene to space are independent of state-based sovereignty, then the agency required to respond to them may need to be premised in an ideology that takes interdependency to heart (Beck 1999: 17). Ironically enough, the very weaknesses of small, marginalized, postcolonial states positioned their leadership to become standard bearers for multilateralist, green ideologies, who exert pressure on their former masters. No doubt motivated by concerns for the security of three Murik villages, which included his own birthplace, as well as by a less ethical posture, the Prime Minister of PNG, Sir Michael Somare, was championing just this kind of thing during the early years of the twenty-first century.

In 2006, he spoke to the General Assembly of the United Nations (UN). Requesting its member states to accept that the world was "in distress," he went on to implore "the industrialized countries to reduce their greenhouse gas emissions." PNG, he vowed, was "prepared to play its part to protect the world's tropical rainforest with the aim of stabilizing the earth's climate" (Somare 2006). The Prime Minister spoke in the chronotopes of modernity and the Anthropocene at the UN. The risk he perceived was palpable. The times were imperiled. The causes of environmental degradation, and the liability, were entirely abstract and disembedded. They were not connected to male or any agency that might have arisen within any Melanesian locality. The relationship of the environment to society, he argued, must be redeemed, but mitigation might only be accomplished in terms of distant, globalized solutions. Appropriate interventions should be based in a premise of interdependency: rich and poor states must cooperate. Obviously, the impact of a speech made to such an *echt*-cosmopolitan audience in such an *echt*-modernist setting, on the Murik community in PNG, with its varied access to mass media, was not uniform. Still, the speech expressed how in that context the Prime Minister understood the tides. Under the influence of Somare and the chronotopes of modernism and the Anthropocene in which he spoke, the employed, Murik middle class also saw the tides as posing risks to the future of the Murik Lakes.

In the parking lot of the Comfort Inn in the national capital, I spoke to Allan Kango, a grandson of an eminent villager who was one of my key informants in the 1980s (see Lipset 1997: 109f), and his father's brother, Elijah, another retired prison warder. Allan is nothing if not cosmopolitan in Merton's terms. He did not grow up in the Murik Lakes, his father having been employed as a teacher in another part of the country during his childhood. In February 2008, he had just returned from a certification course in Brisbane to work as a pharmacist in Australia. I asked him about the tides. "Greenhouse gases," he shot back. Elijah, his "father," in Murik kinship terminology, who was rather less of a cosmopolitan than his nephew, nodded. "Greenhouse gases," he repeated, with no audible conviction. Allan offered nothing else, except to mention the 2008 budget appropriation just announced by the Somare government to compensate customary landowners on whose property three Murik villages might resettle. Whether or not the state was to expand its discipline over these rural communities, the cosmopolitan pharmacist passed no judgment, which I took to imply support of the project, or at least an absence of dissent. The Prime Minister and Allan Ginau spoke in confident, modernist voices. For the two of them, the tides stood for a problem that was both comprehensible and had a plausible solution. Uncle Elijah seemed a little more skeptical. He referred the tides to the absence of a global "other." That is, the tides resulted from a diffuse chain of causes, causes that were abstract, to be sure, operating as they did at a distance from, and out of the control of, any sort of face-to-face agency in time and space. But what in all this worked out to cause rising sea levels on the Murik coast eluded him.

Many villagers also subscribed to the modernist position. I met with a large group of men in a Male Cult House in Mendam village on the eastern edge of the Murik Lakes. In their discussion, one gentleman, of no apparent cosmopolitan appearance, offered his view that the tides "come on their own account. Nature: the tides come and go with the phases of the moon. But now they have become unbalanced." If there was irony in his remarks, it arose from the juxtaposition of the venue, not a parking lot, but a privileged space in the chronotope of archaic masculinity, for example, the sanctum of the Male Cult, with the chronotopes of modernity and the Anthropocene in which he spoke.

In other words, the rival chronotopes of the tides were not separable but combined in ways that gave primary but inconclusive weight to one over another. Its discourse, to borrow Bakhtin's term, was "double-voiced" (1984a: 181), meaning that its unity was simultaneously influenced by and directed toward multiple chronotopes.

THE CHRONOTOPES OF ARCHAIC MASCULINITY AND MODERNITY

In answer to the modernist and the Anthropocenic view of the tides, men talked about the history of rising sea levels which they associated with past *tsunami* events that they understood in terms of the chronotope of archaic masculinity. For example, in response to my asking about the current erosion of the Murik coast, Wanuk, a senior man who lived modestly in Wewak town, was given to compose a list of past storms.

The first one took place before WWII during a large women's initiation that was going on in Darapap [village]. The second time was right after the war. Waves burst through the village and swept a big [wooden] kingpost-spirit out of a new [Male Cult] House that was then being consecrated. The post was retrieved by hereditary [Male Cult] partners from the neighboring village … who … were compensated with a feast [for the service]. In 1951, a huge wave wrecked [the village] and drove the villagers to move to the mangroves. They lost everything. Now is the fourth time.

I want to draw attention to a couple of implications of this man's brief catalogue. First, the current tides, he seemed to be saying, were not new and like past tidal events, they were merely temporary setbacks. Second, resettlement had precedents. Thirdly, but perhaps most significantly, the multiple representations of disrupted space in his list were set amid archaic constructions of masculine time (Leach 1961). That is, the tides had repeatedly interfered with the signifier. They had halted a Female Cult initiation (in which girls sponsored by their fathers become eligible to marry; see Barlow 1995). They cut loose a kingpost-spirit from its moorings during a consecration rite of a Male Cult House. Of the *tsunami* of 1951, Elijah Ginau, the prison warder introduced above, added several relevant details.[9]

> The sea was destroying Darapap [village]. I went with my father and his brother to [process] sago flour and trade for garden produce with inland trading partners. Upon returning to the village, we built and decorated platforms on the beach. We piled up garden produce, sago, cooked pork and fish on the platforms. We left most of it there, but we threw some of it into the ocean for the sea-spirits to eat. In a few months, the beach [recovered] and our fathers planted coconut palms anew.

The men, in other words, made a pact with their ancestors, platforms representing lineages in this region (Meiser 1955; von Poser 2015). A gift of food offered to the sea spirits obliged them to reciprocate work, a magical restoration of the beach (see the story of "Warense's revenge" above). Here was an image of the masculine subject operating in the chronotope of archaic masculinity. The tides were brought to heal, not through a modern "technofix," such as constructing a sea wall or planting a new reef, adaptations that the Prime Minister had been proposing in recent years, but through the intervention of *timiit*, the gendered, personalized and context-specific form of masculine agency.

I subsequently attended a meeting in a Male Cult House in Darapap village, where Mikah Ker (see Chap. 6) inventoried the same storms that Wanuk had recalled above. As a result of the 1951 tsunami, Mikah Ker added, houses had been rebuilt over mangrove roots at a site within the lakes. Seeing him, a longtime leader of the Seventh Day Adventist Mission (SDA), and listening to his narrative reminded me of a version of storm-related events of 1951 that a man called Kangai had told me several decades earlier. Following up a note I made in my field diary to go back to 1981–1982 field notes upon returning to Minnesota, I found his account of early days of the SDA Mission in Darapap.

> We invited the SDA Mission … in 1951 because they promised to open a school for us which the Catholics had not done. The new SDA God then got angry [at us]. Most everyone [had] joined the new Mission. But … [some senior] men went on staging outrigger canoe-consecration rites. A big wave broke over the village, knocking down all the coconut trees but two, ripping up houses, and destroying everything in its path. All the canoes drifted about … The [senior] men … thought the … [ancestors] were telling us to stop making feasts or suffer the wrath of Papa God.

In Kangai's story, the 1951 *tsunami* was an omen: senior men had better bring their worship of the ancestor-spirits to a halt, lest the community suffer a major reckoning from the Christian God of the SDAs, rather than another minor one from their ancestor-spirits. The meaning of the environment had apparently begun to shift. The agency of man in time and space was no longer fully understood in terms of *timiit* magic. The tides were becoming "other" in a new way. Now modern universalisms challenged the agency of the signifier. How did they answer? They erected platforms on the beach, one for each lineage, and propitiated the ancestor-spirits of the sea by giving them a little something to eat.

In 2008, surprisingly enough, rumors of *timiit* magic, and the chronotope of archaic masculinity for which it stood, were still circulating through the villages. One man I spoke to suspected that "somebody had planted a [Cordyline shrub] … to [magically] pull the sea because of one jealousy or another." The "somebody" in question was Makus Murakau, who had since quit the village to take a job in Wewak town as a community sales representative for Garamut Enterprise Limited (see Chap. 2). "The jealousy," as Makus Murakau explained to me, had to do with a property dispute.

> Pame's kin got angry because I built a house on [what they claimed as] their beach [property]. They cut down one of the coconut palms [my father] planted. So I cut down one of their coconut palms. That was where it ended until the sea destroyed the beach and they began to accuse me of bespelling the beach. "No," I objected. "It is nature. It is cyclical. It is seasonal. Ice broke."

Makus repudiated the accusation in the combined terms of modern and Anthropocene chronotopes. The tides, in his denial, were an abstract "other." Their range varied regularly, without connection to human agency, but they had now been altered by global warming. However, as we sat together behind his mother-in-law's betel nut stall alongside the coastal road in Wewak town, Makus did allow that there was more in his philosophy than this modernist view. He had inherited sea magic from his father, he admitted to me, his father having learned it from a sister. This disclosure made his understanding of the tides double-voiced. He both affirmed and denied the chronotope of archaic masculinity while he also affirmed and denied the chronotopes of modernity and the Anthropocene. If the archaic steersman, Warense's destruction of Gaut village and the drowning of Puralima depict the signifier in its suspension in the time and space of the other, how, if at all, did this allegation reflect that vulnerability, or in Lacanian terms, that lack?

Murik men also talked about another *timiit* spell they called Serai Soil. The power of Serai Soil was said not to destroy, but rather to restore, an eroded beach. This magic had been imported to the Murik Lakes from the Sissano Lagoon area during the late colonial era. I asked Wangi, a retired policeman, about it, and then Wanuk, who had given me the initial chronology of past tidal events. Separately, they recited a story about an evil spirit-man, called Masangi, whose death had created this magic.

> Masangi lived on an island [offshore Serai village]. When the wind came up, he set sail. Everyone [on the mainland] saw him coming. The [village] men fell asleep on the beach. Masangi had [love magic]. [He] had intercourse with each of their wives and sisters. This went on for a long time.

The story situates the environment squarely in terms of the Lacanian signifier, and *vice versa*, it situates the signifier in regional and local space. *The name of the father* in this case is Masangi. He is a stranger, but his moral distance from the Serai people is limited. His origins are known, his arrival visible. Being a less alienated ancestor-spirit, Masangi can subordinate society to the force of id. He puts husbands to sleep, like babies. But notice that despite his virility and power, he remains unable to arouse the desire of the other without the benefit of love magic. That is to say, Masangi, the great antagonist, is no different from the sleeping husbands. He suffers from the same lack as every man and eventually they are able to get even.

> The men spied what he was doing. They sent their wives to prepare sago flour and make a meal for them to eat together and set a time to retaliate.
> Masangi came ashore. When he began to have sex with the first woman, they threw their spears and killed him. They buried him in haste [in a shallow grave]. One of his legs, bent at the knee, poked out of the ground. Sand gathered about his knee and the beach expanded there, so much so that his burial site [became surrounded by] bush.

In an effort to reclaim time and space as well as their statuses as husbands, the men of Serai must redeem the signifier, which is to say that they must take back the desire of women by asserting *the name of the father*. To do so, they first petition their wives' nurture by having the women feed them. Then, they *spear* Masangi to death while he is having intercourse. Their vengeance is thus depicted not just as a homicide. The men succeed, and by doing so, they make it clear that intercourse is a moment of exquisite masculine helplessness, no less for the ancestors than for living men. The story then goes on to associate Masangi's murder with a body part, the knee of the spirit-man, and the buildup of land about it. In a semiotic sense, the knee not only stands for Masangi's corpse but also for his dispossession from the desire of the other—his symbolic castration at the hands of the husbands whom he dispossessed. The magical substance that emanated from his corpse thus stands for their intervention and makes the beach and land an ambiguous evocation of both the vulnerability and power of their signifier (cf. Dening 1992: 258). Wanuk went on to suggest this complicated association when he discussed how Serai spells are literally cast.

> Today, men take a bit of soil from [Masangi's] grave and throw it about a beach. [If it] is quiet, the land will return. When you make Serai magic, women must be excluded from the space because it was women who started the whole story. Masangi was killed because of them. Women [must] become taboo to keep him from taking back the land.

That is to say, Serai magic must be deployed with a disclaimer. Despite rousting him, casting his magic demands that when the subject tries to regain what has been lost, that is, eroded seashore, the impossibility of masculine desire must be recreated. In addition to potency, agency, and so on, of the signifier, Serai magic calls the phallus into question yet again.

In other words, the power of Serai magic requires that men separate themselves from "the contagion" of female sexuality. Lending credence to the nominalist side of the debate about the efficacy of magic (Mosko 2014), Makus Murakau explained that the power of his tide magic partly depended upon its precise utterance. But no less, he added, did it require the complete isolation of the magician that was meant to help him focus all of his ill will upon his enemy. The meaning of space thus becomes enmeshed in enmity, on the one hand, and in single-sexed masculinity, on the other. Tabooing all proximity to women (see Strathern 1988), *timiit*-related practices, such as Serai Soil and Makus Murakau's tidal magic, are meant to protect the magician from becoming a vulnerable third term in a sexual configuration, but in doing so, of course, the loss of "her" desire to *the name of the father* is resurrected. Rather than agency, casting *timiit* spells thus recreates the signifier's archaic dismemberment and alienation.

THE TIDES IN THE CHRONOTOPE OF ALIENATION

Up to this point, I have been discussing how men understood rising sea levels through the chronotopes of modernity, the Anthropocene and archaic masculinity. It should come as no surprise, given that these chronotopes do not fit together into any kind of a coherent viewpoint, to report one more chronotope in which the meaning of the rising tides was unclear and elusive. What might be called a chronotope of alienation, wherein human agency in time and space was unknown and indeterminate, was no less audible than the other three. For many men, natural cyclicality and climate change were unpersuasive ideas. Nor did they perceive anyone to scapegoat and blame (Douglas 1990: 2). They did not deny that the range of the tides was extraordinary, but they either wanted to ignore them or just did not know what to think or do about them. In such a hugely uncertain moment in time and space, men lacked adaptive, explanatory or predictive powers, and the future was obscure. The beaches, as I said earlier, were littered with the stumps of coconut palms (Fig. 7.2).

Like many village men of modest education, the late Luke Pimi attended closely to the cosmopolitan scene in the province, nation and the world via

Fig. 7.2 Big Murik village. Photo: David Lipset (2014).

radio and conversation. I worked extensively with him over the years and we regarded each other as adoptive brothers while he was alive. Indeed, his reference groups were largely local. As such, his voice may as well stand for this constituency of rural men. One morning in February 2008, as we breakfasted on sago breads and freshly smoked fish in his junior co-wife's house, I asked him about rising sea levels. "The sun has become hot," he answered, "and ice broke, so the sea level rose … We say it is 'nature.' But we are in the middle. There is not one man who believes it is true." Luke's simultaneous acknowledgment of, and skepticism about, global warming summed up the inconclusive ambivalence with which he viewed the present circumstances. But his attitude only expressed one dimension of men's uncertainties.

No less than colonial history and modernity in contemporary PNG, the Anthropocene has exposed what Lacan in later years might have called "the real" or the moral emptiness of the signifier that resists symbolization (Žižek 1989: 163). I encountered acknowledgment of this lack while visiting some men whom I found chatting amiably on a quiet Saturday afternoon in a Male Cult house in Karau, Sir Michael Somare's home village. The moment, so a senior man offered, differed from the past.

> We used to say rising tides [were caused by] sea magic, but today the sea has its own way. Nature or magic. If a man was jealous, he could make sea magic that would make the sea destroy a village … We do not have Serai magic to build up the beach. We do not have the magic our fathers had. So we wait and cannot do anything, except move.

In the chronotope of archaic masculinity, the sea levels did not rise either because of climate change or nature. The tides rose because the signifier was caught in the time and space of the other, for example, "a man [who] was jealous … could make sea magic." In the story of Masangi, the other was known. His relationship to the subject was known. His name was known. Now, in the chronotope of alienation, the signifier was caught in a time and space that was under the sway of a less identifiable other.

Conclusion: The Anthropocene and Other Negations of the Signifier

In the global north, the Anthropocene has changed modernity, making it a time and space that is menaced by unpredictable, indefinite risks. Rather than mastered by capitalism and the state, space is threatened regardless of political boundaries and economic expertise. The Anthropocene, that is to say, has exposed the limits of modern agency. On the Murik coast, however, the claims made by the Anthropocene against modernity markedly differ—because modernity in PNG differs. The question that rising sea levels now pose for Murik men was raised long before high tides began to break over the Murik coast in 2007. That question was: "Who is the other?" In the stories of Warense's revenge and the death of Puralima, in constructions of the steersman's paddle, Serai Soil and tide magic, men are deprived, or deprive themselves, of women. Their archaic signifier substituted for, but also recreated, their alienation: the loss of the desire of the other. Colonial institutions then banned the signifier, the Male Cult's right to violence, condemned Murik ancestor-spirits as Satanic and condemned their sexual exchanges as "fornication." In modernity in PNG, lost desire has reappeared in a weak postcolonial state that features little or no development in an economy that provides no market for their small-scale fishery. Now, on top of all this masculine alienation, not only does the Anthropocene threaten to inundate their commons, the Murik Lakes, it imperils their one means of production and source of modern value in the developing economy (Lipset 2014a). Taken together, rising sea levels negate the desire of the other, not to exile men into a Symbolic of language and moral order, but to exile them into a vulnerable space and time in between the chronotopes of archaic Murik masculinity and modernity in PNG.

Perhaps a more general lesson may be taken from the problematic subject position of Murik men. In some circles of contemporary environmental anthropology and the anthropology of religion, considerable theoretical effort has been given over to a project in which the subject is construed as plural rather than uniquely human-centered in nature, cosmology and society. Tim Ingold saw relations among hunters, ancestor-spirits and animals in Mistassini Cree cosmology as making up a single field of what he has called "interagentivity" wherein each possess power in mutual relationships (2000: 47). Similarly, Alfred Gell viewed the agency of persons and objects, such as *kula* valuables in the Massim or *malaggan* statues in New Ireland in PNG, as dispersed fragments of single ancestral embodiment (1998). More recently, Eduardo Vivieros de Castro has argued that relations between animals and persons in Amerindian thought "suppose a spiritual unity and a corporeal diversity" (2012: 46) through which animals and people see, and comprehend, themselves and each other through their own autonomous points of view.

Murik dialogue about rising sea levels and climate change illustrate several chronotopes of human agency in space and time that together make up a much less unified and coherent relationship to the environment than in these instances. Instead of a single field of nature and cosmological power, however autonomous each of its constituent subjects may be, the significance of masculinity in the time and space of the Anthropocene on the Murik coast is that it is part of a dialogue in which men speak through rival chronotopes. What is more, in the combined chronotopes of archaic masculinity and the Anthropocene, we hear voices of alienation rather than mastery and conviction.

In subsequent visits to the Murik Lakes that I made up through 2014, I saw new evidence of the damage the annual wet-season tides of the

Anthropocene had done to the coast and I collected stories of midnight evacuations into the mangroves but also of new channels that the tides breached barrier beaches, channels that then closed up the year later. I tracked the comings and goings of several plans for resettlement either on land purchased for this purpose inland from the lakes or on land coastal trading partners offered that was associated with the Murik migration history (Lipset 2013). None came to pass, and the governmental funds for resettlement "somehow" disappeared. In the meantime, the population of peri-urban settlements in Wewak town exploded, leaving villages abandoned. Most recently, two communities had begun to make plans to move families who agreed to do so to the inland edges of the lakes to spaces where they each claimed property rights.

All of which is to say that the circumstances of masculine alienation that I have been discussing in this chapter persisted and men's dialogue with modernity in PNG and now the Anthropocene continued to go on inconclusively. I will now explore the extent of men's dual alienation elsewhere in the Pacific in a brief Afterword.

NOTES

1. On the anthropology of climate change and the Anthropocene, see Cassidy (2012), Crate (2008, 2011), Crate and Nuttall (2009), Cruikshank (2001, 2005), Kelman and West (2009), Lazrus (2012), and Orlove et al. (2008), Rudiak-Gold (2013) and Gibson and Venkateswar (2015).
2. On the danger rising sea levels pose to the Murik Lakes, see Hughes and Bualia (1990), Sullivan (1990), Pernetta (1993), Legra et al. (2008).
3. Mangroves are historically vulnerable to ecosystem collapse; see Ellison and Stoddart (1991). On mangrove ecology and sea-level rise in the Pacific, see Ellison (2000), Gilman et al. (2006). On this danger in general, see also Kennish (2002).
4. US$1,315,280 were allocated, half for Murik resettlement and the other half for the resettlement of Carteret Islanders. The funds were specifically assigned to the Murik Resettlement Administration which had been created in 2006.
5. *Nagam* is also a kin term that is used to address and refer to great-grandparents.
6. Indeed, the Melanesianist James Weiner has even made the point that "whenever the phallus comes into view in New Guinea—as pearl shell, as pregnant python, flute, drum or bullroarer—we should ask ourselves, what is being cut off from our gaze? What act of ... severing is the phallus covering" (1995: 77).

7. See also Douglas and Wildavsky, who discuss risk to cattle among the pastoral Hima in terms of violations of sexual taboos (1982: 40–48; Eilam 1973).
8. My aims were to inspect the coastal erosion and to do a multi-sited survey of what the environmental crisis meant to people and to ask what they were thinking about the prospect of relocation. I met and talked to Murik in Port Moresby, the national capital, in Wewak, the capital of the East Sepik Province and in four villages where I convened meetings in Male Cult Houses and met with selected informants. I elicited and encountered the views of a range of ordinary villagers, young and old, male and female. I collected perspectives of political actors, both at the state- and local-levels. I interviewed members of the employed, middle-class as well as unemployed urban villagers. What I got was not a comprehensive sample in a quantitative sense, but it did represent the strongest currents of opinion among the main categories of men in the dispersed society. This multi-sited research, I maintain, avoided the banalities or bias that may arise from the mobile sort of methodology that I used because of my longitudinal relationship with Murik society that began in 1981. I knew the main categories of men that needed to be represented, that is to say, and I knew where to find voices that could speak candidly and reliably on their behalf.
9. The National Geophysical Data Center reports that a tsunami event did indeed take place on the north coast of PNG on 2.22.1951, possibly the result of an offshore earthquake. See http://www.ngdc.noaa.gov/nndc/struts/results?t=101650&s=10&d=228,185,186,76,78&nd=display&eq_0=10968&eq_12=3145 (accessed 15 March 2010)

Afterword: Men's Dual Alienation in Other Pacific Modernities

I end this book by summarizing my general argument. And then having done so, I begin to assess its broader analytic value by applying it to several selected cases of masculinities in other Pacific modernities.

Under the influence of the sociologist Connell, masculinity studies have made what amounts to a Marxist and Durkheimian claim. Masculine identities are stratified by degree around their relationship to what she calls the "legitimacy of patriarchy" (Connell 1995: 77). Now, my issue with such a framework is that it assumes that the male subject may be defined by a single hierarchy of value spheres that revolves around one concept of legitimacy, one concept of family structure that extends out to the nation-state and one concept of prestige and power that is associated with its cosmopolitan leadership. The point that I have made abundantly clear in preceding chapters is that male citizens in Papua New Guinea (PNG), like the Murik, are not epitomized by one set of value spheres that culminate in, or trail after, one privileged status. Instead, masculine pluralism prevails. Modern value spheres are superimposed upon archaic, which is to say, traditional, or indigenous, forms of gender identity that coexist in dialogue with them. The archaic does not constitute a single masculinity either. Among the latter are not one but multiple sexual divisions of labor, multiple forms of kinship-based legitimacy and multiple cosmologies in which alternative concepts of the body are entailed, all of which defined and continue to define the masculine and the feminine in important, plural ways (Mead 1935). As such, postcolonial masculinity is polyphonic and inconclusive rather than subordinate to a hegemonic form.

I view relations among these plural masculinities as a Bakhtinian dialogue in two senses. First, men's voices are informed by and oriented toward both archaic and modern value spheres and interlocutors. In Bakhtin's terms, if modernity is authorial and the archaic is men's "own signifying discourse," they are both "objects of authorial discourse but also subjects of their own directly signifying discourse" (1984a: 7). In other words, their voices are dialogized: they combine archaic voices with modernity, and vice versa, modern voices with the archaic, in various tones and weights that are both culturally independent yet conditional. Second, their dialogue is inconclusive. Neither they nor modernity answers with an authoritative last word. Being "unfinalized," to use Bakhtin's term (1984a: 31), their dialogue has no end, no *telos*.

Now, the main theme of that dialogue, and the main topic of this book, is men's dual alienation from both their archaic and modernity. Living in a time and space of the other, both in the past and the present, men are nevertheless not unmanned. The alienation of their gender identity remains endowed with agency in the case of Murik men to marry, to domesticate the meaning of modern goods and technologies and to invent new forms of material culture. For a theory of this contradictory kind of dual alienation, I turned to the semiotics of the psychoanalyst Jacques Lacan (1977b). From Lacan, I adopted a view of subject formation that applies no less to archaic than to modern society, and although it does emphasize what has been lost and is missing, it still conceptualizes agency, unity and joy.

For Lacan, the relationship of the subject to culture is built up on being deprived of the desire of the other. Specifically, the subject is deprived of his prediscursive symbiosis with the desire of his mother, the object of whose desire he calls "the phallus" (1977b). What makes "the phallus" the subject is not the intervention of "the father," as in the Freudian view of Oedipus, but rather the *name of the father*, a nominal presence that exemplifies the cutting edge of the post-Edenic world of cultural order, that is, of language, law and the state, into which "the subject/phallus" is exiled. The *name of the father* stands for, but also imposes, the world of signifiers and signifieds upon the subject. Lacan views what we anthropologists would call "culture" as a condition of alienation—of exclusion, isolation, deprivation and estrangement. Culture, in short, is a time and space of the other. In all that is signified, all moral order and communication, something is missing, namely, "the phallus," the signifier of lost desire. The Lacanian phallus is therefore no metaphor of masculine hegemony. It is not a dominant that defines, determines or transforms the integrity of culture and its component features. It does not even stand for itself. The Lacanian phallus is not the male organ. It is not a penis. It is not suspended in webs of significance of its own creation. Rather, it stands for objects, values and ideologies that are misrecognized as important and consequential (cf. Geertz 1973). It hides a lack that must be kept secret. What is not there? The signified, the desire of the other, is absent. The Lacanian phallus is an image of dismemberment. It is "symbolically castrated" rather than erect and virile. As such, the subject must cleave to an imaginary other whose primary function is to conceal what is missing by creating illusions of fulfilled desire, illusions of unity, moral order and love. At the same time, however, the ethos of the Lacanian subject is not melancholic. No. Illusions of moral agency will do, to a certain extent at least. They do appear to foreclose what Lacan calls "the real," which is that which cannot be signified—the absence of the desire of the other.

By combining the Lacanian view of alienation in signification with Bakhtin's dialogism, I arrived at the conclusion that a group of rural men living in a postcolonial modernity find themselves having to respond not just to one but to a combination of two lacks of desire, one archaic and the other modern, and by doing so, they express alienation from both.[1] We have seen how this conclusion offered theoretical traction for understanding the case of Murik men living on a rather precarious and isolated edge of the global Pacific. But, in keeping with Fred Eggan's old preference for "controlled," or regionally based, comparison (1954: 747–8; see also Boas 1896), what light might it also shed on men's predicaments in other kinds of Pacific modernity? What broader analytical value, or insight, does my framework offer, if any? I shall now discuss four studies of men in differing Pacific modernities: the American state of Hawaii, the independent kingdom of Tonga, the Federated States of Micronesia and the bicultural state of New Zealand/Aotearora. None of the ethnography, I should mention, were originally conceptualized in terms that were at all related to my dual alienation thesis.

I begin with Ty Tengan's ethnography of Hale Mua, a small Hawaiian men's group he joined in the 1990s (2008, 2014). Living in contemporary Hawaii, Tengan reports, working- and middle-class men see themselves caught up in an uncanny time and space, one from which they "feel themselves ... disconnected, disempowered and ... emasculated" but which they also see as the land of their ancestors (2008: 3, 8, 19). One of their late twentieth-century answers was a nationalist movement that also included revitalizationist efforts (Wallace 1956) that Tengan labeled as "sites for re-membering" (referring to memory not to repairing the symbolic castration of the phallus). Some of these efforts involved the installation of new commemorative locales, reenactments, rededications, and so forth, in which acts of unification took place that reasserted "authentic" masculine subject positions in a decolonizing struggle for Hawaiian sovereignty (Tengen 2008: 65–66). In Lacanian terms, in other words, they involved the signifier and its illusions of moral agency.

In one momentous event, Hale Mua men, wearing nothing but loincloths, jumped off a cliff into the night and the ocean some 20 yards below (Tengen 2008: 17). The spot they chose had no little significance: it was where the ancestor-spirits were said to have departed for the afterlife and where a nineteenth-century chief used to dive in order to petition them for rain. "As we jumped," Tengan recalled, "into the night and the realm of the ancestors, the people gathered ... to lift up a prayer for the power and strength needed ... in a familiar fight for ... a future in their past" (2008: 3). The leaping men, amid the voices of their supporters, clearly answered the most vulgar elements—North American militarization and global tourism—of the ambient Hawaiian modernity, an answer that voiced the alienation of their signifier from it (see also Ferguson and Turnbull 1999). Their jump, as Tengan put it, "was ... as much about being a *man* as it was about being Hawaiian or, more specifically, a *Hawaiian man*" (italics his, 2008: 6). I think that to Pacific the men's cliff jump can be viewed as an expression of men's alienation in answer to modernity, but to what degree did it also express their alienation from archaic Hawaiian culture (*kanaka maoli*)?

This latter voice is perhaps more difficult to discern in the aftermath of the long, devastating colonial history Hawaiian people and culture have endured. However, looking for instances or manifestations of alienation from the archaic in the contemporary era at least, we do learn of men's shame about wearing loincloths in public and so forth. And there is this: during a cliff jump, men "stumble and trip as they grope their way along a darkness utterly unfamiliar to them ... [and] when the ground disappears from under their feet, the duration of the fall and the impact of the landing is anything but certain" (Tengen 2008: 4). More intriguing, as a Lacanian moment, is the rededication of the temple at Pu'ukohola, Pu'ukohola being associated with nothing less than the founding of the Hawaiian kingdom in the late eighteenth century by Kamehameha (Tengan 2008: 68–123).

The state's first monarch killed his classificatory brother at this site, after the rival had apparently readied himself for death by lopping off "the end of his penis" (Tengan 2008: 69). Kamehameha placed the corpse on an altar there and won the power of an ancestor warrior-spirit who supported his subsequent struggle to conquer the islanders and bring them under his rule by 1810. From this dark site of homicide and phallic surrender, "the Hawaiian nation was born" (Tengan 2008: 69). What is interesting is the extent to which Hawaiian historians and other authors went on to debate the meaning of Kamehameha's murder of his classificatory brother and his retinue. Did the latter man willingly offer himself on behalf of his brother's political ambitions and his love for him? Or was Kamehameha's sincere attachment to him outweighed by ambition as well as by pressure from councilors and seers who advised him?

Several times during the twentieth century, Kamehameha's historical stature came to stand for the moral worth of hereditary elites more generally in Hawaiian society, and for the renewal of their broken world, via the "re-membering" of sacred sites and so forth. This dialogue culminated in the bicentennial celebration of the site in 1991. Organizers made efforts to dissociate it from violence and sought instead to reframe the site's meaning as a "temple of state for those seeking a new Hawaiian nation" that might help their efforts to reclaim a lost cultural identity, particularly relating to male agency (Tengan 2008: 75). Local historians pored through archival accounts of what happened between Kamehameha and his cousin-brother in 1791 in an effort to reconcile their two lineages and reinterpret the victim's act of phallic self-mutilation as a gesture of self-sacrifice rather than of mystical defiance of his antagonist. In the event, amid criticism from devoutly Christian Hawaiians that such revivals were unacceptable unless they were staged as pageants for tourists, as well as from culturally conservative Hawaiians who expressed doubts about its authenticity, representations of unity and moral order won the day. Descendants of Kamehameha "returned" a cloak to descendants of his victim as a peacemaking gesture. Debates about authenticity have nevertheless gone on since then in connection to annual "Establishment Day" celebrations staged at the site.

Out of this initiative, the Hale Mua men's group was formed with the goal of reinventing a Hawaiian warrior identity—for men who wore the loincloth and knew how to carve and use spears, spears being "the ultimate symbol" of Hawaiian masculinity that, by the fact of their very manufacture, constitutes a "life-giving process" (Tengan, 2008: 137). Donning the archaic clothing and carrying the weaponry, as well as fighting with padded clubs in mock battles and spending time in casual solidarity with a cohort of *braddahs*, answered, or was thought to answer men's alienation, the alienation that arose from the abolition of male-female commensality taboos in 1819 (Tengan 2008: 239; see also Sisson 2014). In archaic times, the *Hale Mua* had been a kind of male cult, an initiation society for youth that answered men's lack of the desire of the other by recreating secret figurations of masculine agency and presence (see Chap. 6). In the contemporary moment, the new men's group answered the modern other, who belittled them in the classroom, for example, as lazy. At the same time that it was meant to afford men lost forms of Hawaiian agency, the group was also meant to offer them a safe place that was also not "overwhelmed by women" (Tengan 2008: 141). In addition, it clearly offered its senior members a kind of virility, that is, a sense of being objects of desire by younger students who they expected to make them and their teaching live on into the future. And what did they teach? A kind of cultural revisionism according to which Ku, the ancestor-spirit of war, became a source of masculine rationality—discipline, courage and well-being—and Hawaiian cosmology more generally was seen as a balanced and complementary harmony of male and female spirits rather than one differentiated by taboos, hierarchy, or today by domestic abuse, suicide and other contemporary symptoms of masculine alienation. That is, they taught a vision of moral unity that rejected modernity, but also rejected the archaic.

Having begun to illustrate some of the analytic dividends that my dual alienation thesis might pay to the study of masculinity in another Pacific modernity, I will now move on to a second setting. The independent, sovereign Federated States of Micronesia consist of a string of low-lying atolls about 2400 miles southwest of Hawaii. There, the men of the Marshall Islands also inhabit a time and space that has been overrun by an American other. But instead of being emasculated by foreign workers, tourism and colonialism, Marshallese appetites are fed by expired American goods, their space is degraded by pollution from American nuclear testing in the 1950s and their future is threatened by rising sea levels (see Chap. 7).

In his ethnography of Marshallese views of climate change, Peter Rudiak-Gold (2013) has pointed to a trickster figure of dual alienation in their mythology (see also Carucci 1986). Letao, a "grandson of the creator god Lowa" (Rudiak-Gold 2013: 31), is said to have travelled throughout the islands at one point introducing fire to the subsistence economy by convincing a boy that cooking food will make it tastier. But lighting up a fire, Letao burns down the child's house. That is, Letao offers new, transformative technology but also destroys and deceives. In another, oft-told tale, he sails to the Gilbert Islands, where, demonstrating his superior capacity to feed society living there, he flimflams a chief, getting the leader to bury himself alive in an earth oven, which not only kills him but leaves the community with nothing to eat. Having demonstrated the failure of local-level authority, in some versions, Letao then flees to the USA, where he invested the people there with his superior powers and capacity for dishonesty—but also his nuclear "fire" (see also McArthur 2008: 277).

In my terms, I don't think that it is too much a stretch to propose that in contemporary Marshallese modernity, Letao expresses islanders' alienation, particularly from the American state, with which they identify him, but also from its monetized economy that has cast a kin-based society adrift in a time and space pervaded and perverted by all kinds of shortages. With the impact of American goods and its market economy, Marshallese society has been deprived of the means of production, an autonomous ability to provide for themselves from the land. What about the desire of the other?

Needless to say, there are stories in which Letao is credited with the "invention" of masculine desire, or at least, the desire of the other, which is depicted as nothing less than female genitalia. In one version, Letao is a child who gives a little "toy" to a woman who is somehow termed his "mother" in the story. He asks her to keep an eye on it while he goes to play on the beach where he then encounters an older man at work on a new canoe. Ever busy, his "mother" puts the toy under her arm, as she becomes preoccupied with her daily round. Sitting down, she then places it in between her legs where she finds that it "fits" perfectly and becomes her vagina. She goes to bring a snack to the man her son met on the beach. Letao, having now turned into that man, flirts with her, "joking and telling meaningless tales ... until he finally convinced ... her to sleep with him" (Carucci 1986: 165).[2] For Lacan, the intervention of *the name of the father* dismembers the "phallus" from the desire of the other. In this Marshallese fantasy, this scene is reversed; the desire of the other, the vagina, appears to originate from the pleasure of the trickster son, that is, from his "toy." So how is this woman Letao's mother in the first place if she has no vagina before he "gives" her his "toy" to look after? The "phallus" then appears to take an unalienated form when the father/son seduces his "mother."

In a related episode, this fantasy is revised in more familiar terms. Letao visits a married couple at work harvesting pandanus fruit in their garden. The wife climbs up a tree and standing below her, the husband looks up, sees red blood beneath her matted skirt and worries that she has been injured in some way. Letao bids the husband to go find his wife herbal medicines on the other side of the atoll. He then has intercourse with the woman, teaching her how to do so in the process. The husband returns and discovers what has happened. Feeling jealous and fooled by Letao, he nevertheless becomes a willing "student" of his wife from whom he learns how to have sex. In other words, Letao "invents" the desire of the other but foundationally that desire is divided rather than exclusive.

Rudiak-Gold argues that Letao has become a template of contemporary Marshallese ambivalence about modernity. Like the trickster, modernity has created desire while it has left men uncertain and mistrustful, or, in my term, alienated. The sheer power of Western science, for example, to land men on the moon, or predict a solar eclipse, is breathtaking to them. But at the same time, it was scientists who forced them to have to live amid the environmental aftermath of nuclear tests. Modernity, they feel, lured them away from the virtues of custom and led them to desire foreign values and goods. Rising sea levels also make this same kind of trickster's sense to them. It is but another dimension of Letao's duplicity—his penchant for giving while taking away. Like Letao, Marshall Islanders cleave to a kind of terminal resiliency. They vehemently reject the prospect of resettlement, which they dread as little better than an incurable disease, while insisting that they are partly to blame for climate change (Rudiak-Gold 2013: 177; see Chap. 7). They thus appeal to sustainable resources, such as coconut biofuel and solar power, while reviving customary adaptations, like palm-frond seawalls. Instead of "adapting to climate change," Rudiak-Gold observes, with no little irony, "Marshall Islanders are adapting climate change to themselves" (2013: 177), a claim that simultaneously admits to the vulnerability of time and space just as it seeks "to save Marshall Islanders from modernity" (2013: 142, 175). In their climate change dialogue, the paradox of the Lacanian signifier, of a masculine presence based in the lack of desire, is quite clearly expressed. The signifier, if the Letao tales reflect the subject position of archaic Marshallese masculinity at all, was empty before modernity and the Anthropocene.

Although the political context of the Kingdom of Tonga differs somewhat from Hawaii and the Marshall Islands, Tonga being the one state in the region that never was a European or an American colony, the history and contemporary influence of global modernity are no less encompassing than in these previous two cases. Their constitutional monarchy, modeled on Westminster, was in dialogue with Polynesian hierarchy but today that dialogue has been challenged by commoners espousing democratic ideals. The society is thoroughly internationalized and depends on remittances from diasporas in New Zealand, Australia and the USA. Under the impacts of consumer capitalism, the subsistence economy has become dysfunctional, and the value of men's contribution to it, land tenure and labor, has depreciated. An annual agricultural show has been replaced by two beauty pageants, one of which is for transgender men. Needless to say, missionary Christianity damaged the cosmological agency of Tongan men nearly beyond recognition. In assessing the dialogue of Tongan masculinity with Tongan modernity, I rely on Niko Besnier's ethnography of what he refers to as "anxieties" in urban "sites of modernity" where men struggle to "straddle the edge of the global" (2011: 1).

One of these sites are pawnshops that began to open in Nuku'alofa, the national capital, in 2006. Their owners, for the most part, were men who had been the beneficiaries of retirement checks the government was handing out in an effort to cut back on the civil service in the country. The shops were alienated spaces, to say the least, into which women slunk in, estranged by feelings of shame and the stigma of being too poor to fulfill ceremonial obligations to kin. To their reciprocal disgrace, the pawnbrokers would try to capitalize on their customers' desire for anonymity by locating shops as far out of the way as they could and by avoiding doing business with kin, if at all possible. At the same time, public opinion criticized them for rejecting the "Tongan way" and its value of "mutual empathy" (Besnier 2011: 121). The pawnbrokers become what Besnier dubs "local others" who live in dual alienation—on the margins of not just Tongan modernity but of the Tongan archaic as well.

Needless to say, their estrangement calls their masculine identity into question. Women bring mats and barkcloth to the pawnbrokers, thereby creating a gendered reversal of role: "Women customers worry about money, while male owners worry about possessing women's objects and expertise" (Besnier 2011: 122; see Mead 1935). This turnaround shames them to such an extent that at least one proprietor was led to deny ownership of his business and claim that it belonged to his wife. Other pawnbrokers dismiss what they do as merely one business in an ongoing series in their entrepreneurial careers as men.

Pawnshops are one evident site of the dual alienation of Tongan masculinity. There, the missing desire of the other is expressed, or repressed, in the sentiment of shame. Elsewhere, however, that very desire appears in the foreground of two annual beauty pageants. The Heilala Festival was began in the 1980s by the tourist industry in the country. As I mentioned, it replaced a traditional agricultural show that had been in decline. The event brings together many Tongan voices. State sponsored parades of royals take place during it. School and church choirs perform. And sports tournaments are held that draw both commoners and elites. There is also a garland competition. But the culmination of the festival, according to Besnier, is the rival beauty pageants in which Miss Heilala is crowned and a Miss Galaxy "queen" is chosen. The former celebrates young, educated women who appear as objects of both modern and Tongan desire. They speak English and walk with a model's gait; and they try to appear as poised modern women. They also dress as virgin princesses, speak Tongan and perform local dances. The Miss Galaxy pageant, by contrast, celebrates transgender men, as ambivalent objects of desire in society. In this latter contest, participants are poor, low-ranking men who mock hegemonic masculinity in Tonga. They are not hypermasculine and virile but effeminate. They are egalitarian and outrageous rather than respectful. They even adopt foreign identities at one point during the contest, dressing, for example, as Miss Switzerland or Miss Rarotonga, rather than as Tongan princesses. They take English stage names but are hardly cosmopolitan. And thus society dismisses them as sham women, sham men, sham moderns and sham Tongans.

If symbolic action and things in Lacanian time and space stand for the lost desire of the other—or, the alienation of the signifier—then note how these two beauty pageants defy one of the master signifiers of lack in traditional Tongan moral order. This is the brother-sister relationship whose norms are extended throughout society, across generations and ranks, and to the opposite sex as a whole. In its prototype, which is an avoidance, respect relationship, the self should behave with acute circumspection in the presence of the cross-sex other. Inhibited by shame and discretion, the self is forbidden by decorum not to arouse the desire of the other. Now these two beauty pageants are carnivalesque inversions that feature open and public expressions of desire performed before audiences that may include spectators of higher rank, cross-sex siblings and, inevitably, men. That is to say, participants flaunt rather than repress the self and transgress tradition in a way that may be dismissed as "festival" rather than "real" immodesty but which nevertheless makes kin sufficiently uneasy to such an extent that they may choose not to attend a program or act in ways that "desexualize ... the ... contestants" (Besnier 2011: 130). In other words, no less than pawnshops, the Heilala and the Miss Galaxy festivals alienate men and women both from Tongan norms and modernity.

Another striking site where men engage in dialogue with the "Tongan way" and modernity is the one gym in the country. While women by and large go on actively working in their gardens and families, that is to say, in their village economies, men "work out" there. So, such "work" is not "real work," but is rather an answer to having become marginalized from the traditional means of production, in other words, from land and kin. Moreover, bodybuilding is also an answer to the big and corpulent bodies valued in archaic Tongan culture as a sign of well-being, that is, as a sign of *belonging* and having access to the desire of the other and her collective and material capital—to her nurture. By contrast, the goal of maintaining a hypermasculine body as an end in itself is an expression of modern individualism, an expression in this context of a lack of the other's desire. Thus, their longings and hopes for recognition by modernity as men take a desperate and shameless tone. They are obsessed by what Besnier calls a "millenarian" desire to become famous and make their fortunes as international rugby players or weightlifters (2011: 194). In the street, he saw groups of young bodybuilders parading about town seeking the desire of the other less abstractly. They dressed in tank tops and shorts that revealed rather "more thigh than rules of decency would normally allow" (2011: 199).

I would say that differences of the political history of Tongan men in modernity as compared with PNG, the Marshall Islands and Hawaii are more apparent than real. The characteristic form of men's alienation from both the "Tongan way" and modernity, the lack of the desire of the other in the middle of their gender identity, certainly recalls the dual estrangement and disaffection of the masculine subject in these other Pacific modernities. I want to add two more brief examples of the dialogics of dual alienation of men in a Pacific society where yet another kind of political sovereignty prevails—the bicultural state of New Zealand/ Aotearora.

In the first, Toon van Meijl (2006) studied a vocational training program located on a *marae*, a Māori community center, where unemployed, undereducated youth enrolled to learn computer skills, among other topics. To qualify, they were also required to take a supplementary class in the Māori vernacular as well as in various forms of expressive culture—the latter obligation being an outgrowth of a cultural renaissance movement begun in the 1970s. Most trainees associated Māori with lack, that is, with living in the time and space of the other. "Māori," as an identity, had meant little more than living with the stigma of being tracked with other Māori children as "slow learners" in school. Now this force-feeding of the "*marae* model" of Māori culture did no more than reinforce the feeling "that they belonged neither to European domains nor [to] ... typical Māori domains of ... society" (van Meijl 2006: 918). The young people spoke no Māori, knew little about ritual practice, much less about genealogy and had rarely visited a *marae* before, except perhaps to attend a funeral during childhood. Trainees felt "embarrassment [and] ... resentment" at being confronted with how to live as good Māori. Young men seemed particularly more alienated than the women.[3] They refused to go to class, or else, when they did show up, they sat in the back row and ignored what was going on, preferring instead to talk about rugby, drinking or TV shows. What did they say about what they thought of themselves? They internalized a dialogue of dual alienation. On the one hand, they preferred to view themselves as "human beings" possessing an intrinsic moral worth over and above their citizenship in the bicultural modernity of New Zealand/Aotearora. On the other, they paid lip service to the voices of culturally conservative Māori elders whose criticism left them feeling "bewildered" and disrespected (van Meijl 2006: 920).

Dual alienation was not limited to working-class Māori men. Brandan Hokowhitu, dean of Māori Studies at the University of Waikato, has written extensively about the history of Māori masculinity with particular reference to colonial racism and athletics. However, here I want to limit my focus to a few autobiographical reflections he included in one essay in which he recalls growing up in a small Māori town where his father worked as a schoolteacher, but "lived for sports" (Hokowhitu 2004: 260). Athletic competition, Hokowhitu allows, was his father's way of achieving agency on a level playing field against white rugby teams. Sharing his passion for sports, Hokowhitu recalled the dual alienation of school days when he felt ostracized from his Māori cohort for being academically successful and frustrated by teachers' racist assumptions that Māori students were "inherently physical" and intellectually dim. Today, as an adult, this estrangement has persisted: working-class Māori men ridicule middle-class men such as himself for having effeminate "uncalloused hands" that don't play rugby and don't do manual labor (Hokowhitu 2004: 261). Men who succeed in education they dismiss as bogus, or "plastic" Māori who condescend to and patronize them rather than act in genuine ways.[4] What is more, they hear Hokowhitu's very voice as unmanly. "I find it almost impossible," he admits, "to discuss ... my work ... with ... Māori men because the language I speak is viewed as ... [white] language ... [that] contrasts with the silent, tough and practical Māori masculinity that is distortedly common" (2004: 261).

The dialogue of dual alienation is unmistakable in and between both the working- and the middle-classes of Māori men and modernity in New Zealand/Aotearora. One last expression of it: When Hokowhitu attended his father's funeral, the eulogy upset him because while the man's athletic abilities and accomplishments received praise, the speaker failed to acknowledge the 40 years his father had spent as a teacher (2004: 270). Working-class Māori men celebrate their athleticism as "traditional" and dismiss other moral attributes of their Māori identity, such as compassion and nurture, as "feminine." Centuries of colonial discourse that presumed Māori masculinity to be savage, child-like, violent and incapable of little other than manual labor, in contrast to the more evolved virtue and skills of the Pakeha, the white settlers, had reduced the complexity of Māori masculinity beyond recognition. Today, the spectacle of the Māori athlete performing a *haka* dance before international tournaments attests to the success of a bicultural state that helped them succeed in the one hypermasculine arena in which it permitted men to excel. Hokowhitu expresses his alienation from both in no uncertain terms: he attends his sons' school assemblies where Māori and other Polynesian students are recognized for their athletic accomplishments and writes of feeling "sadness and anger" (2004: 275).

As he seems to suggest, there may be masculine answers, at least possible ones, to both "Māori culture" and modernity not conveyed in the preceding sketches. And surely, this accusation could be leveled at each of the other scenes and figures I have discussed. But incompleteness aside, I think that as a whole my little collection, of the Hale Mua society in Hawaii, Letao, the trickster ancestor of Marshall Islanders, pawnbrokers and others in the Kingdom of Tonga and, lastly, the working- and middle-class Māori in New Zealand/Aotearora, does accomplish two of the things I wanted to do at the end of this book.[5]

First, I have confirmed, or at least begun to suggest, that the dialogue of the dual alienation of masculine desire that I analyzed in contexts in contemporary Murik society, such as the substitutions of outboard motor fiberglass boats for enchanted steering paddles on outrigger canoes, as well as money for sex in Gaingiin Society grade-taking, among many others, is no anomaly in Pacific modernities. But second, I have also offered a glimpse of how men's dual estrangements differ by degree, I would say, but certainly not in kind, from my PNG case.

Throughout the region, in other words, modernity is an uncanny time and space for Pacific men; it is a familiar yet dreadfully other. What varies seems to have to do with the men's alienation from the archaic whose authenticity and value are contested by both modern and traditional voices. The contribution of my PNG case of the men of the Murik Lakes is therefore this: with its shorter, less devastating and less centrifugal history than elsewhere in Pacific, the alienated voices and subject positions of Murik men in their dialogue with the archaic is clearer. That is to say, their agency defined in terms of their cosmology, land tenure and economies remains more intact in PNG than elsewhere in the Pacific. While inevitably, men's archaic voices answer modernity, they remain unmerged from it, as in the authorship of *Woyon's Mother*, the new piece of Murik folk theater. Or else, they merge in composite "double-voices." For example, marijuana becomes a contested kind of trade tobacco and performance enhancer like magic. Meanwhile, they may also speak in modern, subject-centered voices that they have begun to use on mobile phones or in modern, universalist voices as in their understanding of the relationship of rising sea levels to climate change in the Anthropocene. In other words, male voices and subject positions are not reduced to, or determined by, one privileged model of value expressed in the voices and actions of elites, such as the politician Sir Michael Somare. Center and periphery do not align in terms of the binary, modern self and archaic other, or urban middle classes and rural villagers, in any simple way. In PNG, men have not been dominated by the legacy of any obvious set of political purposes. Rather, masculine desire remains constituted by a dialogue between modernity and the archaic. Thus the men of the Murik Lakes may be disaffected and disempowered, but they are not muted by unequal power relations and hegemonic discourses. Modernity has not silenced them. The alienated desire in their voices remains audible and comprehensible, at least to those of us who make the effort to listen.[6]

Notes

1. Tengan allowed that the members of his men's group "felt a dual sense of alienation, from Hawaiian culture because of their Americanization and class status and from American culture because of their Hawaiian ethnic background and upbring" (2008: 133). This is not the same double alienation as I analyzed among Murik men. Because of the rather shorter, less comprehensive and less emasculating colonial history of the latter men, their alienation to Murik culture was seen to arise from itself rather than from the acculturation of Murik men to modernity.
2. In another version, Letao's mother finds and hides her son's "toy" in various hairy locations on her body. In retaliation, Letao hides himself behind some bushes and watches his mother while she husks a coconut. He extends his erect penis until he is able to have intercourse with her, which she enjoys although she fails to understand what it is she is enjoying. This is the first act of intercourse (McArthur 2008: 269).
3. But the women, after their initial enthusiasm subsided, also complained of feeling overwhelmed by the challenge of learning to be good Māori.
4. Interestingly, the trope of not having "calloused hands" seems to connote the desire of the other. In a footnote, Hokowhitu cites a Māori adage evidently offered to encourage a daughter: "Marry a man with calluses on his hands (2004:fn6)."
5. On masculinity and militarism in Fiji, see Clery (2014); on masculinity and nationalism in Tahiti, see Elliston (2004).
6. Obviously, cultural anthropologists, at least in their prime, not only took pains to encounter men like the Murik who live in out-of-the-way places and times but bent over backwards to talk to them in egalitarian settings in which they would feel comfortable and willing to speak in their dialogical voices and metaphors (cf. Spivak 1988).

BIBLIOGRAPHY

Abu-Lughod, Lila. 1990. Shifting Politics in Bedouin Love Poetry. In *Language and the Politics of Emotion*, ed. Catherine A. Lutz and Lila Abu-Lughod, 24–45. Cambridge: Cambridge University Press.

Abu-Lughod, Lila, and Catherine A. Lutz. 1990. Introduction: Emotion, Discourse and the Politics of Everyday Life. In *Language and the Politics of Emotion*, ed. Catherine A. Lutz and Lila Abu-Lughod, 1–23. Cambridge: Cambridge University Press.

Adam, B. 1990. *Time and Social Theory*. Cambridge: Polity.

Adger, Neil W., Jouni Paavola, Saleemul Huq, and M.J. Mace. 2006. *Fairness in Adaptation to Climate Change*. Cambridge: MIT Press.

Ahearn, Laura M. 2001. *Invitations to Love: Literacy, Love Letters and Social Change in Nepal*. Ann Arbor: University of Michigan Press.

Akin, D. 1999. Cash and Shell Money in Kwaio, Solomon Islands. In *Money and Modernity: State and Local Currencies in Melanesia*, ed. D. Akin and J. Robbins. Pittsburgh: University of Pittsburgh Press.

Akin, D., and J. Robbins, eds. 1999. *Money and Modernity: State and Local Currencies in Melanesia*. Pittsburgh: University of Pittsburgh Press.

Allen, B.J., R.M. Bourke, and J. Gibson. 2005. Poor Rural Places in Papua New Guinea. *Asia Pacific Viewpoint* 46 (2): 201–2017.

Andersen, B.A. 2013. Tricks, Lies and Mobile Phones: "Phone Friend" Stories in Papua New Guinea. *Culture, Theory and Critique* 54 (3): 318–334.

Antonelli, C. 1991. *The Diffusion of Advanced Telecommunications in Developing Countries*. Paris: OECD.

Appadurai, Arjun. 1986. *The Social Life of Things: Commodities in a Cultural Perspective*. New York: Cambridge University Press.
———. 1995. The Production of Locality. In *Counterworks. Managing the Diversity of Knowledge*, ed. R. Fardon, 204–223. London and New York: Routledge.
———. 1996. *Modernity at Large: Cultural Dimensions of Globalization*. Minneapolis, MN: University of Minnesota Press.
Asad, Talal. 2003. *Formations of the Secular: Christianity, Islam, Modernity*. Stanford, CA: Stanford University Press.
Auerbach, Erich. 1957. *Mimesis: The Representations of Reality in Western Literature*, trans. Williard Trask. New York: Doubleday Anchor.
Babcock, B. 1993. At Home, No Women Are Storytellers: Ceramic Creativity and Politics of Discourse in Cochiti Pueblo. In *Creativity/Anthropology*, ed. S. Lavie, K. Narayan, and R. Rosaldo, 70–99. Ithaca: Cornell University Press.
Bainton, Nicholas A. 2008. Men of Kastom and the Customs of Men: Status, Legitimacy and Persistent Values in Lihir, Papua New Guinea. *The Australian Journal of Anthropology* 19(2): 194–212.
Bainton, N.A., and M. Macintyre. 2016. Mortuary Ritual and Mining Riches in Island Melanesia. In *Mortuary Dialogues: Death Ritual and the Reproduction of Moral Community in Pacific Modernities*, ed. David Lipset and Eric K. Silverman, 110–134. New York: Berghahn.
Bakhtin, M. M. 1981. Forms of Time and of the Chronotope in the Novel. In *The Dialogic Imagination: Four Essays*, ed. Michael Holquist, Caryl Emerson and trans. Michael Holquist, 84–258. Austin: University of Texas Press.
———. 1984a. *Problems in Dostoevsky's Poetics*, trans. Caryl Emerson. Minneapolis: University of Minnesota Press.
———. 1984b. *Rabelais and His World*, trans. Helene Iswolsky. Bloomington: Indiana University Press.
Bakker, E.J. 1999. Mimesis as Performance: Rereading Auerbach's First Chapter. *Poetics Today* 20 (1): 11–25.
Ball, C. and N. Harkness. ed. 2015. Kinship Chronotopes: A Special Issue of *Anthropological Quarterly*. *Anthropological Quarterly*, 88 (2).
Balme, C. 2007. *Pacific Performances: Theatricality and Cross-Cultural Encounter in the South Seas*. New York: Palgrave Macmillan.
Bamford, S. 2007. *Biology Unmoored: Melanesian Reflections on Life and Biotechnology*. Berkeley: University of California Press.
Barker, J. 2008. *Ancestral Lines: The Maisin of Papua New Guinea and the Fate of the Rainforest*. Peterborough: Broadview Press.
Barker, J., E. Harms, and J. Lindquist. 2013. *Figures of Southeast Asian Modernity*. Honolulu: University of Hawaii Press.
Barma, N.H. 2014. The Rentier State at Work: Comparative Experiences of the Resource Curse in East Asia and the Pacific. *Asia and the Pacific Policy Studies* 1 (2): 257–272.

Barlow, Kathleen. 1985a. The Social Context of Infant Feeding in the Murik Lakes of Papua New Guinea. In *Infant Care and Feeding in the South Pacific*, ed. L.B. Marshall, 137–154. New York: Gordon and Breach.
———. 1985b. The Role of Women in Murik Trade. *Annual Review of Research in Economic Anthropology* 7: 95–122.
———. 1992. Dance When I Die!: Context and Role in the Clowning of Murik Women. In *Clowning as Critical Practice*, ed. W. Mitchell, 58–87. Pittsburgh: University of Pittsburgh Press.
———. 1995. Achieving Womanhood and the Achievements of Women in Murik: Cult Initiation, Gender Complementarity and the Prestige of Women. In *Gender Rituals: Female Initiation in Melanesia*, ed. N.C. Lutkehaus and Paul Roscoe, 121–142. London: Routledge and Kegan Paul.
———. 2010. Sharing Food, Sharing Values: Mothering and Empathy in Murik Society. *Ethos* 38(4): 339–353.
Barlow, Kathleen, and David Lipset. 1997. Dialogics of Material Culture: Male and Female in Murik Outrigger Canoes. *American Ethnologist* 24(1): 4–36.
Barlow, K., Lissant Bolton, and David Lipset. 1988. Trade and Society in Transition along the Sepik Coast: Technical Report on Regional Research in the East Sepik and Sandaun Provinces, Papua New Guinea for the Sepik Documentation Project. Sydney: Australian Museum.
Bashkow, Ira. 2006. *The Meaning of Whitemen: Race and Modernity in the Orokaiva Cultural World*. Chicago: University of Chicago Press.
Bataille, George. 1962. *Eroticism*, trans. Mary Dalwood. London: John Calder.
Bateson, G. 1936/1956. *Naven: A Survey of the Problems Suggestsed by a Composite Picture of the Culture of a New Guinea Tribe from Three Points of View*. Stanford: Stanford University Press.
———. 1973. *Steps to an Ecology of Mind*. New York: Ballantine.
Baudrillard, Jean. 1981. *Simulacra and Simulation*, trans. Sheila F. Glaser. Ann Arbor: University of Michigan Press.
Bazbaban, A. 2000. Anthropology, Nationalism and 'The Invention of Tradition'. *Anthropological Forum* 10: 131–155.
Beck, U. 1981/1992. *Risk Society: Towards a New Modernity*. London: Sage.
———. 1999. *World Risk Society*. Cambridge: Polity Press.
———. 2006a. Living in the World Risk Society. *Economy and Society* 35(3): 329–345.
———. 2006b. *Cosmopolitan Vision*. Cambridge: Polity Press.
Beck, Ulrich, and Elisabeth Beck-Gernsheim. 1995. *The Normal Chaos of Love*. Cambridge, MA: Polity Press.
Becker, H. 1953. Becoming a Marijuana User. *American Journal of Sociology* 59: 235–242.
Bell, Jim. 1995. Notions of Love and Romance Among the Taita of Kenya. In *Romantic Passion: A Universal Experience?* ed. William Jankowiak, 152–165. New York: Columbia University Press.

Bell, Joshua. 2006. Marijuana, Guns, Crocodiles and Submarines: Economies of Desire in the Purari Delta. *Oceania* 76: 220–236.
Bergendorff, S. 1996. *Faingu City: A Modern Mekeo Clan in Papua New Guinea*. Lund: Lund University Press.
Berger, P.L., B. Berger, and H. Kellner. 1973. *The Homeless Mind: Modernization and Consciousness*. New York: Random House.
Bernardi, Bernardo. 1985. *Age Class Systems: Social Institutions and Polities Based on Age*. Cambridge: Cambridge University Press.
Berndt, Ronald M. 1962. *Excess and Restraint: Social Control among a New Guinea Mountain People*. Chicago: University of Chicago Press.
———. 1976. *Love Songs of Arnhem Land*. Chicago: University of Chicago Press.
Besnier, Niko. 1995. *Literacy, Emotion and Authority*. Cambridge: Cambridge University Press.
———. 2002. Transgenderism, Locality, and the Miss Galaxy Beauty Pageant in Tonga. *American Ethnologist* 29(3): 534–566.
———. 2011. *On the Edge of the Global: Modern Anxieties in a Pacific Island Nation*. Stanford: Stanford University Press.
Bloch, M., and J. Parry, eds. 1989. *Money and the Morality of Exchange*. Cambridge: Cambridge University Press.
Boas, F. 1896. The Limitations of the Comparative Method of Anthropology. *Science* 4: 901–908.
Bourke, R.M., and T. Harwood, eds. 2009. *Food and Agriculture in Papua New Guinea*. Canberra: ANU E Press.
Brison, Karen. 1995. Changing the Constructions of Masculinity in a Sepik Society. *Ethnology* 34: 155–176.
Bruett, T., and J. Firpo. 2009. *Building a Mobile Money Distribution Network in Papua New Guinea*. Pacific Financial Inclusion Programme. International Finance Corporation.
Brunton, R. 1980. Misconstrued Order in Melanesian Religion. *Man* (NS) 15 (2): 112–128.
Burbank, Victoria. 1995. Passion as Politics: Romantic Love in an Australian Aboriginal Community. In *Romantic Passion: A Universal Experience?* ed. William Jankowiak, 187–196. New York: Columbia University Press.
Burridge, K. 1969. *New Haven, New Earth*. New York: Harper and Row.
Butler, Judith. 1990. *Gender Trouble: Feminism and the Subversion of Identity*. London: Routledge.
Butt, L., and R. Eaves, eds. 2008. *Making Sense of AIDS: Sexuality and Power in Melanesia*. Honolulu: University of Hawaii Press.
Campbell, Shirley. 2001. The Captivating Agency of Art: Many Ways of Seeing. In *Beyond Aesthetics: Art and the Technologies of Enchantment*, ed. C. Pinney and N. Thomas, 117–136. Oxford: Berg Publishers.
Campbell, Scott, and Yong Jin Park. 2008. Social Implications of Mobile Telephony: The Rise of Personal Communication Society. *Sociology Compass* 2(2): 371–387.

Cancian, Francesca. 1987. *Love in America: Gender and Self-Development*. Cambridge: Cambridge University Press.
Carrier, J., and A. Carrier. 1989. *Wage, Trade and Exchange in Melanesia: A Manus Society in the Modern State*. Berkeley: University of California Press.
Carrigan, T.R., R.W. Connell, and J. Lee. 1985. Toward a New Sociology of Masculinity. *Theory and Society* 14(5): 551–604.
Carucci, L. 1986. Sly Moves: A Semiotic Analysis of Movement in Marshallese Culture. *Semiotica* 62 (1–2): 165–177.
Cassidy, R. 2012. Lives With Others: Climate Change and Human-Animal Relations. *Annual Review of Anthropology* 41: 21–56.
Castells, M. 1996. *The Rise of the Network Society, The Information Age: Economy, Society and Culture*. Vol. 1. Malden, MA: Blackwell Publishers.
de Certeau, M. 1983. Lacan: An Ethics of Speech. *Representations* 3: 21–39.
Chakrabarty, D. 2009. The Climate of History: Four Theses. *Critical Inquiry* 35: 197–222.
Clark, J. 1989. The Incredible Shrinking Men: Male Ideology and Development in a Southern Highlands Society in Culture and Development in Papua New Guinea. *Canberra Anthropology* 12(2): 120–143.
Clery, T.N. 2014. Masculinities, Militarism and the Construction of Gender in Contemporary Fiji: Performances of Parody and Subversion as Feminist Resistance. *Pacific Studies* 37 (3): 202–221.
Clifford, James. 1988. *The Predicament of Culture: Twentieth Century Ethnography, Literature and Art*. Cambridge: Harvard University Press.
Codere, H. 1950. *Fighting With Property*. New York: American Ethnological Society.
Cohen, J.E. 2007. Creativity and Culture in Copyright Theory. *UC Davis Law Review* 40: 1151–1205.
Collier, Jane Fishburne. 1974. *From Duty to Desire: Remaking Families in a Spanish Village*. Princeton: Princeton University Press.
Connell, R.W. 1987. *Gender and Power*. Sydney, Australia: Allen and Unwin.
———. 1990. An Iron Man: The Body and Some Contradictions of Hegemonic Masculinity. In *Sport, Men and the Gender Order*, ed. M. Messner and D. Sabo. Champaign, IL: Human Kinetics Press.
———. 1993. The Big Picture: Masculinities in Recent World History. *Theory and Society* 22(5): 597–623.
———. 1995. *Masculinities*. Berkeley: University of California Press.
———. 2005. Globalization, Imperialism and Masculinities. In *Handbook of Studies on Men and Masculinities*, ed. Michael S. Kimmel, Jeff Hearn, and R.W. Connell, 90–113. Thousand Oaks, CA: Sage.
———. 2014. Rethinking Gender from the South. *Feminist Studies* 40(3): 518–539.
Connell, R.W., and J.W. Messerschmidt. 2005. Hegemonic Masculinity: Rethinking the Concept. *Gender and Society* 19(6): 829–859.

Connolly, B., and R. Anderson. 1988. *First Contact: New Guinea's Highlanders Encounter the Outside World.* London: Penguin Books.

Coombe, R. 1998. *The Cultural Life of Intellectual Properties: Authorship, Appropriation, and the Law.* Durham, NC: Duke University Press.

Cornwall, Andrea, and Nancy Lindisfarne. 1994. *Dislocating Masculinity: Comparative Ethnographies.* London: Routledge.

Cox, John. 2013. The Magic of Money and the Magic of the State: Fast Money Schemes in Papua New Guinea. *Oceania* 83 (3): 175–191.

Cox, John, and Martha Macintyre. 2014. Christian Marriage, Money Scams and Melanesian Social Imaginaries. *Oceania* 2: 138–157.

Crate, Susan. 2008. Gone the Bull of Winter: Grapplilng with the Cultural Implications of and Anthropology's Role(s) in Global Climate Change. *Current Anthropology* 49 (4): 569–595.

———. 2011. Climate and Culture: Anthropology in the Era of Contemporary Climate Change. *Annual Review of Anthropology* 40 (1): 175–194.

Crate, Susan, and Mark Nuttall. 2009. *Anthropology and Climate Change: From Encounters to Action.* Walnut Creek, CA: Left Coast Press.

Creighton, Millie R. 1991. Maintaining Cultural Boundaries in Retailing: How Japanese Department Stores Domesticate 'Things Foreign'. *Modern Asian Studies* 25(4): 675–709.

Cruikshank, Julie. 2001. Glaciers and Climate Change: Perspectives from Oral Tradition. *Arctic* 54: 377–393.

———. 2005. *Do Glaciers Listen? Local Knowledge, Colonial Encounters, and Social Imagination.* Vancouver: University of British Columbia Press.

Crutzen, P.J. 2002. Geology of Mankind. *Nature* 415: 23.

Cuddihy, John Murray. 1987. *The Ordeal of Civility: Freud, Marx, Levi-Strauss, and the Jewish Struggle with Modernity.* Boston: Beacon Press.

Cunha, D. 2015. The Anthropocene as Fetishism. *Mediations* 28 (2): 65–77.

Curry, G.N., G. Koczberski, J. Lummani, S. Ryan, and V. Bue. 2012. Earning a Living in PNG: From Subsistence to a Cash Economy. In *Schooling for Sustainable Development: A Focus on Australia, New Zealand and the Oceanic Region*, ed. M. Robertson. Dordrecht: Springer Science and Business.

D'Andrade, Roy. 1995. *The Development of Cognitive Anthropology.* Cambridge: Cambridge University Press.

Dening, Greg. 1992. *Mr. Bligh's Bad Language: Passion, Power and Theatre on the Bounty.* Cambridge: Cambridge University Press.

Derham, D. 1963. Law and Custom in the Australian Territory of Papua and New Guinea. *The University of Chicago Law Review* 30: 495–506.

Dernbach, K.B., and M. Marshall. 2001. Pouring Beer on Troubled Waters: Alcohol and Violence in the Papua New Guinea Highlands during the 1980s. *Contemporary Drug Problems* 28 (1): 3–47.

Derrida, J. 1981. Plato's Pharmacy. In *Dissemination*, trans. B. Johnson. London: The Athlone Press.
Diggens, John Patrick. 1974. *The Ordeal of Civility: Freud, Marx, Levi-Strauss and the Jewish Struggle with Modernity*. New York: Basic Books.
Dinnen, Sinclair. 1995. Raise the Lord and Pass the Amunition—Criminal Group Surrender in Papua New Guinea. *Oceania* 66(2): 103–118.
———. 1998. Law, Order and State. In *Modern Papua New Guinea*, ed. L. Zimmer-Tamakoshi, 333–350. Kirksville, MO: Thomas Jefferson Press.
———. 2000. Breaking the Cycle of Violence: Crime and State in Papua New Guinea. In *Developing Cultural Criminology: Theory and Practice in Papua New Guinea*, ed. C. Banks, 51–78. Sydney: Sydney Institute of Criminology Monograph Series 13.
———. 2001. *Law and Order in a Weak State: Crime and Politics in Papua New Guinea*. Honolulu: University of Hawaii Press.
Dinnen, S., and A. Ley, eds. 2000. *Reflections on Violence in Melanesia*. Annendale: Hawkins Press.
Douglas, Mary. 1966. *Purity and Danger*. London: Routledge and Kegan Paul.
———. 1975. *Implicit Meanings: Essays in Anthropology*. London: Routledge and Kegan Paul.
———. 1990. Risk as a Forensic Resource. *Daedalus* 119(4): 1–16.
Douglas, Mary, and Aaron Wildavsky. 1982. *Risk and Culture: An Essay on the Selection of Technical and Environmental Dangers*. Berkeley: University of California Press.
Dumont, L. 1986. *Essays on Individualism: Modern Ideology in an Anthropological Perspective*. Chicago: University of Chicago Press.
Durkheim, Emile. 1964. *The Division of Labour in Society*, trans. G. Simpson. Glencoe, IL: The Free Press.
———. 1972. *Selected Writings*, ed. A. Giddens. Cambridge: Cambridge University Press.
———. 1912/1995. *The Elementary Forms of Religious Life*. Trans. Karen E. Fields. New York: The Free Press.
Eggan, F. 1954. Social Anthropology and the Method of Controlled Comparison. *American Anthropologist* 56 (5): 743–763.
Ehrenzweig, A. 1967. *The Hidden Order of Art. A Study in the Psychology of Artistic Imagination*. London: Weidenfeld & Nicolson.
Eilam, I. 1973. *The Social and Sexual Roles of Hima Women: A Study of Nomadic Cattle Breeders in Nyabushozi Country, Ankole, Uganda*. Manchester: Manchester University Press.
Ellis, David M. 2003. Changing Earth and Sky: Movement, Environmental Variability, and Responses to El Nino in the Pio-Tura Region of Papua New Guinea. In *Weather, Climate, Culture*, ed. Sarah Strauss and Benjamin S. Orlove, 161–180. London: Berg.

Elliston, D. 2004. A Passion for the Nation: Masculinity, Modernity and Nationalist Struggle. *American Ethnologist* 31 (4): 606–630.
Ellison, Joanna C. 2000. How South Pacific Mangroves May Respond to Predicted Climate Change and Sea-Level Rise. In *Climate Change in the South Pacific: Impacts and Responses in Australia, New Zealand and Small Island States*, ed. A. Gillespie and W. Burns, 289–301. The Netherlands: Kluwer Academic Publishers.
Ellison, Joanna C., and David R. Stoddart. 1991. Mangrove Ecosystem Collapse during Predicted Sea-Level Rise: Holocene Analogues and Implications. *Journal of Coastal Research* 7(1): 151–165.
Eng, D.L., and D. Kazanjian. 2003. *The Politics of Mourning*. Berkeley: University of California Press.
Epstein, S. 1968. *Capitalism, Primitive and Modern*. Canberra: Australian National University Press.
Epstein, A.L. 1999. *Gunantuna: Aspects of the Person, the Self and the Individual Among the Tolai*. Bathurst: Crawford House.
Eriksen, T.H. 2004. Creolisation and Creativity. *Global Networks* 3(1): 223–238.
Errington, F., and D.B. Gewertz. 1992. The Historical Course of True Love in the Sepik. In *Contemporary Pacific Societies: Studies in Development and Change*, ed. Victoria S. Lockwood, Thomas G. Harding, and Ben J. Wallace, 233–248. Englewood Cliffs, NJ: Prentice-Hall.
———. 1995. *Articulating Change in the 'Last Unknown'*. Boulder: Westview Press.
Evans-Pritchard, E.E. 1940. *The Nuer*. Oxford: Clarendon Press.
———. 1962. *Social Anthropology and Other Essays*. New York: The Free Press.
Eves, Richard. 2003. AIDS and Apocalypticism: Interpretations of the Epidemic from Papua New Guinea. *Culture, Health and Sexuality* 5 (3): 249–264.
Eves, Richard. 2010. Masculinity Matters: Men, Gender-Based Violence and the AIDS Epidemic in Papua New Guinea. In *Civic Insecurity: Law, Order and HIV in Papua New Guinea*, ed. Vicki Luker and Sinclair Dinnen, 47–79. Canberra: Australian National University Press.
Ewing, Katerine P. 1997. *Arguing Sainthood: Modernity, Psychoanalysis, and Islam*. Durham, NC: Duke University Press.
Fabian, J. 1983. *Time and the Other: How Anthropology Makes Its Object*. New York: Columbia University Press.
Featherstone, Mike. 1998. Love and Eroticism: An Introduction. *Theory, Culture and Society* 15(3–4): 1–18.
Ferguson, K.E., and P. Turnbull. 1999. *Oh, Say, Can You See? The Semiotics of the Military Hawaii*. Minneapolis: University of Minnesota.
Filer, C. 2012. The Development Forum in Papua New Guinea: Evaluating Outcomes for Local Communities. In *Community Futures, Legal Architecture: Foundations for Indigenous Peoples in the Global Mining Boom*, ed. M. Langton and J. Longbottom. Oxford, UK: Routledge.

Finney, Ben. 1973. *Big-Men and Business: Entrepreneurship and Economic Growth in the New Guinea Highlands.* Honolulu: University of Hawaii Press.
Fleetwood, Lorna. 1984. *A Short History of Wewak.* Wewak: Wirui Press.
Fong, M.W.L. 2009. Technology Leapfrogging for Developing Countries. IGI Global. http://journalistsresource.org/wp-content/uploads/2013/04/Technology-Leapfrogging-for-Developing-Countries.pdf. Accessed 15 March 2012.
Fortes, M. 1938/1970. Social and Psychological Aspects of Education in Taleland. In *From Child to Adult,* ed. J. Middleton, 14–74. New York: Natural History Press.
———. 1973. On the Concept of the Person among the Tallensi. In *La Notion de personne en Afrique noire,* no. 544, pp. 289–319. Paris: Colloques Internationaux du Centre National de la Recherche Scientifique.
Fortune, R. 1939. Warfare. *American Anthropologist* 41: 22–41.
Foster, R. 1995. *Social Reproduction and History in Melanesia.* Cambridge: Cambridge University Press.
———. 2002. *Materializing the Nation: Commodities, Consumption and Media in Papua New Guinea.* Bloomington: Indiana University Press.
———. 2005. Commodity Futures: Labour, Love and Value. *Anthropology Today* 21 (4): 8–12.
Foucault, Michel. 1970/1994. *The Order of Things: An Archaeology of the Human Sciences.* New York: Pantheon.
———. 1977/1995. *Discipline and Punish: The Birth of the Prison,* trans. Alan Sheridan. New York: Pantheon.
Frazer, J.G. 1890/2009. *The Golden Bough.* Oxford: Oxford University Press.
Frye, Northrup. 1957. *Anatomy of Criticism: Four Essays.* Princeton, NJ: Princeton University Press.
Gadlin, Howard. 1977. Private Lives and Public Order: A Critical View of the History of Intimate Relations in the United States. In *Close Relationships: Perspectives on the Meaning of Intimacy,* ed. George Levinger and Harold Rausch, 56–70. Amherst: University of Massachusetts Press.
Galison, P. 1994. The Ontology of the Enemy: Norbert Weiner and the Cybernetic Vision. *Critical Inquiry* 21 (1): 228–266.
Garap, S. 2000. Struggles of Women and Girls—Simbu Province, Papua New Guinea. In *Reflections on Violence in Melanesia,* ed. S. Dinnen and A. Ley, 159–171. Annendale: Hawkins Press.
Geertz, C. 1973. *The Interpretation of Cultures.* New York: Basic Books.
Gell, Alfred. 1998. *Art and Agency: An Anthropological Theory.* Oxford: Oxford University Press.
Gennep, Arnold van. 1912/1960. *The Rites of Passage,* trans. M.B. Vizedom and G.L. Caffee. Chicago: University of Chicago Press.
Geshiere, P. 1997. *The Modernity of Witchcraft.* Trans. P. Geshiere and J. Roitman. Virginia: University of Virginia Press.

Gewertz, D. 1983. *Sepik River Societies: A Historical Ethnography of the Chambri and Their Neighbors.* New Haven, CT: Yale University Press.

Gewertz, Deborah, and Frederick Errington. 1991. *Twisted Histories, Altered Contexts: Representing the Chambri in a World System.* Cambridge: Cambridge University Press.

———. 1992. The Historical Course of True Love in the Sepik. In *Contemporary Pacific Societies: Studies in Development and Change*, ed. V.S. Lockwood, T.G. Harding, and B.J. Wallace. Englewood Cliffs, NJ: Prentice-Hall.

———. 1999. *Emerging Class in Papua New Guinea: The Telling of Difference.* Cambridge: Cambridge University Press.

Gibson, H., and S. Venkateswar. 2015. Anthropological Engagement with the Anthropocene. *Environment and Society: Advances in Research* 6: 5–27.

Giddens, A. ed. 1972. *Emile Durkheim; Selected Writings.* London: Cambridge University Press.

———. 1984. *The Constitution of Society.* Cambridge: Polity Press.

———. 1990. *The Consequences of Modernity.* Stanford: Stanford University Press.

———. 1991. *Modernity and Self-Identity: Self and Society in the Late Modern Age.* Stanford: Stanford University Press.

———. 1992. *The Transformation of Intimacy: Sexuality, Love and Eroticism in Modern Societies.* Stanford: Stanford University Press.

Gilberthorpe, Emma. 2013. In the Shadow of Industry: A Study of Culturization in Papua New Guinea. *Journal of the Royal Anthropological Institute* 19: 216–278.

Gillespie, A., and W. Burns, ed. 2000. *Climate Change in the South Pacific: Impacts and Responses in Australia, New Zealand and Small Island States.* The Netherlands: Kluwer Academic Publishers.

Gillis, John R. 1988. From Ritual to Romance: Toward an Alternative History of Love. In *Emotion and Social Change*, ed. Carol Z. Stearns and Peter N. Stearns, 87–122. New York: Holmes and Meier.

Gilman, Eric L., Joanna Ellison, Vainauupo Jungblut, Hanneke Van Lavieren, Lisette Wilson, Rancis Areki, Genevieve Brighouse, et al. 2006. Adapting to Pacific Island Mangrove Response to Sea Level Rise and Climate Change. *Climate Research* 32: 161–176.

Glass, Patrick 1987. Trobriand Symbolic Geography. *Man* (NS) 23(1): 56–76.

Gluckman, M. 1955/1969. *Custom and Conflict in Africa.* New York: Harper and Row.

Goddard, Michael. 1992. Big-Man, Thief: The Social Organization of Gangs in Port Moresby. *Canberra Anthropology* 15(1): 20–34.

———. 1995. The Rascal Road: Crime, Prestige and Development in Papua New Guinea. *The Contemporary Pacific* 7: 55–80.

———. 2001. From Rolling Thunder to Reggae: Imagining Squatter Settlements in Papua New Guinea. *The Contemporary Pacific* 13(1): 1–32.

———. 2005. *The Unseen City: Anthropological Perspectives on Port Moresby.* Canberra: Pandanus Books.

Golub, A. 2015. *Leviathans at the Gold Mine: Creating Indigenous and Corporate Actors in Papua New Guinea.* Durham, NC: Duke University Press.

Goode, William J. 1959/1973. The Theoretical Importance of Love. Reprinted in *Love, Marriage, Family: A Developmental Approach*, ed. Marcia E. Lasswell and Thomas E. Lasswell, 162–169. Glenview, IL: Scott, Foresman and Co.

Goody, Jack. 1998. *Food and Love: A Cultural History of East and West.* London: Verso.

Gregory, C. 1982. *Gifts and Commodities.* New York: Academic Press.

———. 1997. *Savage Money: The Anthropology and Politics of Commodity Exchange.* London: Gordon and Breach.

Griffiths, J. 1986. What Is Legal Pluralism? *Journal of Legal Pluralism* 24: 1–55.

Grossman, L. 1984. *Peasants, Subsistence Ecology and Development in the Highlands of Papua New Guinea.* Princeton, NJ: Princeton University Press.

Gupta, Akhil, and James Ferguson. 1992. Beyond 'Culture': Space, Identity, and the Politics of Difference. *Cultural Anthropology* 7(10): 6–23.

Gutmann, Matthew C. 1996. *The Meanings of Macho: Being a Man in Mexico City.* Berkeley: University of California Press.

———, ed. 2003. *Changing Men and Masculinities in Latin America.* Durham, NC: Duke University Press.

Gutmann, Matthew C., and Mara Viveros Vigoya. 2005. Masculinities in Latin America. In *Handbook of Studies on Men and Masculinities*, ed. Michael S. Kimmel, Jeff Hearn, and R.W. Connell, 114–128. Thousand Oaks, CA: Sage.

Habermas, Jürgen. 1979. *Communication and the Evolution of Society.* Trans. T. McCarthy. Boston: Beacon Press.

———. 1984. *Theory of Communicative Action: Reason and the Rationalization of Society.* Vol. 1. Trans. T. McCarthy. Boston: Beacon Press.

———. 1987. *The Philosophical Discourse of Modernity: Twelve Lectures.* Trans. F. Lawrence. Cambridge, MA: MIT Press.

———. 1989/2001. *The Structural Transformation of the Public Sphere.* Cambridge, MA: MIT Press.

Haley, Nicole. 2008. Sung Adornment: Changing Masculinities at Lake Kopiago, Papua New Guinea. *The Australian Journal of Anthropology* 19(2): 213–229.

Hallowell, A. Irving. 1955. *Culture and Experience.* Philadelphia: University of Pennsylvania Press.

———. 1960. Ojibwa Ontology, Behavior and World View. In *Culture in History: Essays in Honor of Paul Radin*, ed. Stanley Diamond, 19–52. New York: Columbia University Press.

Hallstone, M. 2002. Updating Howard Becker's Theory of Using Marijuana for Pleasure. *Contemporary Drug Problems* 29: 821–844.

Halvaksz, Jamon. 2003. Singing About the Land Among the Biangai. *Oceania* 73: 153–169.

———. 2006. Drug Bodies: Relations of Substance in the Wau Bulolo Valley. *Oceania* 76(3): 235–246.

———. 2013. Mining the Forest: Epical and Novelesque Boundaries along the Upper Bulolo River, Papua New Guinea. In *The Ecotourism-Extraction Nexus: Political Economies and Rural Realities of (un)Comfortable Bedfellows*, ed. B. Buscher and V. Davidov. London: Routledge.

Halvaksz, Jamon, and David Lipset. 2006. Another Kind of Gold: An Introduction to Marijuana in Papua New Guinea. *Oceania* 76(3): 209–216.

Hammar, L. 2010. *Sin, Sex, and Stigma: A Pacific Response to HIV and AIDS*. London: Sean Kingston.

Handler, Richard. 1988. *Nationalism and the Politics of Culture in Quebec*. Madison: University of Wisconsin Press.

Hannertz, Ulf. 1990. Cosmopolitans and Locals in World Culture. In *Global Culture: Nationalism, Globalization and Modernity*, 237–252. London: Sage.

———. 1992. *Cultural Complexities: Studies in the Social Organization of Meaning*. New York: Columbia University Press.

Harley, Christopher, et al. 2006. The Impacts of Climate Change in Coastal Marine Systems. *Ecology Letters* 9: 228–241.

Harris, Bruce. 1988. The Rise of Rascalism: Action and Reaction in the Evolution of Rascal Gangs. Discussion Paper 54. Port Moresby, PNG: Institute of Applied Social and Economic Research.

Harris, Helen. 1995. Rethinking Heterosesxual Relations in Polynesia: A Case Study of Mangaia, Cook Island. In *Romantic Passion: A Universal Experience?* ed. William Jankowiak, 95–127. New York: Columbia University Press.

Harrison, Simon J. 1986. *Laments for Foiled Marriages: Love-Songs from a Sepik River Village*. Boroko, Papua New Guinea: Institute of Papua New Guinea Studies.

———. 1992. Ritual Knowledge as Intellectual Property. *Man* (n.s.) 27(10): 225–244.

———. 2000. From Prestige Goods to Legacies: Property and the Objectification of Culture in Melanesia. *Comparative Study of History and Society* 20(3): 662–679.

———. 1993. *The Mask of War: Ritual and the Self in Melanesia*. Manchester: Manchester University Press.

Hart Nibbrig, N.E. 1992. Rascals in Paradise: Urban Gangs in Papua New Guinea. *Pacific Studies* 151: 115–134.

Hartley, L.P. 1953. *The Go-Between*. London: Hamish Hamilton.

Hatfield, Donald J. 2002. Fate and the Narrativity and Experience of Selfhood. *American Ethnologist* 29(4): 857–877.

Hayes, T. 2003. They Are Beginning to Learn the Use of Tobacco: Cultural Context and the Creation of a Passion in Colonial Papua New Guinea. In *Drugs, Labor and Colonial Expansion*, ed. W. Jankowiak and D. Bradburd, 132–145. Tucson, Arizona: University of Arizona Press.

Heald, S. 1999. *Manhood and Morality: Sex, Violence and Ritual in Gisu Society.* London: Routledge.
Healy, C.J. 1985. New Guinea Inland Trade: Transformation and Resilience in the Context of Capitalist Penetration. *Mankind* 15: 127–144.
Hegel, Georg Wilhelm Friedich. 1948 *Early Theological Writings*, trans. T.M. Knox. Chicago: University of Chicago Press.
Herdt, Gilbert. 1981. *Guardians of the Flutes: Idioms of Masculinity.* New York: McGraw Hill.
Hermann, E., W. Kempf, and T. van Meijl. 2014. *Belonging in Oceania: Place-Making and Multiple Identifications.* New York: Berghahn.
Hertz, Robert. 1907/1960. The Collective Representation of Death. In *Death and the Right Hand*, trans. R. Needham and C. Needham, 122–150. Glencoe, IL: The Free Press.
Hijazi-Omarai, H., and R. Ribak. 2008. Playing With Fire: On the Domestication of the Mobile Phone Among Palestinian Teenage Girls in Israel. *Information, Communication and Society* 11 (2): 149–166.
Hobbes, Thomas. 1651/1972. *Leviathan*, ed. Michael Oakeshott. Oxford: Basil Blackwell.
Hobsbawm, Eric. 1969. *Bandits.* Chicago: Weidenfeld & Nicolson.
Hobsbawm, E., and T. Ranger, ed. 1982. *The Invention of Tradition.* Cambridge: Cambridge University Press.
Hodgson, Dorothy. 1999. 'Once Intrepid Warriors': Modernity and the Production of Maasai Masculinities. *Ethnology* 38(2): 121–150.
———. 2001. *Once Intrepid Warriors: Gender, Ethnicity and the Cultural Politics of Maasai Development.* Bloomington, IN: Indiana University Press.
Hogbin, Ian. 1970. *The Island of the Menstruating Men: Religion in Wogeo, New Guinea.* Melbourne: Melbourne University Press.
Hokowhitu, B. 2004. Tackling Maori Masculinity: A Colonial Genealogy of Savagery and Sport. *The Contemporary Pacific* 16 (2): 259–284.
Horkheimer, Max, and Theodore W. Adorno. 1955. *Dialectic of Enlightenment*, trans. John Cumming. New York: Continuum.
Horst, H., and D. Miller. 2006. *The Cell Phone: An Anthropology of Communication.* London: Berg Publishers.
Horton, John. 1964. The Dehumanization of Anomie and Alienation: A Problem in the Ideology of Sociology. *The British Journal of Sociology* 15 (4): 283–300.
Huber, Mary Taylor. 1988. *The Bishop's Progress: A Historical Ethnography of Catholic Missionary Experience on the Sepik Frontier.* Washington, DC: Smithsonian Institution Press.
Hughes, P., and L. Bualia. 1990. Murik Lakes and the Mouth of the Sepik River, Papua New Guinea. In *Implications of Expected Climatic Changes in the South Pacific Region: An Overview*, ed. J.C. Pernetta and P.J. Hughes, 243–246. Nairobi: UNEP.

Ingold, Tim. 2000. *The Perception of the Environment: Essays in Livelihood, Dwelling and Skill*. New York: Routledge.
INSRRT. 1994. *Intergovernmental Panel on Climate Change 2007*. Climate Report 2007: Synthesis Report, Summary for Policy Makers. http://www.ipcc.ch/ipccreports/ar4-syr.htm (accessed 15 March 2009).
Jacka, J. 2015. *Alchemy in the Rain Forest: Politics, Ecology and Resilience in a New Guinea Mining Area*. Durham, NC: Duke University Press.
Jakobson, Roman. 1971. The Dominant. In *Readings in Russian Poetics: Formalist and Structuralist Views*, ed. Latislav Matejka and K. Pomorska, 23–30. Cambridge: MIT Press.
James, Henry. 1898. *The Turn of the Screw*. New York: Macmillan.
Jameson, F. 1981. *The Political Unconscious: Narrative as a Socially Symbolic Act*. Ithaca, NY: Cornell University Press.
Jankowiak, W., and Edward Fischer. 1992. A Cross-Cultural Perspective on Romantic Love. *Ethnology* 31: 149–155.
Jankowiak, W., and D. Bradburd. 1996. Using Drug Foods to Capture and Enhance Labor: A Cross-Cultural Perspective. *Current Anthropology* 37: 717–720.
Jenkins, C., and M. Alpers. 1996. Urbanization, Youth and Sexuality: Insights for an AIDS Campaign for Youth in Papua New Guinea. *Papua New Guinea Medical Journal* 39: 248–251.
Jeudy-Ballini, Monique, and Bernard Juillerat. 2002. *People and Things: Social Mediations in Oceania*. Durham: Carolina University Press.
Jolly, Margaret. 2012. Introduction—Engendering Violence in Papua New Guinea: Persons, Power and Perilous Transformations. In *Engendering Violence in Papua New Guinea*, ed. M. Jolly, C. Stewart, and C. Brewer. Canberra: ANU E-Press.
Jolly, M., C. Stewart, and C. Brewer, eds. 2012. *Engendering Violence in Papua New Guinea*. Canberra: ANU E-Press.
Jorgensen, D. n.d. *Gespaia: Mobile Phones, Phone Friends and Anonymous Intimacy in Contemporary Papua New Guinea*. Paper presented at the annual meetings of the Canadian Anthropological Association, 30 April 2014.
Katz, J.E., and M.A. Aakhus, eds. 2002. *Perpetual Contact: Mobile Communication, Private Talk, Public Performance*. Cambridge: Cambridge University.
Keesing, Roger, and Robert Tonkinson. 1982. Reinventing Traditional Culture: The Politics of Kastom in Island Melanesia. *Mankind* 13(3): 374–399.
Kelman, I., and J. West. 2009. Climate Change and Small Island Developing States: A Critical Review. *Ecological and Environmental Anthropology* 5 (1): 1–16.
Kempf, Wolfgang. 2002. The Politics of Incorporation: Masculinity, Spatiality and Modernity among the Ngaing of Papua New Guinea. *Oceania* 73(1): 56–78.

Kennish, Michael J. 2002. Environmental Threats and Environmental Future of Estuaries. *Environmental Conservation* 29(1): 78–107.
Kim, K.-K. 2003. *Order and Agency in Modernity: Talcott Parsons, Erving Goffman and Harold Garfinkel*. Albany: State University of New York Press.
Kirsch, S. 2006. *Reverse Anthropology: Indigenous Analysis of Social and Environmental Relations*. Stanford: Stanford University Press.
Klein, M. 1929. Infantile Anxiety-Situations Reflected in Art, Creative Impulse. *International Journal of Psychoanalysis* 10: 436–443.
Klein, Melanie, and Joan Riviere. 1953. Love, Hate, and Reparation. In *Psycho-Analytical Epitomes 2*. London: Hogarth Press.
Kligerman, C. 1980. Art and the Self of the Artist. In *Advances in Self-Psychology*, ed. A. Goldberg, 383–406. New York: International Universities Press.
Koczberski, G., and G.N. Curry. 2004. Divided Communities and Contested Landscapes: Mobility, Development and Shifting Identities in Migration Destination Sites in Papua New Guinea. *Asia Pacific Viewpoint* 45 (3): 357–373.
Kohut, Heinz. 1973. *The Analysis of the Self*. New York: International Universities Press.
Knauft, B. 1987. Managing Sex and Anger: Tobacco and Kava Use Among the Gebusi of Papua New Guinea. In *Drugs in Western Pacific Societies: Relations of Substance*, ed. L. Lindstrom, 73–98. Association for Social Anthropology of Oceania, Monograph #11. Lanham, MD: University Press of America.
———. 2002. *Exchanging the Past*. Chicago: University of Chicago Press.
Kraemer, D. 2015. Do You Have a Mobile': Mobile Phone Practices and the Refashioning of Social Relationships in Port Vila Town. *The Australian Journal of Anthropology*. doi:10.1111/taja.12165. Accessed 15 March 2015.
Kranzfelder, Ivo. 1995. *Edward Hopper, 1882–1967: Vision of Reality*. Koln: Benedikt Taschen.
Kulick, Don. 1993. Heroes from Hell: Representations of 'Rascals' in a Papua New Guinean Village. *Anthropology Today* 9(3): 9–14.
Kuper, Adam. 1988. *The Invention of Primitive Society*. London: Routledge.
Lacan, Jacques. 1977a. Desire and the Interpretation of Desire in Hamlet. *Yale French Studies* 55(56): 11–52.
———. 1977b. *Ecrits: A Selection*, trans. Alan Sheridan. London: Tavistock.
———. 1988. *The Seminar. Book II: The Ego in Freud's Theory and in the Technique of Psychoanalysis 1954–1955*, trans. A. Sheridan. Cambridge: Cambridge University Press.
———. 1981/1993. *The Psychoses 1955–1956: The Seminar of Jacques Lacan, Book III*, ed. Jacques-Alain Miller. Trans. Russell Grigg. New York: Norton.
Laidler, Gita. 2006. Inuit and Scientific Perspectives on the Relationship between Sea Ice and Climate Change: The Ideal Complement? *Climate Change* 78: 407–444.

Lakhani, S. and A.M. Willman (2014) *The Socio-economic Costs of Crime and Violence in Papua New Guinea: Recommendations for Policy and Programs.* Washington, DC: World Bank. https://openknowledge.worldbank.org/handle/10986/18974 License: CC BY 3.0 IGO

Lakoff, George, and Mark Turner. 1989. *More Than Cool Reason: A Field Guide to Poetic Metaphor.* Chicago: University of Chicago Press.

Lal, M., et al. 2002. Future Climate Change and Its Impacts Over Small Island States. *Climate Research* 19(3): 179–192.

Landes, David. 1983. *Revolution in Time: Clocks and the Making of the Modern World.* Cambridge, MA: Belnap Press.

Landes, Ruth. 1937. *Ojibwa Sociology.* New York: Columbia University Press.

Larmour, P. 1998. State and Society in Papua New Guinea. In *Modern Papua New Guinea*, ed. L. Zimmer-Tamakoshi, 21–30. Kirksville, MO: Thomas Jefferson Press.

Lash, Scott, and John Urry. 1994. *Economies of Signs and Spaces.* London: Sage.

Lattas, A. 1993. Sorcery and Colonialism: Illness, Dreams and Death as Political Languages in West New Britain. *Man* (NS) 28(1): 51–77.

Lavie, S., K. Narayan, and R. Rosaldo, ed. 1993. *Creativity/Anthropology.* Ithaca, NY: Cornell University Press.

Lawrence, Peter, and M. Meggitt. 1965. *Gods, Ghosts and Men in Melanesia; Some Religions of Australian New Guinea and the New Hebrides.* Melbourne: Oxford University Press.

Layton, Robert. 2003. Art and Agency: A Reassessment. *Journal of the Royal Anthropological Institute* (N.S.) 9(3): 447–464.

Lazrus, Heather. 2009. The Governance of Vulnerability: Climate Change and Agency in Tuvalu, South Pacific. In *Anthropology and Climate Change: From Encounters to Actions*, ed. Susan A. Crate and Mark Nuttall, 240–249. Walnut Creek, CA: Left Coast Press.

Lea, D. 2005. The PNG Forest Industry, Incorporated Entities and Environmental Protection. *Pacific Economic Bulletin* 20 (1): 168–177.

Leach, Edmund. 1958. Magical Hair. *Journal of the Royal Anthropological Institute* 88(1): 147–164.

———. 1961. Two Essays Concerning the Symbolic Representation of Time. In *Rethinking Anthropology*, 174–186. London: Athone.

Leach, J. 2004. Modes of Creativity. In *Transactions and Creations: Property Debates and the Stimulus of Melanesia*, ed. E. Hirsch and M. Strathern, 151–175. New York: Berghahn Books.

Leach, J., and E. Leach. 1983. *The Kula: New Perspectives on Massim Exchange.* Cambridge: Cambridge University Press.

Legra, Leo, Xingong Li, and A. Townsend Peterson. 2008. Biodiversity Consequences of Sea Level Rise in New Guinea. *Pacific Conservation Biology* 14: 191–199.

Lemish, D., and A.A. Cohen. 2005. Tell Me About Your Mobile and I'll Tell You Who You Are: Israelis Talk About Themselves. In *Mobile Communications: Renegotiation of the Social Sphere*, ed. R. Ling and P.E. Pedersen. London: Springer.
Lepani, Kathleen. 2008. Mobility, Violence and the Gendering of HIV in Papua New Guinea. *The Australian Journal of Anthropology* 19(2): 150–164.
LeVine, R.A. 1973. *Culture, Behavior, and Personality*. Chicago: Aldine.
Levi-Strauss, C. 1955. *Tristes Tropiques*. Trans. J. Russell. New York: Penguin.
———. 1966. *The Savage Mind*. Chicago: University of Chicago Press.
———. 1949/1969. *The Elementary Structures of Kinship*. Trans. J.H. Bell and J.R. von Sturmer. Boston: Beacon Press.
Lindholm, Charles. 2001. *Culture and Identity: The History, Theory, and Practice of Psychological Anthropology*. New York: McGraw-Hill.
Lindsay, L.A., and S.F. Miescher. 2003. *Men and Masculinities in Modern Africa*. Portsmouth: Heinemann.
Lindstrom, L. ed. 1982. *Drugs in Western Pacific Societies: Relations of Substance*. Association for Social Anthropology of Oceania, Monograph 11. Lanham: University Press of America.
Lindstrom, L. 2011. Urban Tannese: Local Perspectives of Settlement Life in Port Vila. *Le Journal de la Société des Océanistes* 133: 255–266.
Ling, R., and L. Haddon. 2003. Mobile Telephony, Mobility and the Coordination of Everyday Life. In *Machines That Become Us: The Social Context of Personal Communication Technology*, ed. J.E. Katz. Transaction: New Brunswick.
Ling, R., and B. Yttri. 2002. Hyper-Coordination via Mobile Phones in Norway. In *Perpetual Contact: Mobile Communication, Private Talk, Public Performance*, ed. J.E. Katz and M.A. Aarkus. Cambridge: Cambridge University Press.
Linniken, J. 1983. Defining Tradition: Variations on the Hawaiian Tradition. *American Ethnologist* 10(2): 241–252.
Lipset, David. 1985. Seafaring Sepiks: Ecology, Warfare and Prestige in Murik Trade. *Annual Review of Research in Economic Anthropology* 7: 67–94.
———. 1989. Papua New Guinea: The Melanesian Ethic and the Spirit of Capitalism, 1975–86. In *Democracy in Developing Countries*, ed. L. Diamond, J.J. Linz and S.M. Lipset, vol. 3, 383–423. Boulder, CO: Lynne Rienner.
———. 1990. Boars' Tusks and Flying Foxes: Symbolism and Ritual of Office in the Murik Lakes. In *Sepik Heritage: Tradition and Change in Papua New Guinea*, ed. Nancy Lutkehaus, Christian Kaufmann, William E. Mitchell, Douglas Newton, Lita Osmundsen, and Meinhard Schuster, 286–298. Durham, NC: Carolina University Press.
———. 1997. *Mangrove Man: Dialogics of Culture in the Sepik Estuary*. Cambridge: Cambridge University Press.
———. 2004a. 'The Trial': A Parody of the Law Amid the Mockery of Men in Post-Colonial Papua New Guinea. *Journal of the Royal Anthropological Institute* (N.S.) 10(1): 63–89.

———. 2004b. Modernity without Romance: Masculinity and Desire in Courtship Stories Told by Young Papua New Guinean Men. *American Ethnologist* 31(2): 205–224.

———. 2005. Dead Canoes: The Fate of Agency in 20th Century Murik Art. *Social Analysis* 49(1): 109–140.

———. 2007. Women without Qualities: More Courtship Stories by Papua New Guinea Youth. *Ethnology* 46(2): 219–232.

———. 2009. A Melanesian Pygmalion: Masculine Creativity and Symbolic Castration in a Postcolonial Backwater. *Ethos* 37: 50–77.

———. 2011. The Tides: Masculinity and Climate Change in Coastal Papua New Guinea. *Journal of the Royal Anthropology Institute* (N.S.) 17: 2–43.

———. 2013. The New State of Nature: Rising Sea-Levels, Climate Justice and Community-Based Adaptation in Papua New Guinea (2003–2011). *Conservation and Society* 11 (2): 144.157.

———. 2014a. Place in the Anthropocene: A Mangrove Lagoon in Papua New Guinea in the Time of Rising Sea-Levels. *HAU: Journal of Ethnographic Theory* 4 (3): 215–243.

———. 2014b. Living Canoes: Vehicles of Moral Imagination Among the Murik of Papua New Guinea. In *Vehicles: Cars, Canoes and other Metaphors of Moral Imagination*, ed. David Lipset and Richard Handler, 21–47. New York: Berghahn.

———. 2015. On the Bridge: Class and the Chronotope of Romance in an American Love Story. *Anthropology Quarterly* 88 (1): 165–186.

———. 2016a. Colonial and Postcolonial Museum Collecting in Papua New Guinea. *The Australian Journal of Anthropology* 27: 333–352.

———. 2016b. The Knotted Person: Death, the Bad Breast and Melanesian Modernity Among the Murik, Papua New Guine. In *Mortuary Dialogues: Death Rites and the Reproduction of Moral Community in Pacific Modernities*, ed. D. Lipset and E.K. Silverman, 81–109. New York: Berghahn.

Lipset, David, and E.K. Silverman. 2005. Dialogics of the Body: The Moral and the Grotesque in Two Sepik River Societies. *Journal of Ritual Studies* 19(2): 18–42.

Lipset, David, and J. Stritecky. 1994. The Problem of Mute Metaphor: Gender and Kinship in Seaboard Melanesia. *Ethnology* 33(1): 1–20.

Lipset, David, and Kathleen Barlow. 1987. The Value of Culture: Regional Exchange in the Lower Sepik. *Australian Natural History* 23(3): 156–168.

LiPuma, Edward. 1999. The Meaning of Money in the Age of Modernity. In *In Money and Modernity: State and Local Currencies in Melanesia*, ed. David Akin and Joel Robbins. Honolulu: University of Hawaii Press.

———. 2001. *Encompassing Others: The Magic of Modernity in Melanesia*. Ann Arbor: University of Michigan Press.

Logan, S. 2012. Rausim! Digital Politics in Papua New Guinea. SSGM Discussion Paper 2012/9. http://ips.cap.aun.edu.au/ssgm. Accessed 15 March 2014.
Lohmann, Roger, ed. 2003. *Dream Travelers: Sleep Experiences and Culture in the Western Pacific*. New York: Palgrave Macmillan.
Lowenthal, David. 1985. *The Past is a Foreign Country*. Cambridge, UK: Cambridge University Press.
Luhmann, Niklas. 1986. *Love as Passion: The Codification of Intimacy*. Cambridge: Harvard University Press.
Luhrmann, T.M. 2010. Stanford Survey Contemplates iPhone Addiction. http://www.macworld.com/article/1146957/iphone_addiction.html. Accessed 3 May 2013.
Luker, Vicki, and Michael Monsell-Davis. 2010. Teasing Out the Tangle: Raskols, Young Men, Crime and HIV. In *Civic Insecurity*, ed. Vicki Luker and Sinclair Dinnen, 81–115. Canberra: Australian National University EPress.
Luker, Vicki, and Sinclair Dinnen. 2010. *Civic Insecurity: Law, Order and HIV in Papua New Guinea*. Canberra: Australian National University Press.
Lusby, S. 2014. Preventing Violence at Home, Allowing Violence in the Workplace: A Case Study of Security Guards in Papua New Guinea. *In Brief* 2014/49. ips.cap.anu.edu.au/ssgm
MacDonald, Fraser and Jonathan Kirami. 2015. Women, Mobile Phones and M16s: Contemporary New Guinea Highlands Warfare. *The Australian Journal of Anthropology*. http://dx.doi.org/10.1111/taja.12175. Accessed 19 January 2017.
MacFarlane, Alan. 1986. *Marriage and Love in England*: 1300–1840. London: Blackwell.
Macintyre, Martha. 2008. Police and Thieves, Gunmen and Drunks: Problems with Men and Problems with Society in Papua New Guinea. *The Australian Journal of Anthropology* 19(2): 179–193.
Macnaghten, P. and J. Urry. 1998. *Contested Natures*. London: Sage.
Macpherson, C.B. 1962. *The Political Theory of Possessive Individualism: Hobbes to Locke*. Oxford: Oxford University Press.
Maggi, Wynne. 2001. *Our Women Are Free: Gender and Ethnicity in the Hindukush*. Ann Arbor: University of Michigan Press.
Malinowski, B. 1922. *Argonauts of the Western Pacific*. New York: E.P. Dutton & Co.
Malinowski, B. 1929/1987. *The Sexual Life of Savages*. Boston: Beacon Press.
Malm, A., and A. Hornborg. 2014. The Geology of Mankind: A Critique of the Anthropocene Narrative. *The Anthropocene Review* 1 (1): 62–69.
Marksbury, Richard A. 1995. Marriage in Transition in Oceania. In *The Business of Marriage: Transformations of Oceanic Matrimony*, ed. Richard A. Marksbury, 3–26. Pittsburgh: University of Pittsburgh Press.
Marland, G., T. Boden, and B. Andres. 2006. *Trends: A Compendium of Data on Global Change*. Carbon Dioxide Information Analysis Center, Oak Ridge

National Laboratory, U.S. Department of Energy. http://cdiac.esd.ornl.gov/trends/emis/top2000.tot [2003, 10/10/2003].

Marrett, A. 2000. Ghostly Voices: Some Observations on Song-Creation, Ceremony and Being in NW Australia. *Oceania* 71(1): 18–29.

Martin, Keir. 2013. *The Death of the Big Men and the Rise of the Big Shots: Custom and Conflict in East New Britain.* New York: Berghahn.

Marx, Karl. 1963. *Karl Marx: Early Writings*, ed. T.B. Bottomore. New York: McGraw Hill.

Marx, Karl. 1867/1990. *Capital: A Critique of Political Economy*, trans. Ben Fowkes, vol. 1. New York: Penguin.

Marx, Karl, and Frederich Engels. 1888/2002. *The Communist Manifesto*. London: Penguin Classics.

Mauss, Marcel. 1954/1967. *The Gift: Forms and Functions of Exchange in Archaic Societies*, trans. I. Cunnison. New York: Norton Library.

McArthur, P.H. 2008. Ambivalent Fantasies: Local Prehistories and Global Dramas in the Marshall Islands. *Journal of Folklore Research* 45 (3): 263–298.

McClintock, A. 1995. *Imperial Leather: Race, Gender and Sexuality in the Colonial Contest.* New York: Routledge.

McCormack, F., and K. Barclay, eds. 2013. *Engaging with Capitalism: Cases From Oceania.* Bingley, UK: Emerald Group.

McGavin, K. 2014. Being "Nesian": Pacfiic Islander Identity in Australia. *The Contemporary Pacific* 26 (1): 126–154.

McGuigan, J. 2005. Towards a Sociology of the Mobile Phone. *Human Technology* 1 (1): 45–57.

McLuhan, M. 1964. *Understanding Media: The Extensions of Man.* New York: New American Library.

Mead, M. 1935/1963. *Sex and Temperament in Three Primitive Societies.* New York: Morrow.

———. 1935/1961. *Coming of Age in Samoa.* New York: Morrow.

———. 1938. The Mountain Arapesh, an Importing Culture. *Anthropological Papers of the American Museum of Natural History* 36, Part 3.

Meeker, Michael, Kathleen Barlow, and David Lipset. 1986. Culture, Exchange and Gender: Lessons from the Murik. *Cultural Anthropology* 1(1): 6–74.

van Meijl, T. 2006. Multiple Identifications and the Dialogical Self: Urban Maori Youngsters and the Cultural Renaissance. *Journal of the Royal Anthropological Institute* 12: 917–933.

Meiser, L. 1955. The "Platform" Phenomenon Along the Northern Coast of New Guinea. *Anthropos* 50: 265–272.

Merton, R.K. 1938. Social Structure and Anomie. *American Sociological Review* 3: 672–682.

———. 1949. Social Structure and Anomie: Revisions and Extensions. In *The Family*, ed. R. Anshen, 226–257. New York: Harper Brothers.

———. 1957a. Continuities in the Theory of Social Structure and Anomie. In *Social Theory and Social Structure*, ed. R.K. Merton, 215–248. New York: The Free Press.

———. 1957b. Patterns of Influence: Local and Cosmopolitan Influentials. In *Social Theory and Social Structure*, ed. R.K. Merton, 441–474. New York: Free Press.

Miller, D. 1997. *Capitalism: An Ethnographic Approach*. Oxford: Berg.

Mintz, S. 1985. *Sweetness and Power: The Place of Sugar in Modern History*. New York: Penguin.

Moore, J.W. 2014. The Capitalocene, Part I: On the Nature and Origins of Our Ecological Crisis. http://www.jasonwmoore.com/uploads/The_Capitalocene__Part_I__June_2014.pdf. Accessed 15 March 2015.

Morauta, L. 1987. *Law and Order in a Changing Society*. Canberra: Department of Political and Social Change, Research School of Pacific Studies.

Morrell, Robert. 2001. *Changing Men in Southern Africa*. Pietermaritzburg: University of Natal Press.

Morell, Robert, and Sandra Swart. 2005. Men in the Third World: Postcolonial Perspectives on Masculinity. In *Handbook of Studies on Men and Masculinities*, ed. Michael S. Kimmel, Jeff Hearn, and R.W. Connell, 90–113. Thousand Oaks, CA: Sage.

Morris-Reich, Amos. 2005. From Autonomous Subject to Free Individual in Simmel and Lacan. *History of European Ideas* 31: 103–127.

Mosko, M. 2014. Malinowski Magical Puzzles: Towards a New Theory of Magic and Procreation in Trobriand Society. *HAU: Journal of Ethnographic Theory* 4(1): 1–47.

Mulvey, Laura. 1985. Visual Pleasure and Narrative Cinema. In *Film Theory and Criticism: Introductory Readings*, ed. G. Mast and M. Cohen, 803–816. New York: Oxford University Press.

Munck, Victor C. de. 1998. Lust, Love and Arranged Marriages in Sri Lanka. In *Romantic Love and Sexual Behavior, Perspectives from the Social Sciences*, ed. Victor C. de Munck, 285–300. Westport, CT: Praeger.

Munn, N. 1986. *The Fame of Gawa: A Symbolic Study of Value Transformation in a Massim (Papua New Guinea) Society*. Cambridge: Cambridge University Press.

———.1986. *Pintupi Country, Pintupi Self: Sentiment, Place and Politics Among Western Desert Aborigines*. Washington, DC: Smithsonian Institution Press.

Myers, Fred. 1979. Emotions and the Self: A Theory of Personhood and Political Order Among Western Desert Aborigines. *Ethos* 7: 343–70.

———. 1986. *Pintupi Country, Pintupi Self: Sentiment, Place and Politics Among Western Desert Aborigines*. Washington, D.C.: Smithsonian Institution Press.

Nicholls, Robert, and Jason A. Lowe. 2004. Benefits of Mitigation of Climate Change for Coastal Areas. *Global Environmental Change* 14: 229–244.

Nobus, Dany. 1999. Theorizing the Comedy of Sexes: Lacan on Sexuality. In *The Klein-Lacan Dialogues*, ed. Bernard Burgoyne and Mary Sullivan, 105–124. New York: Other Press.

Numbasa, G., and G. Koczberski. 2012. Migration, Informal Urban Settlements and Non-market Land Transactions: A Case Study of Wewak, East Sepik Province, Papua Guinea. *Australian Geographer* 43 (2): 143–161.

Nunn, Patrick. 2007. Holocene Sea-Level Change and Human Response in Pacific Islands. *Earth and Environmental Science Transactions of the Royal Society of Edinburgh* 98: 117–125.

Nutall, Mark. 2007. *An Environment at Risk: Arctic Indigenous Peoples, Local Livelihoods and Climate Change*. Berlin: Springer.

Oakes, Guy. ed. 1984. *Georg Simmel: On Women, Sexuality and Love*. New Haven: Yale University Press.

Oldyzko, A. 2000. The History of Communications and its Implications for the Internet. http://www.dtc.umn.edu/~odlyzko/doc/history.communications0.pdf. Accessed 15 March 2012.

Oliver-Smith, Anthony. 1996. Anthropological Research on Hazards and Disasters. *Annual Review of Anthropology* 25: 303–328.

Ong, Aihwa. 1987. *Spirits of Resistance and Capitalist Discipline: Factory Women in Malaysia*. Albany, NY: State University Press of New York.

Orlove, Ben. 2003. How People Name Seasons. In *Weather, Climate, Culture*, ed. Sarah Strauss and Benjamin S. Orlove, 121–140. London: Berg.

Orlove, B., E. Wiegandt, and B.H. Luckman. 2008. *Darkening Peaks: Glacier Retreat, Science and Society*. Berkeley: University of California Press.

Ortner, Sherry. 1981. Gender and Sexuality in Hierarchical Societies: The Case of Polynesia and some Comparative Implications. In *Sexual Meanings*, ed. Sherry Ortner and Harriet Whitehead, 359–410. Cambridge: Cambridge University Press.

———. 1996. *Making Gender: The Politics and Erotics of Culture*. Boston: Beacon Press.

Ouzagane, Lahoucine. 2006. *Islamic Masculinities*. New York: Zed Books.

Ouzgane, Lahoucine, and Robert Morrell, ed. 2005. *African Masculinities: Men in Africa from the Late Nineteenth Century to the Present*. New York: Palgrave Macmillan.

Ovid. 1955. *The Metamorphoses of Ovid*. Trans. M.M. Innes. London: Penguin.

Owen, C. 2005. *Betelnut Bisnis, a Video*. Filmcraft Pacific. http://www.imdb.com/title/tt0800312/. Accessed 15 March 2012.

Patterson, M., and M. Macintyre, eds. 2011. *Managing Modernity in the Western Pacific*. St. Lucia QLD: Queensland University Press.

Paz, Octavio. 1993. *The Double Flame: Love and Eroticism*. New York: Harcourt Brace.

Pernetta, John 1993. *Mangrove Forests, Climate and Sea Level Rise: Hydrological Influences on Community Structure and Survival, with Examples from the Indo-West Pacific.* SADAG, Bellegarde-Valserine, France: International Union for Conservation of Nature and Natural Resources.
Plotnicov, Leonard. 1995. Love, Love and Found in Nigeria. In *Romantic Passion: A Universal Experience?* ed. William Jankowiak, 128–140. New York: Columbia University Press.
Pickles, A. 2014. Bom Bombed Kwin: How Two Card Games Model Kula, Moka and Goroka. *Oceania (Special Issue)* 84 (3): 272–288.
Poirier, S. 1990. 'Nomadic' Rituals: Networks of Ritual Exchange between Women of the Australian Western Desert. *Man* (N.S.) 27(4): 757–776.
von Poser, A.Th. 2015. *The Accounts of Jong: A Discussion of Time, Space and Person in Kayan, Papua New Guinea.* Heidelberg: Universitatsverlag.
Price, Sally. 1989. *Primitive Art in Civilized Places.* Chicago: University of Chicago Press.
Rasmussen, Anders E. 2015. *In the Absence of the Gift: New Forms of Value and Personhood in a Papua New Guinea Community.* New York: Berghahn.
Redfield, Robert. 1951. *The Primitive World and Its Transformations.* Ithaca, NY: Cornell University Press.
Reed, Adam. 2003. *Papua New Guinea's Last Place.* New York: Berghahn.
Rheingold, H. 2002. *Smart Mobs: The Next Social Revolution.* New York: Basic Books.
Riesenfeld, A. 1947. Who are the Betel People? *Internationales Archiv fur Ethnographie* 45: 157–215.
Robbins, Joel. 1998. Becoming Sinners: Christianity and Desire Among the Urapmin of Papua New Guinea. *Ethnology* 37 (4): 299–316.
———. 2004. *Becoming Sinners: Christianity and Moral Torment in a Papua New Guinea Society.* Berkeley: University of California Press.
———. 2005. The Humiliations of Sin: Christianity and the Modernization of the Subject among the Urapmin. In *The Making of Global and Local Modernities in Melanesia: Humiliation, Transformation and the Nature of Cultural Change*, ed. Joel Robbins and Holly Wardlow, 43–56. Burlington, VT: Ashgate.
Robbins, J., and D. Akin. 1999. Introduction to Melanesian Currencies: Agency, Identity and Social Reproduction. In *In Money and Modernity: State and Local Currencies in Melanesia.* Honolulu: University of Hawaii Press.
Robbins, Joel, and Holly Wardlow, ed. 2005. *The Making of Global and Local Modernities in Melanesia: Humiliation, Transformation and the Nature of Cultural Change.* Burlington, VT: Ashgate.
Roberson, James E., and Nobue Suzuki, ed. 2003. *Men and Masculinities in Contemporary Japan: Dislocating the Salaryman Doxa.* London: Routledge Curzon.

Rodman, W. 1991. When Questions Are Answers: The Message of Anthropology, According to the People of Ambae. *American Anthropologist* 93(4): 421–434.
Rollason, W., ed. 2014. *Pacific Futures: Projects, Politics and Interests.* New York: Berghahn.
———. 2011. We Are Playing Football: Seeing the Game on Panapompom, PNG. *Journal of the Royal Anthropological Institute* 17: 481–503.
Rosaldo, R. 1989/1993. *Grief and a Headhunter's Rage. Reprinted in Culture and Truth.* New York: Routledge.
Roscoe, P. 1999. Return of the Ambush: 'Raskolism' in Rural Yangoru, East Sepik Province. *Oceania* 69: 171–183.
Rosi, Pamela, and Laura Zimmer-Takahasi. 1995. Love and Marriage Among the Educated Elite in Port Moresby. In *The Business of Marriage: Transformations of Oceanic Matrimony*, ed. Richard A. Marksbury, 175–204. Pittsburgh: University of Pittsburgh Press.
Rowley, C.D. 1965. *The New Guinea Villager.* Melbourne: F.W. Cheshire.
Rudiak-Gold, P. 2013. *Climate Change and Tradition in a Small Island State: The Rising Tides.* New York: Routledge.
Rumsey, A., and J. Weiner, eds. 2001. *Mining and Indigenous Lifeworlds in Australia and Papua New Guinea.* Wantage: Sean Kingston.
Sahlins, Marshall. 1963. Poor Man, Rich Man, Big-Man, Chief: Political Types in Melanesia and Polynesia. *Comparative Studies in Society and History* 5(3): 285–303.
———. 1972. *Stone Age Economics.* Chicago: Aldine-Atherton.
———. 1985. *Islands of History.* Chicago: University of Chicago Press.
———. 1993. Goodbye to Tristes Tropes: Ethnography in the Context of Modern World History. *Journal of Modern History* 65(1): 1–25.
Sai, Anastasia. 2007. Tamot: Masculinities in Transition in Papua New Guinea. PhD Thesis. Victoria University, Australia.
Salisbury, J.G. 1962. Early Stages of Economic Development in New Guinea. *Journal of the Polynesian Society* 71: 328–339.
Sanders, Todd. 2003. (En)gendering the Weather: Rainmaking and Reproduction in Tanzania. In *Weather, Climate, Culture*, ed. Sarah Strauss and Benjamin S. Orlove, 83–102. London: Berg.
Scheiflin, E.L. 1982. Cultural Dimensions of Alcohol Abuse in a South Pacific Nation. In *Through a Glass Darkly: Beer and Modernization in Papua New Guinea*, ed. M. Marshall, 49–57. Boroko, PNG: Institute of Applied Social and Economic Research.
Schieffelin, E.L., and R. Crittenden, eds. 1991. *Like People You See in a Dream: First Contact in Six Papuan Societies.* Stanford: Stanford University Press.
Schiltz, Marc. 1985. Rascalism, Tradition and the State in Papua New Guinea. In *Domestic Violence in Papua New Guinea*, ed. S. Toft. Port Moresby, PNG: Papua New Guinea Law Reform Commission.

Schmidt, Joseph. 1922–1923. Die Ethnographie der Nor-Papua (Murik-Kaup-Karau) bei Dallmanhafen, Neu-Guinea, trans. K. Barlow. *Anthropos* 18–19: 700–732.

———. 1926. Die Ethnographie der Nor-Papua (Murik-Kaup-Karau) bei Dallmanhafen, Neu-Guinea, trans. K. Barlow. *Anthropos* 21: 38–71.

———. 1933. Neue Beitrage zur Ethnographie der Nor-Papua (Neuguinea), trans. K. Barlow. *Anthropos* 28: 321–354, 663–682.

Schwartz, T. 1975. Cultural Totemism: Ethnic Identity Primitive and Modern. In *Ethnic Identity: Cultural Continuities and Change*, ed. G. De Vos and L. Romanucci-Ross, 106–132. Palo Alto, CA: Mayfield Publishing.

Scott, James. 1985. *Weapons of the Weak: Everyday Forms of Peasant Resistance*. New Haven: Yale University Press.

Seligman, A.B. 1997. *The Problem of Trust*. Princeton: Princeton University Press.

Sexton, L. 1986. Wok Meri: A Women's Savings and Exchange System in Highland Papua New Guinea. *Oceania* 52 (3): 167–198.

Sharp, T. 2016. Trade's Value: Relational Transactions in Papua New Guinea Betel Nut Trade. *Oceania* 86 (1): 75–91.

Sharp, T., J. Cox, C. Spark, S. Lusby, and M. Rooney. 2015. The Formal, the Informal and the Precarious: Making a Living in Urban Papua New Guinea. SSGM Discussion Paper 2015/2. http://ips.cap.anu.edu.au/ssgm

Shaw, G.B. 1913/2003. *Pygmalion*. London: Penguin Classics.

Shipton, P. 1989. *Bitter Money: Cultural Economy and Some African Meanings of Forbidden Commodities*. Washington, DC: American Anthropological Association.

Sillitoe, P. 1994. Whether Rain or Shine: Weather Regimes from a New Guinea Perspective. *Oceania* 64(3): 246–270.

———. 2014. Local Perceptions of Forest, Conservation and Logging in Papua New Guinea. *Revue d'ethnoecologie* 6. https://ethnoecologie.revues.org/1905

Sillitoe, P., and C. Filer. 2014. What Local People Want with Forests: Ideologies and Attitudes in Papua New Guinea. In *Natural Resource Extraction and Indigenous Livelihoods: Development Challenges in an Era of Globalization*, ed. E. Gilberthorpe and G. Hilson. Farnham: Ashgate Publishing Ltd.

Silverman, Eric K. 2016. The Waters of Mendangumeli: A Masculine Psychoanalytic Interpretation of a New Guinea Flood Myth—and Women's Laughter. *The Journal of American Folklore* 129 (512): 171–202.

Silverstone, R., and L. Haddon. 1998. Design and the Domestication of Information and Communication Technologies: Technical Change and Everyday Life. In *Communication by Design: The Politics of Information and Communication Technologies*, ed. R. Silverstone and R. Mansell. Oxford: Oxford University Press.

Simmel, Georg. 1950. *The Sociology of Georg Simmel*. Trans. Kurt H. Wolff. Glencoe, IL: The Free Press.

———. 1978. *The Philosophy of Money*. Trans. K.H. Wolf. Glencoe, IL: The Press Press.
———. 2007. The Philosophy of Lanscape. *Theory, Culture & Society* 24 (7–8): 20–29.
Singh, S. and Y. Nadarajah. 2011. School Fees, Beer and "Meri": Gender, Cash and the Mobile in the Morobe Province of Papua New Guinea. Institute for Money, Technology and Financial Inclusion Working Paper 2011-3. http://www.imtfi.uci.edu/files/blog_working_papers/working_paper_singh.pdf. Accessed 15 March 2012.
Sisson, J. 2014. *The Polynesian Iconoclasm: Religious Revolution and the Seasonality of Power*. Berghahn.
Silverman, Eric K. 1999a. Tourist Art as the Crafting of Identity in the Sepik River (Papua New Guinea). In *Unpacking Culture: Art and Commodity in Colonial and Postcolonial Worlds*, ed. Ruth B. Phillips and Christopher B. Steiner, 51–66. Berkeley: University of California Press.
———. 1999b. Art, Tourism and the Crafting of Identity in the Sepik River (Papua New Guinea). In *Unpacking Culture: Art and Commodity in Colonial and Postcolonial Worlds*, ed. R. Phillips and C. Steiner, 51–66. Berkeley: University of California Press.
———. 2001. *Masculinity, Motherhood, and Mockery: Psychoanalyzing Culture and the Iatmul Naven Rite in New Guinea*. Ann Arbor: University of Michigan Press.
Smit, Dirk, and Soroi Marepo Eoe. 1999. A Festival to Honour the Dead and Revitalize Society: Masks and Prestige in a Gamei Community (Lower Ramu, Papua New Guinea). In *Art and Performance in Oceania*, ed. Barry Craig, Bernie Kernot, and C. Anderson, 107–139. Honolulu: University of Hawaii Press.
Smith, E.B. [Laura Bohannan]. 1964. *Return to Laughter: An Anthropological Novel*. New York: Anchor.
Smith, M.F. 1982. Bloody Time and Bloody Scarcity: Capitalism, Authority and the Transformation of Temporal Experience in a Papua New Guinea Village. *American Ethnologist* 9(3): 503–518.
———. 1994. *Hard Times on Kairiru Island: Poverty, Development and Morality in a Papua New Guinea Village*. Honolulu: University of Hawaii Press.
Somare, Michael. 1975. *Sana: The Autobiography of Michael Somare*. Hong Kong: Niugini Press.
———. 2006. Papua New Guinea Statement to the 61st Session of the United Nations General Assembly. http://www.un.org/webcast/ga/61/pdfs/papua%20new%20guinea-e.pdf (accessed 15 March 2008).
———. 2013. *A Faraway, Familiar Place: Anthropologist Returns to Papua New Guinea*. Honolulu: University of Hawaii Press.

Spiro, Melford E. 1993. Is the Western Conception of the Self 'Peculiar' within the Context of World Cultures? *Ethos* 21(2): 107–153.
Spivak, G.C. 1988. Can the Subaltern Speak? In *Marxism and the Interpretation of Culture*, ed. C. Nelson and L. Grossberg. Urbana: University of Illinois Press.
Standage, T. 1998. *The Victorian Internet: The Remarkable Story of the Telegraph and the Nineteenth Century's On-line Pioneers*. New York: Walker and Co.
Stanley, L. 2008. The Development of Information and Communication Technology Law and Policy in Papua New Guinea. *Pacific Economic Bulletin* 23 (1): 16–29.
Stephen, Michele. 1979. Dreams of Change: The Innovative Role of Altered States of Consciousness in Traditional Melanesian Religion. *Oceania* 50(1): 3–22.
Stewart, S. 1984. *On Longing: Narratives of the Miniature, the Gigantic, the Souvenir, the Collection*. Baltimore: Johns Hopkins University Press.
Stoller, Paul. 2002. *Money Has No Smell: The Africanization of New York City*. Chicago: University of Chicago Press.
Strathern, M. 1979. The Self in Self-Decoration. *Oceania* 49 (4): 241–257.
———. 1988. *The Gender of the Gift*. Cambridge: Cambridge University Press.
———. 2011. Our Man In: A Melanesian "Spring"—The Online Revolution in Papua New Guinea. https://ourmaninproject.wordpress.com/2011/10/18/a-melanesian-spring-the-online-revolution-in-papua-new-guinea/. Accessed 15 March 2012.
Sullivan, Marjorie. 1990. The Impacts of Projected Climate Change on Coastal Land Use in Papua New Guinea. In *Implications of Expected Climatic Changes in the South Pacific Region: An Overview*, ed. J.C. Pernetta and P.J. Hughes, vol. 128, 33–58. Nairobi: UNEP, UNEP Regional Sea Reports and Studies.
Sullivan, N. 2010. Fieldwork Report in Support of an Environmental and Social Management Framework for the World Bank Supported Rural Communications Fund Project in East Sepik and Simbu Pronvinces, Papua New Guinea. Fiedlwork_Report_in_Support_of_an_Envrionmental_and_Social_Management_Framework_for_Rural_Communications. https://www.academia.edu/4492654/. Accessed 15 March 2012.
———. 2011. Our Man In: A Melanesian "Spring"—The Online Revolution in Papua New Guinea. https://ourmaninproject.wordpress.com/2011/10/18/a-melanesian-spring-the-online-revolution-in-papua-new-guinea/.
Suwamaru, J.K. 2014. Personal Experiences with Mixed Methods Research in Papua New Guinea. *Contemporary PNG Studies: DWU Research Journal* 21: 73–85.
Swart, Sandra. 2001. Man, Gun and Horse: Hard Right Afrikaner Masculine Identity in Post-Apartheid South Africa. In *Changing Men in Southern Africa*, ed. R. Morrell, 75–89. Pietermaritzburg, South Africa: University of Natal Press.

Sykes, Karen. 1999. After the 'Raskol' Feast: Youths' Alienation in New Ireland, Papua New Guinea. *Anthropological Forum* 17(3): 213–224.

———. 2000. Raskolling: Papua New Guinean Sociality as Contested Order. In *Developing Cultural Criminology: Theory and Practice in Papua New Guinea*, ed. C. Banks, 174–194. Sydney: Sydney Institute of Criminology Monograph Series 13.

Taga, Futoshi. 2005. East Asian Masculinities. In *Handbook of Studies on Men and Masculinities*, ed. Michael S. Kimmel, J. Hearn, and R.W. Connell, 129–140. Thousand Oaks, CA: Sage.

Taussig, Michael. 1980. *The Devil and Commodity Fetishism in South America*. Chapel Hill: University of North Carolina Press.

Taylor, Charles. 1999. Two Theories of Modernity. *Public Culture* 11(1): 153–174.

Tedlock, B. 1991. The new anthropology of dreaming. *Dreaming: Journal of the Association for the Study of Dreams* 1(1): 161–178.

Telban, B., and D. Vavrova. 2014. Ringing the Living and the Dead: Mobile Phones in a Sepik Society. *The Australian Journal of Anthropology* 25: 223–238.

Temple, O. 2009. *The SMS Serendipity in PNG or sms@upng.ac.pg*. Port Moresby: The University of Papua New Guinea Press.

Tengan, Ty P.K. 2008. *Native Men Remade: Gender and Nation in Contemporary Hawai'i*. Durham, NC: Duke University Press.

———. 2014. The Return of Ku: Re-Membering Hawaiian Masculinity, Warriorhood and Nation. In *Performing Indigeneity: Global Histories and Contemporary Experiences*, ed. L.R. Graham and H.G. Penny. Lincoln: University of Nebraska Press.

Tennov, Dorothy. 1979. *Love and Limerence: the Experience of Being in Love*. New York: Stein and Day.

Thomas, B. 2006. Cannabis in Papua New Guinea. *Papua New Guinea Medical Journal* 49(1–2): 52–56.

Thomas, David S.G., and Chasca Twyman. 2005. Equity and Justice in Climate Change Adaptation Amongst Natural-Resource-Dependent Societies. *Global Environmental Change* 15: 115–124.

Thompson, E.P. 1967. Time, Work-Discipline and Industrial Capitalism. *Past and Present* 36: 57–97.

Thurnwald, Richard. 1916. Banaro Society: Social Organization and the Kinship System of a Tribe in the Interior of New Guinea. *American Anthropological Association Memoirs* 3: 253–391.

Tiesler, F. 1969/1970. Die intertribalen Beziehungen an der Nordkust Neuguineas in Gebiet der kleiner Schouten-Inseln, trans. K. Barlow. Abhandlungen und Berichtet des Statlichen Museums fer Volkerkunde, Dresden, Akademie Verlag.

Tonkinson, Robert. 2003. Ambrymese Dreams and the Mardu Dreaming. In *Dream Travelers of the Western Pacific: Sleep Experiences and Culture in*

Australian Aboriginal, Melanesian and Indonesian Societies, ed. R. Lohmann, 87–105. New York: Palgrave Macmillan.
Trask, H.-K. 1991. *From a Native Daughter: Colonialism and Sovereignty in Hawaii*. Honolulu: University of Hawaii Press.
Trouillot, M.-R. 2002. The Otherwise Modern. In *Critically Modern*, ed. B.M. Knauft. Bloomington: Indiana University Press.
Tsing, A.L. 1993. *In the Realm of the Diamond Queen: Marginality in An Out-of-the-Way Place*. Princeton: Princeton University Press.
Turner, Victor. 1974. *Dramas, Fields, and Metaphors: Symbolic Action in Human Society*. Ithaca, London: Cornell University Press.
———. 1982. *From Ritual to Theatre: The Human Seriousness of Play*. New York: Performing Arts Journal Press.
Tuzin, Donald. 1997. *The Cassowary's Revenge: The Life and Death of Masculinity in a New Guinea Society*. Chicago: University of Chicago Press.
Tylor, E.B. 1873. *Primitive Culture*. London: John Murray.
Umbach, M., and B. Hüppauf, eds. 2005. *Vernacular Modernism: Heimat, Globalization and the Built Environment*. Stanford: Stanford University Press.
Uy-Tioco, C. 2007. Overseas Filipino Workers and Text Messaging: Reinventing Transnational Mothering. *Continuum: Journal of Media and Cultural Studies* 21 (2): 253–265.
Vedwan, Neeraj. 2006. Culture, Climate and the Environment: Local Knowledge and Perception of Climate Change among Apple Growers in Northwestern India. *Journal of Ecological Anthropology* 10: 4–18.
Vivieros de Castro, Eduardo, E. 2012. Cosmological Perspectivism in Amazonia and Elsewhere. HAU: Network of Ethnographic Theory. http://www.haujournal.org/index.php/masterclass/article/view/72/54. Accessed 15 March 2013.
Waddell, Eric. 1975. How the Enga Cope with Frost: Responses to Climatic Perturbations in the Central Highlands of New Guinea. *Human Ecology* 3(4): 249–273.
Wagner, Roy. 1986. *Symbols that Stand for Themselves*. Chicago: University of Chicago.
———. 1991. The Fractal Person. In *Big Men and Great Men: Personifications of Power in Melanesia*, ed. M. Godelier and M. Strathern, 159–173. Cambridge: Cambridge University Press.
Wallace, A.F.C. 1956. Revitalization Movements. *American Anthropologist* 58 (2): 264–281.
Wallerstein, I. 1979. *The Capitalist World Economy*. Cambridge: Cambridge University Press.
Wardlow, Holly. 1999. *All's Fair When Love Is War: Attempts at Companionate Marriage Among the Huli of Papua New Guinea*. Paper Prepared for the Annual Meetings of the AAA.

———. 2006. *Wayward Women: Sexuality and Agency in a New Guinea Society.* Berkeley: University of California Press.

———. 2008. "You Have to Understand: Some of Us are Glad AIDS has Arrived": Christianity and Condoms Among the Huli, Papua New Guinea. In *Making Sense of AIDS: Culture, Sexuality and Power in Melanesia*, ed. Leslie Butt and Richard Eves, 187–205. Honolulu: University of Hawaii Press.

Watson, A.H.A. 2010. Mobile Phones in PNG Villages: An Island Village Experience. QUT Digital Repository. http://eprints.qut.edu.au/. Accessed 15 March 2012.

———. 2011. Early Experience of Mobile Telephony: A Comparison of Two Villages in Papua New Guinea. *Media Asia* 38 (3): 170–181.

———. 2012. Tsunami Alert: The Mobile Phone Difference. *The Australian Journal of Emergency Management* 27 (4): 44–49.

———. 2013. Mobile Phones and Media Use in Madang Province of Papua New Guinea. *Pacific Journalism Review* 19 (2): 156–178.

Weber, Max. 1946/1958a. Religious Rejections of the World and Their Directions. In *From Max Weber: Essays in Sociology*, ed. and trans. H.H. Gerth and C. Wright Mills, 323–362. New York: Oxford University Press.

———. 1946/1958b. *From Max Weber: Essays in Sociology*, trans. and ed. H.H. Gerth and C. Wright Mills. New York: Oxford University Press.

———. 1958c. *The Protestant Ethic and the Spirit of Capitalism.* New York: Scribners.

———. 1978. *Economy and Society*, ed. Guenther Roth and Claus Wittich. Berkeley: University of California Press.

Weiner, Annette. 1978. The Reproductive Model in Trobriand Society. In *Trade and Exchange in Oceania and Australia*, ed. J. Specht and J. Peter White, 175–186. Sydney: Sydney University Press. (*Mankind*; v. 11(3)).

———. 1979. Trobriand Kinship from Another View: The Reproductive Power of Women and Men. *Man* (NS) 14: 328–348.

———. 1980. Reproduction: A Replacement for Reciprocity. *American Ethnologist* 7(1): 71–85.

Weiner, James. 1991. *The Empty Place: Poetry, Space and Being among the Foi of Papua New Guinea.* Bloomington, IN: Indiana University Press.

———. 1995. *The Lost Drum: The Myth of Sexuality in Papua New Guinea.* Madison: University of Wisconsin Press.

Wellman, B. 2001. Physical Place and Cyberplace: The Rise of Personalized Networking. *International Journal of Urban and Regional Research* 215 (2): 227–252.

West, F. ed. 1970. *Selected Letters of Hubert Murray.* Melbourne: Oxford University Press.

West, P. 2006. *Conservation is Our Government Now: The Politics of Ecology in Papua New Guinea.* Durham, NC: Duke University Press.

———. 2008. Tourism as Science and Science as Tourism: Environment, Society, Self and Other in Papua New Guinea. *Current Anthropology* 49(4): 597–626.
———. 2012. *From Modern Production to Imagined Primitive*. Durham, NC: Duke University Press.
Wild, S.1987. Recreating the Jukurrpa: Adaptation and Innovation of Songs and Ceremonies in Warlpiri Society. In *Songs of Aborrigginal Australia*, ed. C. Ross, M.T. Donaldson, and S. Wild, 97–120. Sydney: University of Sydney (Oceania Monograph 32).
Wildavsky, Aaron, and Karl Dake. 1990. Theories of Risk Perception: Who Fears What and Why? *Daedalus* 119(4): 41–60.
Wilde, Charles. 2004a. From Racing to Rugby: All Work and No Play for Gogodala Men of Western Province, Papua New Guinea. *The Australian Journal of Anthropology* 15(3): 286–302.
———. 2004b. Acts of Faith: Muscular Christianity and Masculinity among the Gogodala of Papua New Guinea. *Oceania* 75: 32–48.
Williams, F.E. 1940. *Drama of Orokolo: The Social and Ceremonial Life of the Elema*. Oxford: Oxford University Press.
Winnicott, D.W. 1987. *The Child, the Family and the Outside World*. Reading, MA: Addison-Wesley.
Wolf, E.R. 1982. *Europe and the People Without History*. Los Angeles: University of California Press.
Wood, Michael. 1998. Logging, Women and Submarines: Some Changes in Kamula Men's Access to Transformative Power. *Oceania* 68: 228–248.
Woolgar, S. 2005. Mobile Back to Front: Uncertainty and Danger in the Theory-Technology Relation. In *Mobile Communications: Renegotiation of the Social Sphere*, ed. R. Ling and P.E. Pedersen. London: Springer.
Yamo, H. 2013. *Mobile Phones in Rural Papua New Guinea: A Transformation in Health Communication and Delivery Services in Western Highlands Province*. MA Thesis submitted to the School of Communication Studies, Auckland University of Technology.
Zimmer, Laura. 1987. Gambling with Cards in Melanesia and Australia: An Introduction. Oceania 58(1): 1–5.
Zimmer-Tamakoshi, Laura. 1997. The Last Big Man: Development and Men's Discontents in the Papua New Guinea Highlands. *Oceania* 68: 107–122.
———. ed. 1998. *Modern Papua New Guinea*. Kirksville, Missouri: Thomas Jefferson University Press.
———. 2012. Troubled Masculinities and Gender Violence in Melanesia. In *Engendering Violence in Papua New Guinea*, ed. M. Jolly, C. Stewart, and C. Brewer. Canberra: ANU E-Press.
Žižek, Slavoj. 1989. *The Sublime Object of Ideology*. New York: Verso Press.
———. 1991. *Looking Awry: An Introduction to Jacques Lacan through Popular Culture*. Cambridge: MIT Press.

Index[1]

A
Aakhus, M.A., 95, 98n6
Abu-Lughod, Laila, 51n5
Air Niugini, 85
Akin, David, 57, 151
Andersen, Barbara, 81, 95
Anthropocene, 161, 165, 167, 188, 190
  as chronotope, 166, 167, 178
  as concept of alienation, 166
  and concept of nature/society, 165
  as critique of capitalism, 166
  and global risk, 168
  global warming, 179, 184, 187
  green activism, 165, 179
  greenhouse gas, 180
  and Murik masculinity, 188–9
anthropology
  of climate change, 165–6, 190n1
  environmental, 189
  of masculinity, 2, 24n1
  of modernity, 24n2
  of the Pacific, 126

psychological, 116
of religion, 189
Appadurai, Arjun, 47, 79, 132, 151
archaic, 193–5, 206
Auerbach, Eric, 33
Australian Museum (Sydney), 76n3
  Sepik Documentation Project, 146

B
Bainton, Nicholas, 13
Bakhtin, Mikhail, 5–6
  chronotope, 32–4, 52n9, 109, 166–8
  dialogism, 6, 23–4, 195
  dialogue, 6
  Dostoevsky, 1
  double-voiced discourse, 91, 125, 154, 174, 181, 184, 206
  hidden dialogue, 137
  medieval carnival, 96
Barclay, Kate, 57

---

[1] Note: Page numbers followed by "n" denote notes.

Barlow, Kathleen, 53n17, 101, 139, 146, 147, 159, 174, 176, 182
Bashkow, Ira, 25n5
Bateson, Gregory, 54n20, 98n3, 129, 167
Baudrillard, Jean, 162n1
Becker, Howard, 76n4
Beck, Ulrich, 168
Bell, Joshua, 70
Bernardi, B., 140
Besnier, Niko, 31, 201, 203
betel nuts, 21, 83
Bloch, Maurice, 151
Boas, Franz, 195
Bolton, Lissant, 76n2, 146
Brison, Karen, 151
Burridge, Kenelm, 151
Butt, Leslie, 54n17

C
Campbell, S.W., 95
capital, 3, 4
Carnival (Brazil), 118
Carrier, Achsah, 24n4
Carrier, James, 24n4
Carucci, Laurence, 199
Castells, Manuel, 89
Chakrabarty, Dipesh, 165
Christianity, 114
Clery, Tui N., 207n5
Cohen, Julie E., 104
Connell, R.W., 1–2, 193
  hegemonic masculinity, 1–2, 49, 135
Coombes, Rosemary, 111
copyright law, 111
Crutzen, Paul, 165

D
Dake, Karl, 177
de Certeau, Michel, 105

Dening, Greg, 185
Derrida, Jacques, 162n1
Digicel Company, 79, 80, 92
Dinnen, Sinclair, 10, 25n9
Douglas, Mary, 186, 191n7
Durkheim, Emile, 3, 39
  anomie, 59, 69
  conjugal morality, 71

E
Eggan, Fred, 195
Elliston, D., 207n5
Engels, Frederick, 167
Epstein, E.L., 24n4
Errington, Frederick, 13, 31, 151
Evans-Pritchard, E.E., 175
Eves, Richard, 25n9

F
Fiji, 207n5
Filer, Colin, 25n6
Fortune, Reo, 163n5
Foster, Robert, 95, 151
Foucault, Michel, 116, 162n1
Fowler Museum (UCLA), 111
Freud, Sigmund, 4
  Oedipus complex, 104, 109, 140, 153, 194

G
Garamut Enterprise Ltd., 183
Geertz, Clifford, 105, 195
Gell, Alfred, 122, 189
Gewertz, Deborah, 13, 31, 151
Giddens, Anthony, 29–30, 50n1, 81, 91, 150, 175
Gisu people (Uganda), 2
Glass, Patrick, 174
Gluckman, Max, 118

Goddard, Michael, 10
Goode, William J., 50n2
Goody, Jack, 30
Gregory, Chris, 151
Gutmann, Mathew, 24n1

H
Habermas, Jurgen, 22, 79, 135
Haddon, Leslie, 83
Hallowell, Irving, 3
Halvaksz, Jamon, 25n6, 68, 134n4
Hamlet, 105
Harley, Christopher, 220
Harris, Bruce, 10
Harrison, Simon, 111
Hawaii/Hawaiians, 154
 and American colonialism, 196, 198
 Christianity, 197
 cosmology, 193, 198
 hereditary elites, 197
 Kingdom of, 197
 King Kamehameha, 197
 masculinity; and alienation, 196, 198; dialogue with modernity, 196, 198; dialogue with the archaic, 195, 196, 198; Hale Mua, 195, 198; warrior identity of, 198; and women, 198
 nationalist movement, 196
 nation of, 197
Healy, C.J., 163n8
H.M.S. Titanic, 166
Hobbes, Thomas, 141
Hodgson, Dorothy, 24n1
Homer, 33
Hornborg, Alf, 166
Horst, Heather, 89, 92

I
Ingold, Timothy, 169, 189
intellectual property, 104, 111

J
Jacka, Jerry, 25n6
Jankowiak, William, 31, 59, 77n11
Jolly, Margaret, 25n9
Jorgensen, Dan, 95, 98n5

K
Katz, J.E., 95, 98n6
Kirsch, Stewart, 25n5, 25n6
Klein, Melanie, 121
Knauft, Bruce, 25n5, 38, 65
Kraemer, Daniela, 97
Kulick, Don, 10
Kwakiutl *potlatch*, 12

L
Lacan, Jacques, 4–5, 135, 194, 199
 alienation, 4, 194
 desire, 104–5
 the hour of the other, 172
 the mirror stage, 107, 110–13
 the name of the father, 105, 107, 121, 122, 135, 145, 184, 185, 194, 199
 the phallus, 4–5, 23, 104–6, 108, 135, 148, 149, 173, 194–5; as organ, 109; as signifier, 106, 109–10, 115, 135, 155, 166, 169, 184, 194, 196, 200; symbolic castration, 105, 106, 108, 135, 158, 185, 188, 195, 196
 psychoanalysis of, 101, 104
 the real, 134n5, 188, 195
 signification, 102, 104, 105, 140; chains of, 136, 152
 subject formation in culture, 107, 194; the lack, 4, 9, 131, 137, 148, 155, 160, 174, 176, 194;
 the signifier, 104, 105, 108, 195, 196

Lacan, Jacques (*cont.*)
  the Symbolic, 4, 105, 107, 122,
    135, 140, 145, 149, 189
  time and space of the other, 146,
    167, 172, 173, 184, 188
Landes, David, 168
Lash, Christopher, 167
Lattas, Alexander, 132
Lavie, Smadar, 118
Leach, Edmund, 101, 118, 182
Leach, J., 224
Lindholm, Charles, 31
Lindstrom, Lamont, 74, 81
Ling, Rich, 83, 88, 90
Lipset, David, 14, 16–18, 22, 33, 38,
    39, 41, 47, 53n17, 54n20, 57,
    58, 61, 67, 76n3, 80, 82, 86, 90,
    91, 93, 101, 102, 109, 110, 115,
    117, 118, 121–3, 128–31, 133,
    134n7, 137, 139, 143, 144,
    146, 147, 153, 163n5, 173,
    178, 180, 189
  fieldwork of, 60, 62–9, 71–2, 85,
    89, 102, 111, 127, 133–4, 146,
    147, 151, 177–8, 180–1,
    183–4, 188–90
LiPuma, Edward, 10, 38
Lohmann, Roger, 116
Lowenthal, David, 177
Luhrmann, Tanya, 93

M
Maasai people (Kenya), 2
Macintyre, Martha, 8–9, 13, 25n4
magic, 169
Malinowski, Bronislaw, 31, 50n3, 101,
    111, 169
Malm, Andreas, 166
Mardi Gras, 118
marijuana, 120, 131, 167
Martin, Keir, 13, 25n5, 155, 179

Marx, Karl, 57, 76n1, 152, 193
  alienation, 3, 166
  fetishism, 151
  man and nature, 167
  masculinity, 1–2, 11, 24n1
  alienation, 5, 13
Mauss, Marcel, 151, 162n1
McCormack, F., 57
McLuhan, Marshall, 94
Mead, Margaret, 1, 60, 82, 201
Meiser, Leo, 182
Melanesia, 8, 50, 144, 145, 180
  manhood, 108
  postcolonial, 151
Merton, Robert K.
  leadership, 178
  retreatism as anomie, 59
Mexico, 2
Micronesia, Federated States of,
    198–201
  cosmology; Letao, 199–200
  masculinity and; American nuclear
    testing, 198–9; climate change,
    199, 200; dialogue, of dual
    alienation, 198; dialogue, with
    modernity, 200–1; dialogue,
    with the archaic, 201; rising
    sea-levels, 198, 200
Miller, Daniel, 86, 92
Mintz, Sydney, 74
mobile phones, 18, 21, 23, 167
  apparatgeist of, 98n6
  as commodities, 95
  domestication hypothesis, 85
  hyper-coordination, 90
  in Jamaica, 94–6, 98n7
  micro-coordination, 90
  among Norwegian youth, 90
  perpetual contact, 95, 98n6
modernity, 1–3, 5, 7–14, 20–4
  alienation in, 5, 6, 8, 16, 25
  and the Anthropocene, 170, 188

bureaucracy, 140
capitalism, 38, 49, 57, 74, 165, 167, 188
causation in, 172
chronotope of, 167-8, 178
chronotope of modern romance, 32, 33
chronotope of the Anthropocene, 167, 168, 177, 179-81
creativity, 103
freedom, 103
human exceptionalism, 167, 168
and love, 30-2
men; dual alienation in, 194
moral indeterminacy, 81
Murik concept of (*yabar*), 155
personhood; autonomous agency, 103, 105; citizen-subject, 132; courtship and marriage in, 30; individualism, 29, 30, 48, 49, 70, 71, 203; romantic love and, 29-32, 46
regionally based ethnography of, 2, 7
self, 4, 29, 103, 206; life histories and, 30; reflexive project of, 29, 39, 43; subject-centered voices, 206
the state, 4, 7, 9-11, 16, 21, 23
time and space in, 29
universalism, 131, 206
money, 61, 72, 76n1, 135-63
metaphors of, 150-4, 158
Mosko, Mark, 169
Mulvey, Laura, 128
Munn, Nancy, 16
Murik people (Papua New Guinea), 1
archaic culture, 95, 97
Catholicism, 115, 183; Society of the Divine Word, 34
as citizens; voting, 136
cosmology; ancestor-spirits, 169, 171-3, 177; ancestor-spirits,

afterlife, 122; ancestor-spirits, migration of (*nagam*), 170; ancestor-spirits, propitiation of, 182, 183; bush-spirits, 172; dreams, 169; Kakar-spirits, 70, 173, 175; masks, 111; sea-spirits, 172; sun-spirits, 172; Two Brothers, 87; *yabar*, 154-6; *yabar*, as concept, of modernity, 155; *yabar*, as concept, of white people, 155
dialogue; with modernity, 96; Tokpisin, 131
economy; boats, 158-9; boats, canoes, 17, 110, 131, 171, 174-8; boats, fiberglass boats, 14, 18, 39, 85, 110, 131; boats, outboard motors, 85; division of labor, 14, 16, 171, 178; markets, dispossession, 39; markets, regional, 14; poverty, 58; small-scale fishery, 14, 57-8; trade, conventions of, 123-6; trade, conventions of, arrival, 123-4; trade, conventions of, departure, 124-7; trade, conven-tions of, desire, 124, 125; trade, conventions of, hospitality, 125; trade, conventions of, marriage and brideservice and, 55n24; trade, conventions of, "routes," 60, 64; trade, decline of, 16, 17; trade, regional goods, baskets, 19, 60; trade, regional goods, *canarium* almonds, 83, 84; trade, regional goods, carvings, 16; trade, regional goods, clay pots, 124; trade, regional goods, folk theater, 101, 107, 131, 134n7; trade, regional goods, folk theater, Woyon's Mother, 167, 169; trade, regional

Murik people (Papua New Guinea) (*cont.*)
  goods, shell ornaments, 16; trade, regional goods, tobacco, 60–7, 124; trade, regional goods, tobacco, and gender, 68, 83; trade, regional goods, tobacco regional goods, tobacco, during the colonial era, 73–4; trade, regional goods, tobacco, moral construction of, 65–7; trade, regional goods, tobacco, village marketing of, 60, 64–5; trade, regional goods, wooden dishes, 124
  environment, 14, 16; Anthropocene and, 167, 168, 179–86, 189, 190; beaches, 177, 182, 186; climate change, 24, 186, 188, 189, 199, 200, 206; damage, Casuarina trees, 165; damage, coastal erosion, 165, 177, 181, 186; damage, coconuts, 186; lack of land, 16; lakescape, 173; lake tides, 165; mangroves, 14, 173, 182, 183; rising sea-levels, 20, 161; rising sea-levels, as divine punishment, 183; rising sea-levels, chronotopes of, 179, 181–6; rising sea-levels, magic and, 172, 179, 183–4, 186, 188; rising sea-levels, meaning of, 167, 179, 186; rising sea-levels, past storm events, 172, 183; rising sea-levels, resignation and, 178; rising sea-levels, stoicism and, 177–9; rising sea-levels, uncertainty and, 177, 179, 181; shellfish, clams, 178; shellfish, sand crab, 171
  ethnohistory; ancestors' migration (*nagam*), 170, 190; Gaut village, 170–5, 184; Kumbun and Darua, 36–7; Masangi and Serai soil, 184–6; Puralima and Kakritena, 173–4; Warense's revenge, 170–3, 188
  expressive culture of, 134; Woyon songs, 112–13
  Facebook, 21
  kinship, 19; brothers, 69, 85, 87; father, 69, 71, 92, 123; father's brother, 71, 120; father's mother, 71; mother's brother, 91; sisters, 94; sister's son, 102; son, 69, 70; son's daughter, 71; son's son, 123; terminology (Hawaiian), 180–1; wife's mother, 91
  lineage organization, 19, 123; initiation, 138, 153; insignia (*sumon*), 19, 137, 140, 152; insignia (*sumon*), baskets, 137; insignia (*sumon*), ornaments, 152, 174; insignia (*sumon*), reproduction, 137; insignia (*sumon*), ritual leadership, 137; platforms, 182
  local government, 20
  magic (*timiit*), 169–70; love, 169, 184; rain, 177; sea, 183, 184, 186, 188; Serai soil, 184, 185, 188
  marriage, 23; affines, 102, 114; affines, and marijuana traffic, 68; affines, avoidance, 53n15, 82; breakdown of organization, 69; brideservice, 35, 53n15, 82; bridewealth, 41; courtship, chronotope of Homeric romance, 33, 39–46, 52n11, 68; courtship, gift-giving and,

38; divorce, 72; domestic violence, 70–2; elopement, 37; Female Cult and, 36; infidelity/adultery, 31, 35; love magic and, 36–7; Male Cult and, 34, 37; Male Cult and exchange of wives' sexual services in, 38; mobile phone use, 84, 88–9; postmarital residence, 77n8; sexual jealousy (scandal), 72, 82, 90; sister-exchange, 34, 38
men and masculinity, 1, 14–24; canoe, as Lacanian signifier, 137; chronotopes of, alienation, 167, 179, 186–8; chronotopes of, archaic masculinity, 167, 170, 173, 174, 179, 181–6, 189; chronotopes of, Homeric romance, 170; chronotopes of, modernity, 178–81; chronotopes of, the Anthropocene, 167–8, 179–81, 189, 190n1; dialogue, of dual alienation, 57, 70, 97, 135, 140, 151, 152, 154, 155, 158, 159, 206; dialogue, with modernity, 79, 135, 140, 150, 151, 155, 158–60, 206; dialogue, with the archaic, 70, 206; double-voiced discourse of, Gaingiin Society, 206; double-voiced discourse of, marijuana discourse, 206; double-voiced discourse of, mobile phones, 206; double-voiced discourse of, rising sea-levels, 206; double-voiced discourse of, romance narratives, 23; double-voiced discourse of, Woyon's mother, 206; and folk theater, *Woyon's Mother*, and colonial rule, 104, 107; and folk theater, *Woyon's Mother*, and modernity, 108, 122; and folk theater, *Woyon's Mother*, and status rivalry, 131; and folk theater, *Woyon's Mother*, and the Lacanian signifier, 104–5, 108; and folk theater, *Woyon's Mother*, and the Male Cult, 10, 111, 112; and folk theater, *Woyon's Mother*, as dialogue of, alienation from modernity, 113, 120, 122, 126, 129, 132; and folk theater, *Woyon's Mother*, as dialogue of, alienation from the archaic, 104, 109, 114, 120, 122, 132; and folk theater, *Woyon's Mother*, as dialogue of, dual alienation, 104, 107, 109, 114, 123–30; and folk theater, *Woyon's Mother*, as Pygmalion, 102, 104, 108; and folk theater, *Woyon's Mother*, authorship of, 102, 103, 113–22; and folk theater, *Woyon's Mother*, dreams and, 115–16, 118, 119, 132; and folk theater, *Woyon's Mother*, exchange of, 16, 19, 82; and folk theater, *Woyon's Mother*, exchange of, as lineage initiation, 111, 112; and folk theater, *Woyon's Mother*, exchange of, performances, magic and stagecraft, 111, 120; and folk theater, *Woyon's Mother*, exchange of, performances of, 102, 127, 129; and folk theater, *Woyon's Mother*, exchange of, performances of, and desire, 111, 127–8, 133; and folk theater, *Woyon's Mother*, lyrics, 129–32; and folk theater,

Murik people (Papua New Guinea) (*cont.*)
Woyon's Mother, masks, 103, 121; and folk theater, *Woyon's Mother*, masks, butterfly motif, 119–20, 130, 134n7; and folk theater, *Woyon's Mother*, masks, fish motif, 119–20, 130, 134n7; and folk theater, *Woyon's Mother*, mourning and, 115–18, 120, 122, 132; Gaingiin Society, 20, 23, 66; Gaingiin Society, age-grades in, 140–5, 147, 153; Gaingiin Society, age-grades in, skipping, 149; Gaingiin Society, dialogue with modernity, 136, 150, 151; Gaingiin Society, exchange of sexual services ("skirts"), 136, 145, 146, 151, 153, 158, 163n5; Gaingiin Society, fictive kinship in, 144–6; Gaingiin Society, grade-taking in, 140, 144, 146, 150, 152; Gaingiin Society, grade-taking in, substitution of money in, 149–50, 152; Gaingiin Society, initiation in, 148, 149, 152, 153; Gaingiin Society, installation of coconut harvest taboo, 142, 146–7; Gaingiin Society, masks in, 136, 140–6, 153; Gaingiin Society, maternal norms in, 137; loss of magical agency, 58; loss of moral agency, 57, 69; and Male Cult, 19, 62, 73, 141, 143, 147, 149, 156, 157, 163n5; and Male Cult, adoption, 120; and Male Cult, Arake, mother of the Kakar, 110; and Male Cult, decline of, 23; and Male Cult, in the 20th century, 110; and Male Cult, in the 20th century, fiberglass boats and, 110, 131; and Male Cult, in the 20th century, initiation, 110; and Male Cult, in the 20th century, male cult house construction, 170, 172; and Male Cult, in the 20th century, male cult house construction, consecration rites of, 172, 182; and Male Cult, in the 20th century, outrigger canoes, 106, 131; and Male Cult, in the 20th century, outrigger canoes, consecration rites, 182; and Male Cult, in the 20th century, outrigger canoes, the steersman, 108; and Male Cult, in the 20th century, outrigger canoes, the steersman, shipwreck, 176; and Male Cult, in the 20th century, outrigger canoes, the steersman's paddle, 159, 174–7; and Male Cult, in the 20th century, outrigger canoes, the steersman, wife of, 176; and Male Cult, joking partnerships, 90–1, 102, 108–9, 173–4, 178; and Male Cult, Kakar spear-spirits, 19, 109; and Male Cult, sexual exchange, 106, 173; and Male Cult, sexual exchange, as symbolic castration, 110; marijuana discourse, 79; marijuana discourse, and domestic violence, 71–2; marijuana discourse, and legal system of Papua New Guinea, 73; marijuana discourse, consumption discourse, 65–71, 74; marijuana discourse, moral construction of, 62, 64, 65, 68; marijuana discourse, traffic

discourse, 62–5, 69; marijuana discourse, vernacular name of, 65; and material culture, substitutions in, end of mourning gifts, 158; and material culture, substitutions in, lighting hearth fires, 156–7; and material culture, substitutions in, lime power containers, 155; and material culture, substitutions in, moiety exchange in the Male Cult, 149, 156–7; and material culture, substitutions in, outrigger canoes, 159–60; and material culture, substitutions in, outrigger steering paddles, 159; and material culture, substitutions in, pillows and sleeping bags, 158; senior men, marijuana discourse of, 59, 62, 66, 67, 69, 75; and trade, 101, 175, 176; young men and, alcohol use, 74; young men and, alcohol use, beer, 74; young men and, athletics, 62; young men and, athletics, soccer, 68; young men and, card playing, 67; young men and, courtship narratives, 23, 33, 39–46, 50; young men and, courtship narratives, and masculinity, 49; young men and, dialogue with modernity, 38, 39, 43, 50; young men and, dialogue with modernity, marijuana discourse, 23, 59, 61, 62, 68–9, 72–4; young men and, mobile phone use, 59, 91; young men and, overseas trade, 47
mobile phones and, 36, 38; conflict, 85–8, 90; feigned misrecognition, 87; hyper-coordination of relationships, 90; micro-coordination of daily life, immoral, 88–90; micro-coordination of daily life, moral, 84, 87, 90; overseas trade, 82
moral community; ethos of reciprocity, 70
Papua New Guinea and, 178–9, 183
personhood; canoe-body of, 82, 115–16, 137, 140; canoe-body of, as spirit-passenger, 140; death, 114, 115, 121; death, custody disputes and, 120, 123; death, explanation of, 118; death, mourning, pollution, 115, 117; death, mourning, taboos, 115–17; death, mourning, Washing Feast, 115, 117; moral agency, 58, 69, 71; narration rights of, 102; subjective self-disclosure, 68; succession, 140
resettlement, 190
Seventh Day Adventism (SDA), 18, 40, 42, 67, 84, 113, 115, 150, 183
time; archaic year, 174; and ceremonial exchange, 175; knots, 175; the morning star, 175; winds and tides, 174
urban diaspora, 21, 79, 81–4, 88, 92, 94, 165, 182, 183; views of, civil society, 82; views of, modern (urban) life, 82, 96; views of, the state, 88, 97
villages; Big Murik, 177, 187; Big Murik, Wokumot hamlet, 123; Darapap, 40, 43, 45, 73, 113; Karau, 169, 188; Mendam, 165, 181
women; Female Cult, 19, 147, 149, 156, 182; illness, 71

N

nature/culture binary, 165
New Zealand/Aotearora, 203–5
  Māori, 203–5; cultural renaissance of, 204; cultural renaissance of, *marae* model of, 204; masculinity, dialogue of dual alienation with, modernity, in athletics, 205; masculinity, dialogue of dual alienation with, modernity, in athletics, rugby, 205; masculinity, dialogue of dual alienation with, modernity, in school, 204; masculinity, dialogue of dual alienation with, the archaic, *haka* dance, 205; masculinity, dialogue of dual alienation with, the archaic, in ritual practice, 204; masculinity, dialogue of dual alienation with, the archaic, the vernacular, 204; masculinity, Hokowhitu, Brandan, 204; masculinity, Hokowhitu, Brandan, dual alienation, at his father's funeral, 205; masculinity, Hokowhitu, Brandan, dual alienation, at son's school assemblies, 205; masculinity, Hokowhitu, Brandan, dual alienation, in school, 204; women, 204
Nobus, Dany, 105

O

Odysseus, 33
Ovid, 106, 114, 133

P

Pacific Islanders, 154
  dual alienation of, 24

Pacific modernity, 193, 195, 198, 203, 206
Pacific Soccer Club Championships, 68–9
Papua New Guinea (PNG), 1, 5–13, 193
  Aitape town, 76n2
  athletics; canoe-racing, 13; rugby, 12
  Australian colonial rule of, 88
  Biangai people, 134n4
  Bogia town, 62
  Christianity in, 8, 11, 12
  civil society, 8
  concept of citizenship, 136
  crime in, 7, 10
  development in, 8
  Duna people, 11
  economy; national, 7; relationship to global, 168
  Finchhafen, 83
  Gawa people, 101
  Gebusi people, 65
  Gogogala people, 12–13
  Highlands, 44, 62, 81, 97n1
  independence, 89
  infrastructure, 7
  kina (national currency), 150, 152
  kinship and society, 7–8
  Lae town, 42
  languages, 7; English, 7; Tokpisin, 7, 39; vernaculars, 7
  Lihir Island, 13
  local-level leadership; bigmen, 10, 11; *bigshot*, 13
  Madang town, 62
  Manam Island, 114
  Maprik people, 69
  masculinity, men; and alienation, 5–13; crime, 7–8, 10; dialogue of, dual alienation, 206; employment in, as

entrepreneurs, 8; employment in, as security guards, 8; employment, in extraction industry, 8; as fathers, 8; history of, 206; as husbands, 9; magic, 12; Massim region, 101; mobile phones, 88; mobile phones, and joking, 89–91, 94; mobile phones, and urban youth, 88–90, 94, 96; mobile phones, calls, and infidelity (marriage), 82, 89, 91, 94; mobile phones, calls, and sorcery, 94; mobile phones, calls, and the modern subject, 91–4; mobile phones, calls, from ghosts, 81; mobile phones, calls, harassment of women, 81; mobile phones, calls, phone friendships, 81, 95; mobile phones, calls, prank, 95; mobile phones, calls, and sorcery, 94; mobile phones, credit units, 80, 83, 89, 95; mobile phones, moral panic, 81; mobile phones, the voice, and subject-centered personhood, 90, 92, 94, 97; mobile phones, the voice, archaic modes of talk, 92; mobile phones, the voice, individuation of, 79; mobility of, 9; modernity in, 5–13, 39, 48, 49, 60, 79, 81, 82, 84, 85, 88, 90, 91, 94–7, 101, 107, 109, 113, 120, 122, 129–32, 150, 153–5, 167, 188–90, 206; modernity in, carbon cowboys, 82; modernity in, fast-money schemes in, 9; modernity in, marijuana, 11, 61; modernity in, marriage, 8; and violence, 9; youth, 39, 48; youth as rascals (*raskol*), 10–11, 59

Massim region, 189
and Murik resettlement, 190n4
Muschu Island, 60
national elections of 1982, 136
National Fisheries Authority, 110
New Ireland; *malaggan* statues, 189
North Coast, 58, 76n2, 101, 119, 146, 170
political institutions, 7
as postcolonial state, 39; lack of development projects, 189
Sepik, 40, 41, 53n17, 54n20, 60, 73, 76n2–4, 80, 101, 109, 119, 124, 129, 134n3, 146, 150, 159, 163n5, 170, 172, 191n8; Bin village (PNG), 73; But village, 76n2; Marienberg, 150; Sub village, 60; Wewak town, 41–2, 55n25, 76n2, 81, 83, 85, 92, 94; Wewak town, Dagua market, 40; Wewak town, Kreer market, 42; Yakamul people, 76n2; Yangoru people, 70
Sissano Lagoon, 184
stratification, 7
Sub village, 60
symbolics in; archaic, 6, 11; modern, 6
Tolai people, 13
Trobriand Islands, 169
2008 budget, 169
Urapmin people, 11–12
Park, Y.J., 95
Parry, Jonathan, 151
Paz, Octavio, 48
personhood
  estrangement of, 3
  moral agency, 3
Propoetides, 106
Pygmalion and Galatea, 102, 104, 106–9, 114, 122, 130, 132–4

R
Rasmussen, Anders E., 179
Rheingold, H., 95
Riviere, Joan, 121
Robbins, Joel, 8, 11, 12, 24n4, 25n5, 25n10, 57, 109, 150, 151, 161n2, 163n8
Rodman, Margaret, 126
romance, 29–33, 40, 43, 46, 47, 51n4, 51n5, 52n9–11, 53–4n17
Rosaldo, Renato, 134n8
Rudiak-Gold, Peter, 179, 190n1, 199, 200

S
sago, 68, 72, 124, 127, 142, 145, 148–50, 152, 182, 185, 187
Sahlins, Marshall, 154
Salisbury, J.G., 163n8
Schmidt, Father Joseph, 34, 35, 53n14
Scott, Michael, 96
Seligman, A.B., 81, 150
Shaw, George Bernard, 39
Shipton, Parker, 151
Silverman, Eric K., 54n20, 129, 144
Simmel, Georg, 4, 29, 96, 150
Smith, Michael French, 126
Somare, Sir Michael, 21, 53n15, 73, 120, 129, 130, 156, 168, 169, 180, 188, 206
  and climate change, 180
  at the United Nations (UN), 180
Spivak, Gayatri C., 207n6
Stephen, Michelle, 116
Strathern, Marilyn, 108, 151
Sullivan, Nancy, 81, 97n2

T
Tahiti, 207n5
Taussig, Michael, 151
technological leapfrogging, 79

Tedlock, Dennis, 116
Telban, Borut, 80
Tengen, Ty, 126, 195
Thompson, E.P., 175
Thurnwald, Richard, 38
Tiesler, Frank, 16
Tonga, kingdom of, 201–3
  and global modernity, 201
  and masculinity; dual alienation of, as pawnbrokers, 201–2; dual alienation of, from the Tongan Way, 201, 203; dual alienation of, in gyms, 203; dual alienation of, in the Miss Galaxy Pageant, 202–3
  modernity and; remittance economy, 201
Trask, H.-K., 126
Turner, Victor, 118
Tuzin, Donald, 25n10, 109, 150, 154

U
Urry, John, 167

V
van Gennep, Arnold, 82
van Meijl, Toon, 204
Vanuatu, 69
Vavrova, Daniela, 80, 81
Vivieros de Castro, Eduardo, 189
von Poser, Alexis, 182

W
Wallace, Anthony, 196
Wardlow, Holly, 8, 9, 25n4, 25n9
Watson, Amanda, 81
Weber, Max, 3, 97, 105, 151, 166
Weiner, Annette, 140, 163n6
Weiner, James, 24n3, 25n6, 173, 190n6

Wentworth, Chelsea, 98n5
West, Paige, 25n4, 25n7
Whig history, 167
Wildavsky, Aaron, 191n7
Wilde, Charles, 12, 13
Wolf, Eric, 74
Woolgar, Stephen, 85

Y
Yttri, B., 88, 90

Z
Zimmer-Tamakoshi, Laura, 24n4
Žižek, Slavoj, 5, 105, 188

The manufacturer's authorised representative in the EU is Springer
Nature Customer Service Centre GmbH, Europaplatz 3, 69115 Heidelberg,
Germany. If you have any concerns regarding our products, please
contact ProductSafety@springernature.com

Printed and bound by CPI Group (UK) Ltd, Croydon, CR0 4YY
23/03/2026
02076735-0007